W9-BBC-712

The State of the Earth

The State of the Earth

Environmental Challenges
on the Road to 2100

Paul K. Conkin

THE UNIVERSITY PRESS OF KENTUCKY

Publication of this volume was made possible in part by a grant
from the National Endowment for the Humanities.

Copyright © 2007 by Paul K. Conkin

Scholarly publisher for the Commonwealth,
serving Bellarmine University, Berea College, Centre College of Kentucky, Eastern
Kentucky University, The Filson Historical Society, Georgetown College, Kentucky
Historical Society, Kentucky State University, Morehead State University, Murray
State University, Northern Kentucky University, Transylvania University, University
of Kentucky, University of Louisville, and Western Kentucky University.
All rights reserved.

Editorial and Sales Offices: The University Press of Kentucky
663 South Limestone Street, Lexington, Kentucky 40508-4008
www.kentuckypress.com

11 10 09 08 07   5 4 3 2 1

Library of Congress Cataloging-in-Publication Data

Conkin, Paul Keith.
  The state of the Earth : environmental challenges on the road to 2100 / Paul
K. Conkin.
      p. cm.
  Includes bibliographical references and index.
  ISBN-13: 978-0-8131-2411-7 (hardcover : alk. paper)
  ISBN-10: 0-8131-2411-5 (hardcover : alk. paper)
  1. Environmental responsibility. 2. Environmental education. 3. Environmental
policy. I. Title.
  GE195.7.C66 2006
  333.72--dc22   2006032085

This book is printed on acid-free recycled paper meeting the requirements of the
American National Standard for Permanence in Paper for Printed Library Materials.
∞ ✸

Manufactured in the United States of America.

Member of the Association of
American University Presses

Contents

Illustrations

Preface

I suspect few people regret the passing of the twentieth century. It is impossible to forget the troubled events from 1914 to 1945: international turmoil, two great wars, a worldwide depression, the rise of two totalitarian ideologies and regimes, the cruelty of the Holocaust, and total warfare encompassing civilian populations. Just as remarkable, and possibly even more momentous in long-term consequences, was the unprecedented, and almost incomprehensible, growth of human populations and human consumption during that century.

After growing from 1.7 billion to 3 billion from 1900 to 1960, the world population doubled, from 3 billion to just over 6 billion, from 1960 to 2000. The United Nations Population Division estimated a population of almost 6.5 billion in 2005. By most estimates, the world's population will be around 9 billion by 2050. Of the necessary conditions for this population explosion, two are all but obvious. One was the development and worldwide dissemination of new knowledge and new technologies in the prevention and cure of diseases. This increased life expectancy in all parts of the world, but with the most dramatic consequences in much of Africa and Asia. The other necessary condition was the dramatic increase of human economic productivity, with the most critical improvement in agriculture. This resulted from a continued but accelerated use of new knowledge and more efficient tools. The energy for this productivity explosion came largely from the controlled burning of organic materials.

The economic growth exceeded that of population. Estimates here are not exact, but in rough terms the world domestic product and energy use rose by at least twelve times in the twentieth century. Most of this increase was in the twenty-five wealthiest countries, but some growth occurred in all areas of the world. Humans used more fossil fuels in this one century than in all past history. This accompanied a near tenfold increase in water use. As with population, most of this growth came

vii

after World War II, in what turned out to be an almost frenzied period of growth in all areas.

This growth in both population and consumption, with all its rewards, has led to a twofold problem that can only worsen as the new century progresses. One is regional scarcities of essential resources—soil, water, and energy—or scarcities already suffered in much of the underdeveloped areas of the earth. The other is the burden placed on the earth and on other species by what humans have done—by polluting air, water, and soil, by stealing essential living space away from other species, and by contributing to such major changes in our atmosphere and in the oceans as to threaten major climate change. Compounding these problems is a huge ethical dilemma. The gap in incomes between the top one-fourth of humanity and the lower three-fourths is wide. By almost any calculation, the earth does not have the basic resources needed to raise the poorer people of the world to living standards even close to that of the top twenty-five countries. And if, by some miracle, everyone in the world could consume what Americans do, the earth could not long absorb the pollution and growing burden of waste products.

It is difficult to imagine a rate of growth in either population or consumption in the twenty-first century that comes even close to that in the twentieth. What if the earth's population did quadruple, and thus move up to 24 billion? What if resource use and consumption increased by twelve times? Neither will happen, for the earth could not begin to sustain either increase. Thus, the great challenge: either stabilize populations and limit consumption, or find new ways of coping with both types of growth. Population growth is not a problem for affluent countries, but their present pace of growth in production and consumption, if continued, will soon lead to major resource scarcities and problems of pollution. Even if rapid consumptive growth continues yet awhile in wealthy countries, such growth will require a further draw down of resources, such as oil, from the poorer areas of the world. This will invite continued political tensions, and make more difficult any narrowing of the present gap between living standards in rich and poor countries.

At present, knowing what we now know with some degree of assurance, it is almost impossible to be sanguine about the state of the earth, and thus the overall human prospect, by the end of this century. In so many areas one can cite the problems but not identify any clear or politically feasible solutions. It is easy to suggest that the people in the underdeveloped world should curtail population growth. Birthrates are now declining in most counties, but not rapidly enough to stabilize the world's population before 2050, and by most forecasts not before 2100. It is easy to suggest that people in wealthy countries, where populations are often stable or in decline, should change patterns of consumption or even lower their level of material consumption. But to persuade them to do so would require radical changes in the very structure of their societies.

These problems, these challenges, are what I have tried to address in this book. I worry about them all the time. I know most other people share these concerns. In this book, it is my purpose to help them better understand the challenges that lie ahead. I hope I have offered such an understanding of the earth and of life on earth as to enable laypeople to understand the planet's vulnerability to human activities. I have tried to survey the road that led to the major environmental issues that humans face today. I want to help people understand why we need to attend to these problems, but also to understand the risks and costs of such efforts.

This is no easy task. The issues are complex, and involve the insights developed by almost every academic discipline. I need to be clear, but not at the expense of being over-simplistic. The literature on environmental issues is now monumental, and growing exponentially every year. No one can read it all. No one can have the technical knowledge to understand it all. My task has been to try to gain an understanding of the issues, and to communicate that understanding in a way that will inform a broader audience than is addressed by most experts, and without the political agenda that accompanies most books and articles by committed but often deeply divided environmentalists.

I write as an old man. I will not be around much longer. The challenges I cite will largely affect my grandchildren and great grandchildren. They will almost certainly have to cope with a much warmer earth. They will have to find solutions to such other global problems as ocean pollution, much higher costs for fossil fuels, and regional scarcities of food and water. But what will be most revolutionary, and completely unprecedented in the last two thousand years, they will have to adjust to a world in which the present pattern of rapid growth—in population, in production and consumption—will no longer be possible. In the twentieth century, the ability of humans to shape the world around them grew at an unprecedented rate. Technological advances surpassed in one century all that had come before. But the cost has been very high, for the growth has not been sustainable because of the draw down of finite resources. In so many areas, the growth, and the material abundance it has yielded, has created environmental debts that humans will have to pay during this century if they are to make it safely and securely to 2100. This may be the greatest challenge they have ever faced.

Acknowledgments

To some extent any book reflects the contributions of many people. Because of the diversity of disciplines involved in this project, most contributors to the content, and more specifically the scientific content, have been people I do not know personally, but whose books and articles I have read. Many of these are cited in the endnotes.

I am much in debt to Professor Jonathan M. Gilligan, Senior Lecturer in Earth and Environmental Sciences at Vanderbilt University. He is an expert on global warming as well as on many environmental issues. He read my chapters on climate change, referred me to many needed sources, and identified mistakes or unclear analysis.

I did almost all my research and writing in a study within the Central Library of the Jean and Alexander Heard Library at Vanderbilt. As always, the staff of both the Central and the Science and Engineering libraries were helpful in finding or borrowing needed books.

The maps, charts, and graphs for this book derived from the sources identified below. I gratefully acknowledge these sources, and the permission to print black-and-white versions of the illustrations.

Figures 3–8 and 16 are from a publication prepared by the United Nations Department of Economic and Social Affairs for the Johannesburg Summit on Sustainable Development in 2002, *Global Challenge, Global Opportunity, Trends in Sustainable Development* (2002).

Figures 1, 2, 9, and 17 are from Worldwatch Institute, *Vital Signs 2005*, www.worldwatch.org.

Figures 10 and 12–15 are from the Intergovernmental Panel on Climate Change, *Climate Change 2001, The Scientific Basis* and *Climate Change 2001, Synthesis Report* (Cambridge, U.K.: Cambridge Univ. Press, 2001). Many of these illustrations appear in the other two volumes of *Climate Change 2001*, and in all cases in brilliant color versions.

Figure 11, a map labeled *Last Glacial Maximum*, was specially prepared by C. R. Scotese in 2006, but derived from his PALEOMAP PROJECT (www.

scotese.com). A version of this map appears on page 52 of C. R. Scotese, *Atlas of Earth History*, vol. 1, *Paleogeography* (Arlington, Texas, 2002).

Table 1, the International Union for Conservation of Nature and Natural Resources 2006 Red List of Threatened Species (www.iucnredlist.org), was downloaded on May 25, 2006.

PART ONE

The Setting and the Challenge

Humans live on a wondrous planet. No other may be like it. No other may support self-conscious forms of life. The earth is in no early danger of losing its life-supporting assets. At least, we are aware of no such danger, in spite of remote concerns about a colliding asteroid. But we do live in a period of rapid extinctions, and could in the near future face rapid changes in climate. To a greater extent than ever before, one species of life—Homo sapiens—already plays a major role in effecting changes in the earth's life-support system. In this sense, humans are not only the only species that can know about the past history of the earth, or understand the complexity of its biosphere in the present, but also are the only species able to take responsibility for its future health. In chapter 1, I offer readers a short, summative account of how the earth came to support not only primitive forms of life, but very complex forms.

In chapter 2, in very broad terms I assess the present challenges to a life-sustaining earth, and particularly an earth that can allow humans, everywhere, to live an abundant life. We already can anticipate the great squeeze. An unprecedented surge in population, and an even faster growth in human consumption, will soon increase what is already a reality for over half the earth's population—scarcities in such vital resources as productive soils, water, and energy, and so much pollution of air, water, and land as to threaten the survival of thousands of species. But the challenges vary immensely, from those faced by wealthy, high-energy, high-consumption societies to those suffered by the three-fourths of humans that live in relatively poor to very poor countries. This means that equity issues haunt all discussions of environmental problems.

Our Green Planet

The earth supports life. From all that we now know, it is the only such planet in our solar system, although it is possible that, in the past, one or more of the other eight planets, or their satellites, sustained life. It is even conceivable that life migrated to the earth from neighboring planets, with Mars the most likely candidate. It is also conceivable that living organisms reached the earth from comets or asteroids. At least a rich mixture of organic chemicals so reached the earth, and still do. In any case, the background to all environmental challenges of today is the living earth.

THE ORIGIN AND EVOLUTION OF LIFE ON EARTH

It is difficult to stipulate a definition of life that satisfies everyone, or that is useful in all contexts. But living organisms, even if with a very different, even unimaginable, chemical makeup than those on earth, may well exist on planets that circle other stars, in our own galaxy or in other galaxies. We now know, through indirect but compelling evidence, that planets circle up to 5 percent of the stars in our Milky Way galaxy, which is only one of around 100 billion galaxies. Since the likely number of stars in our universe numbers in the quadrillions, and since many stars have characteristics close to that of our sun, it would seem highly likely that other planets, perhaps millions or even billions of other planets, support life. But as yet we have no evidence of such life, and short of extraterrestrial intelligent life (organisms with a symbolic language that would allow interstellar communication), we will not soon, if ever, have any way to know about life beyond our solar system. Even in our galaxy, such communication will not be easy. The closest star to the sun is four light years away. In a reasonable limit for present electronic communication (one thousand light years), we have about 10 million stars, many comparable to our sun. Even at one thousand light years, any electronic communication might well be from intelligent beings already extinct.

The primitive earth not only provided a suitable home for early life, but it would, from that point on, be profoundly shaped by life. It is almost impossible, today, to speak about any aspect of the earth's history without implicating life, which above all created the present level of atmospheric oxygen. Even the hot gases in an erupting volcano contain carbon that once was part of living organisms. Thousands of chemical reactions involve organic molecules, including those that contribute to the weathering of rocks and the creation of soils. With the early development of photosynthesis, life began a slow process of cooling the earth's early hot temperature. It did this by absorbing carbon dioxide, in most cases temporarily in biomass, more permanently in carbon-rich deposits on the ocean floor. In these ways, and more, life itself slowly prepared a more and more hospitable environment for much more complex forms of life, all the way to mammals. Our green planet is the result. The present Mars is a likely model of an earth without life. In no literal sense is the inanimate part of the earth a living organism, but the earth as a whole is so full of life, so inseparably tied to life, that one may be inclined to so characterize it, as does James Lovelock in his highly speculative Gaia hypothesis (see chapter 10).

The influence of life on the earth had to be minimal in the first billion years after its still inexplicable beginnings. A detailed history of life on earth is beyond our knowledge, at least at present. One likely candidate for its place of origin are the deep sea vents along mid-ocean ridges. It is clear that for two billion years the only life on earth consisted of microscopic organisms, with cell-like structures that contained no nucleus (such organisms are called prokaryotes) and thus no concentrated DNA. Most were bacteria, but some in what seem almost impossible environments (super hot vents, very salty water, or very acidic water) are today classified as a separate order, the archaea. Only about 1.5 billion years ago did the first eukaryotes (organisms such as the amoeba with cellular nuclei) evolve. These were the distant progenitors of all plants and animals.

We cannot know whether early life had single or multiple origins. We do now understand how it evolved through time. Charles Darwin grasped the rather simple principle, while later geneticists have revealed the dynamics of organic change. What is essential to any definition of life is reproduction. Living organisms contain no distinctive elements. What constitutes them are certain chemicals, with carbon and hydrogen most important, organized in a pattern, an identity that continues from one generation to another. Early, prokaryotic reproduction involved a type of cloning. One organism, guided by the dispersed DNA, split into two, and so on indefinitely. Each succeeding organism copied its parent. But not always perfectly. Then as now, the old and new strands of DNA did not always match at every point. Copying errors led to small changes, or mutations. This opened the door to variation and, in times of rapid environmental change, to a sometimes rapid shift in certain traits. At times, copying mistakes made it less likely that an individual would survive. In rare cases, mutations meant that an organism had better chances of surviving or reproducing, or in a time of rapid environmental shifts, the only chance of surviving. With sexual reproduction, the recombination of strands of DNA in meiosis (the production of sperm and eggs) increased exponentially the possibility of variations from one generation to the next, but only mutations allowed completely new patterns.

Sun and Earth

Despite the seeming possibilities, or the statistical probabilities, of life elsewhere, one has to note not only the many circumstances on earth that made life possible, but even more those that made more complex forms of life possible, including mammals. So much had to be just right, and as one locates each fortunate circumstance the odds against another planet with even close to the same life-supporting traits grows exponentially.

Organisms on earth are fortunate to be near the right star. Our sun is a young to middle-aged star, still radioactive but reasonably stable. It is, in brief, a huge fusion reactor, born out of the remnants of earlier stars just over 4.5 billion years ago. It provides almost all the energy for life on earth (the small exception is the heat from beneath the earth's crust). As a late developing star in the larger universe, which we now believe began in the big bang over 13 billion years ago, it gained many heavy elements from the fusion that took place during the dramatic deaths of earlier stars (supernovas), thus implicating earlier generations of stars and galaxies in its life-supporting role. Because of the surface temperature of the sun, most of the energy that makes it to the earth is in the near middle spectrum of electromagnetic waves, with a preponderance in the narrow spectrum of visible light (visible that is to a human eye). Were the sun much hotter, it would radiate largely shorter waves, those dangerous to life (it does radiate some such energy, but not enough to overwhelm the protective barriers to shortwave radiation in our atmosphere). If the sun were an aged star, it would not be hot enough to support life on earth. By most calculations, the sun today is 25–30 percent hotter than when the earth formed, and will be hotter still in the future. Our fusion reactor has not yet started to wind down.

The earth is a very special planet. Its age may not be critical for life-support (it is around 4.5 to 4.6 billion years old), but the fact that it is a radioactive planet is necessary for the type of life that now inhabits the earth. Notably, neither of the two nearby planets—Venus and Mars—have such a radioactive core, although Mars probably had such a core, and the magnetic fields it creates, early in its history. Radioactive decay helps heat the interior of the earth. Also, the highly compressed, very hot, ferrous inner core of the earth generates both heat and electrical activity in the fluid, largely ferrous outer core, and this electrical energy and heat, joined with that produced by radiation, is transferred to the largely silicate mantle, which reaches up to the earth's crust. In a sense, the fluid outer core acts as an electrical generator, or what some call the geomagnetic dynamo. The generator effect may be increased by what seems a slower revolution of the inner core and lower outer core than for the rest of the earth. In any case, the dynamics of the outer core creates electrical currents that pervade the mantle and reach the earth's surface. These electrical currents produce the main magnetic field around the earth.

The chemical composition of the earth is critical for life-support. In the universe as a whole, the two most plentiful elements are hydrogen and helium. Not so on earth. Formed from the debris of a coalescing sun, the earth has a high proportion of heavy elements, beginning with the most prevalent, iron. It contains more than its share of elements critical to life, beginning with carbon. It is also rich in nitrogen and oxygen. Much of the early earth's hydrogen and helium probably escaped the planet's atmosphere, with the most plentiful surviving hydrogen locked up in water (at present, the only element to escape from our atmosphere is hydrogen, but this loss may be balanced by the hydrogen in the water present in incoming meteors).

The earth has at least its share of other life-supporting elements, such as sulphur, phosphorus, potassium, and calcium. But it would be the hydrogen and carbon, and a critical medium, water, that made the type of life we know on earth possible, whether it originated on earth or not. Water is a wonderful medium, lighter when frozen than as a liquid, thus floating on the oceans. If ice were heavier, most of the oceans would have gradually frozen over, and the earth would have been too cold for life, not just because of all that ice, but because the icy surface would have reflected so much solar energy back into space.

The varied relationships between the sun and earth are critical to life. Life does not depend on any set distance between a star and a planet. Distance is a covariable along with orbit, axial orientation, speed of revolution, and above all with atmosphere. But given the earth's atmosphere, the sun is the perfect distance from the earth, allowing a mean earth temperature consistent with a preponderance of liquid water. Even the placement of other planets around the sun, and particularly the large gaseous planets far out from the earth, helped make life possible on earth, for they, particularly Jupiter, have enough gravity to pull most asteroids and comets away from paths that would otherwise allow them to bombard the earth with life-extinguishing force.

The orbit is critical. The earth has only a slightly elliptical orbit, which gradually changes in its eccentricity over a cycle of ninety-five thousand years, which means the sun's distance from the earth varies only slightly from year to year (only 3 million miles around the average of 93 million). The slight shifts in the amount of the sun's energy received by the earth may trigger major climate changes, but in itself this eccentricity does not change surface temperatures even by $1\,°C$.

The rapid revolution of the earth on its axis (or the length of the day) is also a critical variable. A much slower revolution, given the existing distance and exiting atmosphere, would at least considerably reduce the inhabitable portion of the earth, for a slower revolution would lead to much colder nights and hotter days. Such a change is inevitable in the distant future, for the earth's spin has gradually slowed from the time of its origin. The faster revolution that prevailed in the distant past minimized the temperature change from night to day, and with this the differential between day and night temperatures on the earth's surface, which meant lower wind speeds and less severe storms.

The earth has a life-enhancing, and only slightly varying, axial inclination (from 21.8° to 24.4°, but now approximately 23.5°). This is the degree to which the axis departs from perpendicular to the flow of energy from the sun. We now believe an early collision between the young earth and a smaller planet not only created this inclination, but also resulted in an exploding mass that coalesced as our moon. The inclination causes the seasons and allows a larger proportion of the earth's surface to be conducive to life. Were the inclination greater, the seasons would be more extreme as the sun would annually move to higher latitudes. With less inclination, the tropics would be much hotter, the high latitudes much colder.[1]

PLATE TECTONICS

The earth has a clearly demarcated crust. It rests on top of the mantle. The crust includes a relatively thin layer of rock underneath oceans, and a deeper layer of lighter rock in land areas. Sections of this crust, which we call plates, move about on the surface of the mantle at a glacial pace, but over millions of years such movement has led to major changes in the location of both continents and oceans. In areas where moving plates converge, the enormous force pushes the surface of the crust upward (folds it) into mountains or more gently elevates large expanses of land (warps it). Converging ocean plates, being heavier, push beneath continental plates. Part of the subducted crust of oceans is thus gradually absorbed back into the molten mantle. But the convergence creates cracks or fault lines in both the ocean and continental crusts, allowing magma to push upward in a process called vulcanism, which helps create new land. In comparatively rare cases, continental plates crunch into each other, creating the most dramatic folding and thus the highest mountains. Today, this is occurring only where the Asian subcontinent (or the Indo-Australian plate) pushes against the Eurasian plate, as dramatically illustrated by the still-rising Himalayan chain. The Indian subcontinent is moving north at the comparatively rapid rate of six and a half feet each century. At other places, large plates separate, creating rift valleys and lakes or new inland extensions of oceans and seas. Along oceans, land continually erodes into the sea, but at approximately the same rate as new land forms from the deposits of rivers (deltas) and from vulcanism. Thus the surface of the earth reveals a complex, dynamic equilibrium of competing forces.

Today, the starting point for understanding the crust of the earth is what we call plate tectonics. This was not true even sixty years ago. Until the twentieth century, if anything seemed certain to geologists it was the stability of continents. Yet, historians have discovered a surprising number of geographers and geologists who noted the jigsaw-like puzzle fit of the eastern hump of Brazil with the large indentation in the western coast of Africa. A few even speculated that the past convergence of the two continents explained the peopling of the Americas. But no one had a provable explanation of how the two continents separated, and when and how quickly. Until the nineteenth century, given the widespread belief in the foreshortened chronology supported by the Christian Bible, it had to be a very rapid shift, perhaps even instantaneous and miraculous, or a god's way of dispersing humans across the whole earth. In 1912, a German geologist, Alfred Wegener, argued that the present continents had drifted apart in the past (continental drift), from the breakup of a huge super continent, which he called Pangaea. He gained almost no support for this theory, and faced ridicule as late as his death in 1930. One problem he faced was how to account for such continental movement. What could push whole continents about?

After World War II new information about the ocean floor finally vindicated Wegener. The discovery of the mid-Atlantic ridge, and the dating of rock near it, revealed that nearby rock was of very recent origin, and the age of more distant rock proportionate to the distance from this ridge. The crust in the mid-Atlantic was slowly separating. Later observations of such mid-ocean ridges revealed frequent vents (small extrusions of heated gases) along the separating ridges, and the gradual filling in of new crust. The lay of crystals in magma helped date their origin, since we now can date past reversals in the magnetic field that orients such crystals as they cool. This proved that many continents were now thousands of miles from where they had been in the past. Such paleomagnetism allowed geologists to map past continental movements. Even here Wegener had been prescient, for as recently as about 200 million years ago most (but not all) of the landmass of the earth clustered together, and this at the beginning of the separation that slowly created the Atlantic Ocean.

The movement of continents meant that the earth's crust is not of a piece, but cut up into many large plates and some smaller ones. The major plates are as large as continents or oceans. At the juncture of plates are major cracks or fault lines, with many minor fault lines in the interior of plates. The plates seem to be in continuous motion, although not at the

same speed. These discoveries revolutionized geology. So much that had
been puzzling was now clear, including the location of areas of intense
vulcanism (on or near plate boundaries), the dynamics of earthquakes
(along plate boundaries or major faults), and the source of the energy
that led to major crustal folding and thus mountain ranges.

Why do the plates move? The only persuasive theory is that they are
pushed by convection currents in the mantle. That is, uneven heating,
caused by movement and friction near the core, or by localized radioac-
tivity in the mantle, lead to up-swelling currents in the semi-fluid mantle, much as water boils in a pot. These currents, in areas of the most
intense boiling, push the surface plates in patterns that have obviously
shifted through time. It is likely that convection patterns, in the future,
will bring the continents back together. Over the last billion years, several
such major shifts are now identifiable.

The convective currents that redistribute continents also nourish
earthquakes and vulcanism. Magma pushes up near the surface, or breaks
through completely in volcanoes. This thermal activity creates new land
at a pace that matches the loss of land by erosion or by the plunging
downward of plates (subduction) at points of convergence. More important, if the earth were a radioactively dead planet, without an internal
source of electricity, uneven heating, and convective currents, it would
have a different atmosphere and very different magnetic fields. Without
vulcanism, the continents would eventually dissolve in the oceans, leaving no land. In a sense, one secret of life on earth is both the heat within
and the sun's heat without, and how they mesh in the earth's crust.[2]

OUR MAGNETIC SCREENS

Even more critical for life than what happens inside the earth is what surrounds the surface of the planet—its magnetic fields and its atmosphere.
Moving electrical charges (moving relative to a stationary observer) create magnetic fields. The earth is surrounded by a very complex array of
magnetic fields, and these in turn have a vital relationship to life on earth.
It is impossible, in a short space, and without a background of very technical knowledge, to describe the causes, the lay, and the effects of magnetic fields. In fact, much of this knowledge is very recent in origin, and
much is still very speculative. It is now generally accepted that the earth's
main magnetic field, the one dominant at the surface and in the lower

atmosphere, is almost entirely produced by electrical currents (most concentrated around the equator) generated by the geomagnetic dynamo referred to above. Above the main magnetic field, and in the most minuscule remnants of our atmosphere (in the ionosphere or thermosphere, from sixty to six hundred miles above the earth) there are other sources of electricity and at least three other magnetic fields, none of which has the rather stable, dipolar (meaning two poles of opposite charge) lay of the main field. These ionospheric fields deflect, or trap, most of the deadly shortwave radiation that enters the earth's atmosphere. Without their screening effect, most types of life that we have on earth would be impossible, including all surface life.

The dipolar orientation of the main magnetic field raises critical issues that may relate to human welfare and survival. This magnetic field is similar, in its lay, to that of a bar magnet near the earth's axis, with a positive charge on one end, and a negative on the other. In the short term, this magnetic field is fairly stable, but year by year the magnetic axis, which is today about $11°$ of inclination away from the geographical axis, moves about. Practically, this means that the two magnetic poles move, requiring annual adjustments in compasses. The effects of such movement on life are not clear, if there are any at all.

This is not true for what has happened many times in the past—a reversal of poles. At present, and for the last 775,000 years, the positive pole has been at the south. It may soon reverse. Such reversals occur at irregular intervals, with most past reversals occurring at an average of about every 200,000 years. Thus, a reversal is now overdue. No one can yet fully explain such reversals, but only speculate that something about the core, or its geomagnetic dynamo, may be responsible. The past changes are revealed in the residual magnetism in rocks, and in the orientation of crystals in basalt and other forms of lava. It is such crystals that provided the clinching proof of continental drift, for we can date the movement of continents by such crystalline orientation, given our knowledge, from other sources, of past shifts in the magnetic field. A reversal could have a major impact on life, although we have no proof of such during past reversals (all before the emergence of Homo sapiens). It seems that a reversal takes place during a period of up to five thousand years. The force of the main, dipolar magnetic field first weakens, with various anomalies and at times multiple poles to replace the normal dipolar orientation (a compass would go crazy). After a period with little or no magnetism, the magnet reforms with an opposite orientation. Presently, the field is weakening, suggesting that we are in the early stages of what will, possibly within a few hundred or thousand years, be another reversal. This is a matter of some concern. In the period when the dipolar field is weakest or not present, more shortwave particles will reach the earth's surface, for the main magnetic field is a final screen for such particles. This does not mean that all life would be endangered, for the ionosphere will still trap most such particles. But it would mean increased radiation, with a likelihood of more cancer, possibly major genetic effects, and the likely extinction of some species. In other words, it may pose a problem for humans comparable to present ozone depletion, a thinning which, because of chemical reactions in the stratosphere, it will enhance. The reversal is a problem beyond human control. At present, no one has identified any correlation between such reversals and other phenomenon, such as rapid climate change.

It is easier to seek such climate correlates in periodic disturbances or storms that impact ionospheric magnetic fields. In truth, the ionosphere is never completely stable, only more stable at some periods than others. Floods of solar particles (the solar wind) are continuously interacting with upper atmospheric particles, creating ionized and deadly forms of radiation. The first interaction of the earth's magnetic fields with these incoming particles occurs well outside of what most consider the upper reaches of the earth's atmosphere, or even conventional definitions of the ionosphere. Some now refer to this zone as a magnetosphere. Here, as if trapped between magnetic fields, charged particles accumulate, with greatest concentration over the equator, and thinning toward each pole (in a sense, they bounce back and forth between the stronger magnetic fields over each pole). First identified with satellites, these are now called the Van Allen radiation belt. This zone of trapped and intensely radioactive particles is not sharply limited, either in space or altitude, but does display two zones of highest concentration. They are roughly between ten thousand and twenty-three thousand miles, with the most intense concentration toward the lower height, and the next most intense toward the top. This makes up what could be called two doughnuts, each very dangerous to any space explorers. The lower belt may be unique in capturing cosmic rays, the shortest and most deadly form of radiation, and in this case radiation mostly from the larger universe, not the sun. The magnetic field converts such radiation into electrons and protons, and traps most of the heavier protons. The outer belt contains particles that originate from the sun or the earth's atmosphere, most being ionized forms of helium. These belts, however dangerous to humans who enter them, form what is probably the first, and maybe the most important, screen that protects the earth from harmful radiation, although the role of the Van Allen belts joins with the screening that takes place among other magnetic fields in the ionosphere and the screening out of ultraviolet waves by ozone in the stratosphere (see chapter 5 for a full discussion of the role of ozone).

Magnetic storms result largely from the solar wind. This is not a type of electromagnetic radiation, but particles (largely protons) emitted from the sun at great speeds (but far less than the speed of light). These particles collide with the earth's magnetic fields, creating shock waves. The source of the most intense bombardment of particles are solar flares, or very hot spots that develop on the sun's surface. At the point of a flare, the surface heat of the sun soars from $11,000°$ to 3.6 million°F. Visual sunspots result from localized cooling on the sun's surface caused by the clouds of gas and the magnetic storms that accompany flares. Other bursts of the solar wind result from thin areas of the sun's surface (solar holes). It is the more intense bursts of solar wind that not only shift and distort global magnetic fields, but spur more localized and often very intense disturbances (substorms). It is the latter that humans are most aware of, in the aurora (northern and southern lights), in increased radiation at the earth's surface, in radio interference, even in distortions of electrical transmission. Fortunately, the most intense solar activity is periodic and somewhat predictable. What is not known is whether the roughly eleven-year cycles were similar in the past. These magnetic storms may, because of the increased radiation, pose a danger to human health, but the extent of the danger is not clear. At present, some speculate that global warming might, in part, be caused by increased solar radiation tied to solar flares. Any increase in the frequency or the intensity of such storms would, quite clearly, increase temperatures on the earth's surface.[3]

The Earth's Atmosphere

The earth's atmosphere is critical to life. By atmosphere, I mean the gases that exist above the earth's surface, and the fluids (water droplets in fog and clouds, and various other droplets, with sulfates most prominent) and solids (ice crystals, soot, pollen, spores) suspended in these gases.

It is impossible to set any limits to the outer reaches of the atmosphere. Hydrogen atoms are present not only beyond the magnetic belts, but also in interplanetary space. Above about sixty miles, or the top of the meso- sphere (thirty-five to sixty miles), is the ionosphere. Here the gases are in the form of individual atoms, and so thin as to have almost no effect on spaceships. Yet, the outer parts of our atmosphere, as indicated above, are critical to life. Even more so is the atmosphere closest to the earth's surface, or the troposphere (the air up to an average of about ten miles, and marked by a gradual cooling of temperatures with altitude) and the stratosphere (a layer of thinning air, from about ten to thirty-five miles, where temperatures increase with altitude, largely because of the absorp- tion of ultraviolet light by ozone). All weather phenomena occur in the troposphere.

The early earth had an atmosphere that, at least, allowed life to de- velop. But in most ways it was not very congenial to life. It was very different than today. It was largely made up of carbon dioxide, methane, hydrogen sulfide, and ammonia. It was probably less dense or heavy than today. It included almost no oxygen. Without oxygen, there could not be any ozone, a molecular form of oxygen. Thus, at the beginning of life, few if any forms of life could withstand the ultraviolet bombardment at the surface of oceans or land. But nonetheless this early atmosphere was essential to life, because of its effect on climate. It helped keep the earth warm, or almost too warm. The carbon dioxide and methane, joined with water vapor, intercepted and absorbed and reflected back longwave radiation from the earth's surface, thus warming the nearby atmosphere and the earth's surface. Without this greenhouse effect, most solar energy would have returned to space, and the earth would have steadily cooled until all water froze (think of Mars). But it screened almost too well, with the earth much too hot (possibly near the boiling point of water) for most forms of life as we know it today. If this early level of greenhouse gases had not diminished, the gradual increase in solar radiation might have eventually evaporated all the oceans, and life, even if already present, might not have survived (think of Venus).

Nitrogen is the main component of the present atmosphere, but probably not so at the beginning, when carbon dioxide was most likely the most plentiful gas. Nitrogen now makes up over 78 percent of the stable and uniform gases (this calculation does not include nongaseous suspended components or such variable gases as water vapor and carbon dioxide). Nitrogen is a very stable gas, and within the range of normal surface temperatures on earth an inert gas (it does not chemically interact with other elements or compounds). But it does largely account for the weight of the air, and thus air pressure. Nitrogen gas does react chemically at high temperatures, forming various compounds. Thus, lightning in storms converts nitrogen into nitrates, which mix with falling rain and help enrich the soil. Certain organisms also interact with nitrogen, in some cases releasing nitrogen from compounds (the probable source of most atmospheric nitrogen), in other cases converting nitrogen into nitrates (as do the nodules of nitrogen-fixing bacteria on legumes). Through artificial means, humans use heat to convert atmospheric nitrogen into nitrates used in explosives and fertilizers.

Argon, the third major ingredient of air (just less than 1 percent), is also inert. Not so the second largest component, oxygen (almost 21 percent). It readily forms chemical bonds with many elements and compounds, is a necessary support for combustion, and is also a necessary component of life (but not always as atmospheric oxygen). At least a hundred minor gases account for less than 0.01 percent of stable gases. Some of these are important, for they are greenhouse gases (see chapter 8).

The two most concentrated, and important, variable gases are water vapor and carbon dioxide. In various ways, they are critical to life on earth. Water vapor is necessary for condensation and precipitation, and thus a part of the vital hydrologic cycle. It remains in the atmosphere for only a few days, is highly variable in concentration (as anyone who suffers high humidity is aware), and can make up as much as 4 percent of the atmosphere in hot and humid climates (warm air can hold more water vapor). Carbon dioxide is necessary for plant metabolism, and, next to water vapor, is the most important greenhouse gas, although in too high concentrations it is deadly for animals (by displacing oxygen). It varies in concentration over time, but today is exceptionally high, at least in comparison to the last 120,000 years, making up over one-third of 1 percent of the atmosphere. Suspended aerosols and particles are also critical, for some of these provide the needed nucleus for raindrops. Many dust particles have a human origin, as do a large proportion of the sulfates that contribute to acid rain.

Oxygen now seems a stable component of the atmosphere. But free oxygen is decreasing, although in comparison to its volume in minute amounts each year. The cause is the increased burning of fossil fuels (the oxygen used in combustion combines with carbon to create carbon dioxide). When the earth first formed, over 4.5 billion years ago, solar debris fused together through gravity, and perhaps only fortuitously settled into a stable orbit around the sun (a balancing of gravity and centrifugal force). Other planets were also forming, the solar environment was turbulent, and meteorites and comets continuously bombarded the new planets. Life, as we know it, could not have existed in the first 600 million years, but fortunately for what came later, the maturing earth very early, after its gigantic collision with a smaller planet, gained a solid crust and increasing amounts of water (vulcanism freed water from deep within the earth, while meteors and comets brought water from outer space). Early life had to originate underground or deep in oceans. Only life itself would eventually produce the present level of oxygen, and with it the stratospheric ozone needed to make the surface of the earth habitable.

Life on earth began comparatively early, almost as soon as the deadly meteorite bombardment slackened, or possibly as early as 3.9 billion years ago. We have no actual fossils of microscopic life going back this far, but early rock formations contain organic chemicals that have all the distinctive characteristics of a living source. Most early life found its home in water, primarily the oceans, and would remain water-bound until comparatively recently, or to about 500 million years ago. Only then was enough oxygen present to support animal life and to provide ozone protection. By 2.7 billion years ago, or possibly much earlier, ocean organisms had begun to use light (photosynthesis) to separate the hydrogen and oxygen in water. A product of this process was free oxygen, which bubbled up from the oceans. By 2 billion years ago, the atmosphere contained increasing amounts of oxygen, although not enough to sustain combustion. Soon, some still-microscopic ocean organisms became dependent on free oxygen. They were the prototype of later animals. By 1.5 billion years ago, organisms with cell nuclei (eukaryotes), containing concentrated strands of DNA, had developed, and soon thereafter began sexual reproduction. But only in the immediate pre-Cambrian era (around 700 million years ago) did multicelled organisms evolve (worms, sponges, jellyfish). Then, in the Cambrian era (570 million years ago), life radiated out in a rich profusion of multicelled organisms, or the progenitors of most later fungi, plants, and animals, but most still remained in the oceans. With better ozone screening, such organisms began moving to the surface and on land after 500 million years ago. Land plants, insects, even early reptiles were just ahead. In the midst of the age of dinosaurs, the first small mammals evolved (by 250 million years ago), or the progenitors of humans. From the abundance of plant life, which depended upon atmospheric carbon dioxide, issued more and more oxygen, with the quantity in the atmosphere eventually reaching today's level.[4]

The earth's atmosphere is just right for life, given the distance from the sun and the quantity of solar radiation that reaches the earth. Over half the sun's energy at the earth's surface is visible light, a narrow part of the total radiation spectrum. Visible light is just on the shortwave side of this spectrum. Most, but not all, of these short waves are able to penetrate the atmosphere. Slightly over half of solar radiation is reflected back into space (by clouds or white surfaces), or absorbed by the gases in the upper atmosphere, helping heat them. The light waves that penetrate heat the surface of the earth, but the warmed earth radiates heat waves (infrared light) back toward space, releasing too much heat to allow for a life-supporting temperature were it not for a final magical aspect of our atmosphere. Water vapor and dozens of minor gases (carbon dioxide is the most important of these) are transparent to most shorter light waves, but not to the long heat waves radiated up from the earth. Thus, largely in the middle and upper troposphere, these gases absorb these heat waves and, like a warm blanket, radiate a part of this heat back to the surface, further warming it.

Except in areas with thick clouds, which are like mirrors and reflect a large percentage of sunlight, the lower atmosphere during the daytime transmits the sun's energy that has not been absorbed, scattered, or reflected by the upper atmosphere. No more than 10 percent of the heating of the atmosphere is a direct result of absorbed sunlight. The other 90 percent of warming reflects the direct warming of the surface by solar radiation, plus the heat waves radiated back to the surface by greenhouse gases. This surface heating is all important. It is an uneven heating. Dark soil or vegetation absorbs more light rays, and heats more rapidly. Light surfaces reflect most of the energy, and heat slowly if at all (snow is an excellent reflector). Land warms more rapidly than water, particularly deep areas of water. Water absorbs most solar energy only when the sun is overhead or at a high angle; it reflects most slanted light waves. When the energy does penetrate the surface, the water is largely transparent to light, and thus the light waves penetrate deeply, warming a much thicker layer than it can on opaque land. Thus, a given area of surface water heats less.

Water moves and mixes, thus further dissipating heat. It takes up to five times as much energy to heat a unit of water as for most soil or rock. This means that the 71 percent of the earth's surface that is now covered by water (it covered less during the height of the late Wisconsin glacier) makes a great thermostat. In the summer months, ocean water may gain only a fifth of the heat of nearby land. The reverse is true in the winter, when it radiates five times less heat. Thus, the variation of water temperatures from winter to summer, in the oceans, may be only ten degrees, while at the same time land differentials are as high as fifty degrees or more. If it were not for moving currents in the oceans, which help equalize temperatures between tropical and arctic areas, and the movement of wind over oceans and onto the land, the land areas of the earth would be much hotter in the summer and much colder in the winter. The greatest extremes of temperature thus exist at the heart of large, temperate zone continental landmasses, those least affected by oceans.[5]

The unequal heating of earth surfaces accounts for regional differences in air pressure and for moving air, or wind. Wind, plus unequal heating and bottom sea topography, help create ocean currents. The complex, often vast circulation patterns of wind and ocean waters affect the various climates on earth. But the energy behind all this is always from the sun. (See chapter 7 for a fuller discussion of climate.)

THE MAGIC OF CHLOROPHYLL

Why did it take over 3 billion years for life on earth to move from single-celled organisms to all the complex plants and animals of today, all of which evolved in only 500 million years? In a relatively brief period of less than 100 million years, in the early Cambrian, all present orders of life radiated out in all directions, creating an ecology almost as rich as what we know today. Before Darwin, and before we knew very much about pre-Cambrian life, it was easy for those in the Semitic religious tradition to posit a creative act by a god as the miraculous source of all forms of life, even when they conceded a subsequent amplification through natural processes. What is now clear is that it was pre-Cambrian life that, over a very long time, finally created the environment needed to support more complex eukaryotes like ourselves. That is, such new and more complex forms of life needed a cooler earth (less CO_2 in the atmosphere), enough free oxygen to support animal metabolism, and, for surface life, enough stratospheric ozone to screen out most ultraviolet light. Of course, much more is involved than this. But such changes were necessary conditions for the Cambrian explosion. And at the heart of all these three modifications of the earth's environment was one complex but rather small organic molecule (or four very closely related molecules). We call it chlorophyll.

We do not know when the first chlorophyll formed, probably from precursor molecules that were light sensitive. We think that the earliest (and still prominent) photosynthesizers were cyanobacteria. They first turned parts of the ocean green, and they still contribute much of the oxygen released into the atmosphere each year. Their origin may go back 3 billion years or more. Before photosynthesis, bacteria had gained all their energy not directly from the sun, but chemically from minerals that contained oxygen. For all early bacteria, which lived in an atmosphere without oxygen, any free oxygen would have been a deadly enemy, as it still is. Such bacteria today live in oxygen-free, or nearly oxygen-free environments (an example are the bacteria that convert nitrogen into nitrates in air-tight nodules on the roots of legumes). But free oxygen was no problem at the beginning of photosynthesis. It did not yet exist, but was a product of the complex process fueled by photons of light. In time, the process led to present levels of oxygen, but charting the amount at any time in the distant past is all but impossible. Note that until oxygen became at least 10 percent of the atmosphere, combustion was impossible. If it rises above 25 percent, fire is an ever-present danger, and by 35 percent almost all hydrocarbons will spontaneously combust and terrestrial life will become impossible. Note also that until life-created hydrocarbons accumulated there was only minute amounts of fuel for combustion. It is in this sense that life created the foundations of most present energy use—the controlled burning of hydrocarbons, from the sugars burned in the bodies of animals to the gasoline burned in the pistons of automobile engines.

The most important chlorophyll molecules are attached to the walls of bacteria or, in multicelled plants, to leaf cells. These 120-atom molecules are umbrella shaped, with a flexible stem. They collect photons of light (two per second) and feed them into a reaction center (like a small factory) in the cell. They absorb most of the light spectrum, except green, which yields the color of chlorophyll. In the reaction center, with other chlorophyll molecules playing a role, the solar energy is used to break water into its components of hydrogen and oxygen, which is no mean feat. Left over from this process are free electrons, which provide the energy for the synthesis that follows. Also unneeded at this point is much of the freed oxygen, which is in fact very dangerous to anaerobic life, which can live only in an oxygen-free environment. The cell uses the preserved energy to fuse carbon dioxide, available from air or water, with hydrogen to create carbohydrates $(C_6H_{12}O_6)$, which in turn are the main source of energy for the organism. The same energy also creates the amino acids and proteins needed for body structures. Thus, photosynthesizers absorb carbon dioxide, use the carbon as the main structural component of often very complex hydrocarbon molecules, and expel oxygen. Such photosynthesis, for the first time, made possible new forms of microscopic life. As atmospheric oxygen increased to a certain level, in about 200 million years, the first oxygen-using organisms evolved, the progenitors of later animal life. They complemented the photosynthesizers by absorbing oxygen and respiring carbon dioxide.

Atmospheric oxygen created a hazard for photosynthesizing microbes and later plants. The new, free oxygen easily combined with some of the carbon in cells, or a type of plant respiration, which limited the amount of carbon that could go into sugars and enzymes. At present, most plants cycle about a third of the carbon dioxide used in photosynthesis back into the atmosphere. Present levels of oxygen and carbon dioxide reflect a near equilibrium between photosynthesis and respiration. Note that any severe reduction of photosynthesizers, and particularly those in the ocean, could gradually lower the level of oxygen in the atmosphere, while global warming could speed up photosynthesis and increase atmospheric oxygen unless it led to an increase in animals that consume oxygen.[6]

THE CYCLES THAT SUSTAIN LIFE

Recycling is a vital aspect of life. In fact, it is necessary for the abundance and diversity of life-forms now on earth. For example, without cycling, the earth would not retain enough available carbon in the form of carbon dioxide. If 99.5 percent of the carbon dioxide used in photosynthesis and converted into organic hydrocarbons was not, through the work of worms, fungus, and bacteria, consumed and recycled back into the atmosphere, the process would have soon exhausted the supply of carbon dioxide in the atmosphere. As it is, only 0.05 percent of the carbon dioxide involved in photosynthesis is permanently removed from the atmosphere. It is eventually deposited on the bottom of the ocean as carbonates or, when blended with calcium-rich shells, as calcium carbonate or limestone. If all had become rock, life would, at best, have settled into a limited niche, drawing energy either from chemicals (as along deep sea vents) or from a very limited photosynthesis fed by the annual net gain of usable carbon dioxide contributed by vulcanism. Even the limited life supported by this natural input would have been precarious, because an atmosphere stripped of most of its carbon dioxide, a major greenhouse gas, might be too cold to support any life. Also, the oxygen contributed by this limited photosynthesis would not have reached the threshold of combustion and animal metabolism. We would not be here.

Here in such cycling we confront one of the hundreds of factors that sustain complex forms of life, or what has always seemed to many people the contrivances of a divine mind. For scarce elements needed by life, such as nitrogen (in the form of usable nitrates), the cycling ratio is even higher than for carbon (at least five hundred atoms of nitrogen used by plants are recycled back into water or air for every one sequestered). Without nitrogen-fixing bacteria, mostly in ocean waters, there would not be enough nitrates for the present volume of life on earth. For elements with a more plentiful supply, such as phosphorus, the ratio is only forty-six to one, while for calcium, which is abundant, the ratio is one to one, with little or no recycling. Human-induced changes in the supply of the different elements or nutrients required for life can alter a whole community of organisms. The use of fertilizer, to increase yields, and to maintain yields year after year, is one example. Another, perhaps more momentous example is the rapid using up of fossil fuels, which has led to major shifts in the earth's atmosphere.

The earth is the only green planet that we know about, because it is the only known planet with life. In thousands of ways, life and the inorganic part of the earth interact, mutually shaping each other. As I have emphasized, life has helped shape our atmosphere, and various forms of cycling maintain it at its present near-equilibrium. Life vitally influences climate, and even local changes in weather. Life enormously speeds up the mechanical and chemical weathering of rocks, which creates the base of soils, while living organisms are a critical component of productive soils. Microorganisms insure the decay of most organic matter, including human waste. All our fossil fuels are a deposit of past life. Less obvious, life even provides some of the components of the magma extruded by volcanoes.

Today, the role of life in shaping the earth's evolution has taken on a new aspect. Of all the interactions between life and inorganic matter, the most extensive now involves purposeful actions by humans, the only self-conscious form of life. Never before has one species had such enormous control over natural processes. What this may mean for the future, what major environmental problems human actions have already created, is the subject of the rest of this book.[7]

Population, Consumption, and the Environment

A lmost any consideration of the earth's present health, or its prospects during the next century, has to begin with the human population. The doubling of the world's population between 1960 and 2000, the 6.5 billion people on earth in 2006, and the prospect of 9 billion by 2050 raise innumerable issues about available resources, about the level of pollution and waste, about massive extinctions, and about the quality of human life in crowded cities. Countries with nearly stable or even declining populations do not face some of these problems, but these are the very countries with the highest levels of consumption, resource use, and emissions. They also have economies that are predicated on a continued growth in living standards. The pressures on the earth thus come from both directions, from the multiplying poor and the indulgent rich.

POPULATION AND RESOURCES

It is much too early to assess with any degree of assurance the consequences of the present population explosion. Such a new surge of population growth is not new, but its pace has been unprecedented. The first surge may have begun even before the evolution of Homo sapiens, when humanoids first learned to control fire. The second surge in population began when humans moved from hunting and gathering to the domestication of animals and to the cultivation of crops. The present surge was only the climax of a more gradual expansion of population in the modern era, particularly in the nineteenth century. What changed is that after

1950 so many trend lines turned sharply upward. One example is what happened to agriculture in the developed countries, and particularly in the United States, where productivity almost doubled from 1950 to 1970 because of increased uses of chemicals for fertilizer and pest control, new and more productive varieties of crops, and the use of fossil fuels to power larger and more efficient machines. The green revolution spread. Since 1970 the world's production of food has more than doubled. Without this agricultural revolution, the earth simply could not feed the present population, and in a sense is not even feeding it well in the present (over 800 million people are hungry because they have to survive at less than an optimum level of nutrition).

After past introductions of new technologies, the subsequent growth of population soon leveled off. In effect, larger populations eventually probed the existing limits of subsistence. Will the present population explosion soon level off? Obviously, the growth rate cannot continue at present levels, and is already slowing in most countries, with worldwide annual growth rates down from 2.1 percent in 1970 to 1.14 percent in 2004 (see figures 1 and 2). Even the 9 billion expected by 2050 reflects more than a 50 percent decrease in the rate of growth from that of the last half of the twentieth century. In 2003, in the wake of the AIDS epidemic, the United Nations Population Division lowered its median estimate for 2050 from 9.3 to 8.9 billion. But in its 2004 revision, its medium projected 2050 population is back up to 9.1 billion. Even 9 billion people will present new problems. In fact, two-thirds of the world's population is already pressing against such intractable resource scarcities, and such environmental degradation, as to make even low incomes difficult to increase. In the poorest countries, the growth of population has pushed beyond the limits of economic growth, with a bleak future for such populations in the future. At least eighteen countries, most in central Africa, have suffered a negative per capita income growth in the last decade, and at least thirty other countries have enjoyed little if any growth, with an AIDS pandemic aggravating already desperate economic challenges.

One may object that the present problems in poor countries result not primarily from population growth, but from low productivity based on a variety of problems that are, in principle, correctable—unstable governments, a lack of educational opportunities and thus a shortage of human capital, the suppression of women, a lack of modern technology and thus great economic inefficiency, and a primitive agriculture. Demographers

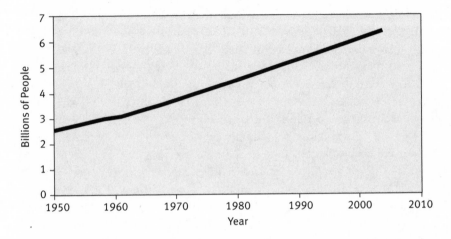

Fig. 1. World population, 1950–2004 (data from Census Bureau). (Worldwatch, *Vital Signs* 2005, 65.)

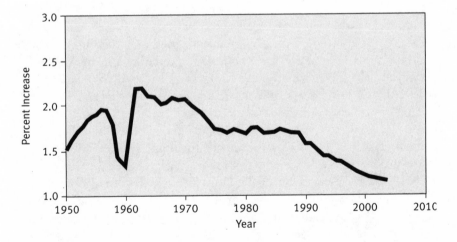

Fig. 2. Annual growth rate in world population, 1950–2004 (data from Census Bureau). (Worldwatch, *Vital Signs* 2005, 65.)

have long predicted, or at least hoped, that the same demographic transition that occurred in Europe and North America—from high mortality and birthrates, to technological changes that led to both prosperity and lowered mortality rates, to a final stage with low mortality and the present low fertility rates—would be duplicated elsewhere. But it may not be possible to duplicate such a transition in much of central Africa and southern Asia. By coercion, China has come close to such a transition to low fertility despite low per capita incomes. Elsewhere, lowered fertility rates have accompanied higher incomes, but have dropped only slowly or not at all for very low-income families. The transition has taken place only among elites. The only likely way to gain something close to replacement level fertility in much of the world seems to depend on rapid economic growth. But it is simply impossible to imagine the natural resources—water, soil, energy—that would allow these crowded countries to gain living standards comparable to those in western Europe, at least short of magical new technologies, such as cheap and plentiful fusion energy. And even if they attained such a level of prosperity, and their population leveled off at no more than a third above present levels, one wonders about the quality of life possible in such a crowded world.

From a worldwide perspective, the earth probably has enough resources to feed 9 billion people, even with present agricultural knowledge and tools. This may be small consolation to poor countries that have no way to meet their own food needs. The earth has enough fossil fuels to last for the next fifty years, even at the present annually increased rate of use. This may be small consolation to the two-thirds of the earth's population that have, so far, consumed a small share of such fuels, but have been direly affected by the global impact, including recent warming, due to the production and consumption in wealthy countries.

With the sole exception of the United States, the population of the twenty-three wealthiest countries, or those with a 2002 per capita Gross National Income (GNI) of over $15,000, or approximately 15 percent of the total, is stable or declining. The U.S. Census Bureau predicts that by 2025 all the net population increase will be in the recently poorer countries, and until then 98 percent will be in such countries (much of the other 2 percent will be in the United States). By then the 20 percent of the world population now living in what the United Nations designates as developed countries (roughly those with a present per capita GDP of over $10,000) will drop to 15 percent.

This means that present demographic imbalances will increase, with a very high percentage of people over sixty-five years old in affluent countries, a very small base of youth under fifteen, and a shortage of working-age people. In poorer countries, at present, from 40 to 50 percent of the total population is under fifteen years old, with the population over sixty ranging from only 3 to 7 percent. Over 90 percent of their dependent population is under fifteen. The huge bulge of child-bearing women in the near future assures a continued population growth for the next three decades despite declining birthrates. Conversely, in the most affluent countries the population under fifteen is only 14–20 percent, except in the United States (21.8 percent), the population over sixty from 20 to 25 percent, except in the United States (16.1 percent). The only means of correcting such demographic imbalances would be a speedup of the present outsourcing of work to underdeveloped countries and a major migration of working-age people from the underdeveloped countries into the labor-short developed world, a migration that has already had a major influence on the population of the United States.[1]

SUSTAINABLE DEVELOPMENT

Today the verbal mantra "sustainable development" is a loaded phrase. Everyone supports it, but few define it in exactly the same way or honestly probe its implications. The central idea is an old one, at least among economists. If people are to remain prosperous over a long time, they must develop and preserve their tools of production, or capital. Otherwise, they will soon use up capital and face declining returns and ultimately bankruptcy. Today, environmentalists have extended this understanding of the vital role of human-made tools to non-human-created goods, such as soil, water, air, and fuels. Economic growth, both in developed countries and poor countries, will be self-defeating if it involves a using up of nonrenewable resources, such as fossil fuels, or a steady draw down of renewable resources, such as forests or soil nutrients.

For nonrenewable resources, with fossil fuels by far the most important, humans cannot avoid a continued draw down, at least in the near future. In this case, the mandate of sustainability requires enough research and development in the present to find renewable replacements for fossil fuels before they are exhausted. Finally, humans must not emit more pollutants than the environment can safely assimilate. Today, in no area of the world are economies even close to meeting these goals. Poor countries, by necessity, are rapidly using up renewable resources, while the wealth of affluent countries depends upon the past and continuing exploitation of the world's dwindling reserve of fossil fuels.

The goals of sustainability are not new. Human concerns about scarce resources, and about environmental degradation, reach back to the dawn of civilization. Prehistoric people at times were unable to adjust to environmental change, such as cycles of drought, or pressed too strongly against scarce resources and suffered famine, population decline, and cultural bankruptcy. Few present environmental concerns are new, except those created by new technologies (such as ozone-depleting chemicals). But because of the population explosion, never before have so many environmental problems been global in their implications (global warming, massive extinctions of species, rain forest destruction, acid rain, ocean pollution) and so difficult both to understand and to mitigate.

Sustained development, to the extent that it means economic growth, poses the most difficult challenge for poorer countries. In 2004, the most wealthy twenty countries, with a per capita Gross National Income (GNI, or what was formerly called GNP) of over $25,000 in current U.S. dollars (excluding tiny nations like Lichtenstein), made up less than 15 percent of the world's population, but they controlled 72 percent of the world's total income. The United States alone accounted for 30 percent of this income. The list of the twenty most wealthy countries includes the United States and Canada, Australia, fifteen western European countries, and only Japan and Hong Kong in Asia. It includes no countries in Africa or Latin America, and no country from the former Soviet bloc. In fact, none of these areas have any countries among the additional nine nations with incomes above $15,000, or nations usually included among lists of "developed" countries. Slovenia, from the former Yugoslavia, is among the short list of six countries with incomes between $10,000 and $15,000, or countries sometimes listed as either developed or emerging.

Comparisons of per capita GNI is necessarily tied to world prices and to exchange rates among world currencies. The per capita GNI of Sierra Leone, for example, reflects how many products an average citizen could buy on the international market, and in this case very few, for its per capita GNI is only $190. On the basis of per capita GNI, around seventeen countries have incomes between $5,000 and $10,000. A few of those are growing rapidly, and may soon cross the $10,000 threshold, particularly the Czech Republic, Hungary, and Mexico. All the roughly 130 countries with incomes below $5,000, or less than an eighth of the income in the United States, are relatively poor, but among the nineteen with incomes over $3,000 are some major world powers, including Russia, Turkey, South Africa, and Brazil. The remaining 110 countries, all with incomes under $3,000, include over two-thirds of the world's total population, for China ($1,500) and India ($620) are among them, as well as such other populous countries as Indonesia, Pakistan, Bangladesh, Nigeria, and Sudan. At the very bottom are those fifty or so countries with incomes below $500.[2]

Yet, the ranking of countries on the basis of GNI can be very misleading. This is obvious when one tries to determine how anyone could survive in the approximately thirty-five countries with incomes of less than $400 a year, or in the lowest of all, Burundi, on $90 a year. In the United States, a person could not survive for a week with that income. Thus, today, the fairest and increasingly most often cited income figure is what is called the Purchasing Power Parity income, or what I will refer to as PPP. Instead of currency exchange rates, this is based on a survey of the cost of hundreds of goods and services in the local currency. It includes statistical conversions that come as close as possible to estimating the real income among countries. In poor countries, generally, the cost of local foodstuffs, and above all of human services, tends to be very low, unbelievably low when translated into dollars. In terms of local purchasing power and living standards, such currencies are drastically undervalued in exchange rates. The PPP corrects for this, and for most poor countries it is as much as five times higher than the per capita GDP. For example, in India the GDP in 2004 was only $620, but the PPP was $3,100; in booming China the GDP was $1,500, while its PPP was $5,890. At the higher incomes, the changes from GDP to PPP are small, and in some cases the PPP lower (dramatically so for Norway and Switzerland). But as one moves down the GDP, the gap between GDP and PPP becomes more pronounced.

In 2004, approximately thirty countries had a PPP over $20,000 (only twenty of these had a population of over 1 million, but notably, some tiny countries are among the most wealthy, with Luxemburg always at the top). These most affluent countries generally duplicate the present thirty countries that are members of the Organization of Economic Cooperation and Development (OCED), but not exactly, since some lower income countries (Mexico, Turkey) are in this elite organization. Twenty-two additional countries, some very small, had a PPP of over $10,000, or roughly the poverty level for a single person in the United States. This means that their living standards range from one-fourth to one-half that of the United States (which has a PPP of just under $40,000). These two groups total just over 1.222 billion, or barely 18.5 percent of the world's total population. At least most of these are generally listed as developed or industrialized countries. The exception would be a few countries that gain a high rank in incomes only because of the exportation of oil. But some countries almost always listed among industrialized or developed countries are not in the above $10,000 PPP group, and this includes Russia. Also note that much of this data is based upon the self-reporting of countries, and may slightly overestimate incomes. Also, in some nations, particularly oil-rich countries, incomes are so skewed toward a few at the top as to leave the great mass of citizens at very low incomes.

Around forty countries have a PPP of $5,000 to $10,000. This means that living standards range from one-eighth to one-fourth of those in the United States. Some of these countries are often listed as having emerging economies, for some may soon cross the threshold of $10,000 (Russia, Mexico, Brazil, Thailand, and Turkey are the best candidates). Other quite populous countries in this list (Philippines, Ukraine) are far from this goal of $10,000, as are the 1.3 billion people of China, who have PPP incomes near $6,000. These forty countries, ranging from near poor to emergent, contain 2.34 billion people, or 36 percent of the world's population (over half in China).

Almost 3 billion people have PPP incomes of under $5,000 in ninety-two countries, some very small. Whatever the euphemisms used to describe them (such as underdeveloped), those countries are simply poor. Most have little early prospects of moving above $5,000 PPP. But even here, those close to $5,000 are worlds apart from those at the lowest level. None of these aspirants are in sub-Saharan Africa. Albania, Armenia, El Salvador, and Paraguay are above $4,500, with Egypt, Guatemala, Jamaica, Jordan, Morocco, and Surinam above $4,000. India is a special case. Its 1.08 billion people make up over a third of those with incomes below $5,000. By its own accounting, its PPP had risen to $3,100 in 2004, and its annual growth rate is very high. It is conceivable that, in another decade or so, it will reach the $5,000 level. A total of forty countries have incomes between $2,000 and $5,000, while fifty-two countries are below $2,000. These make up the poorest of the poor, with thirty-two in sub-Saharan Africa, about a dozen in Asia, and only Haiti in the Western Hemisphere. The others are small island republics. Fifteen African countries are at $1,000 or below (Sierra Leone and Somalia are at the bottom at $600). The two most populous African countries—Nigeria and Ethiopia—are in this group. It is difficult to conceive of people surviving on one-fortieth the average purchasing power of Americans. Compounding the problem is that incomes in these poorest countries are often concentrated in small elites.

Average PPP levels may be very misleading if one is concerned about the overall welfare of a population. Vitally important is income distribution, or the degree of income equality. The best indicator of the general welfare of a population might be the average per capita PPP of those who suffer the lowest 20 percent of incomes. Unfortunately, income inequality is usually greater in poor countries than it is in affluent ones (see figure 3). Welfare includes several factors, some not tied to income.

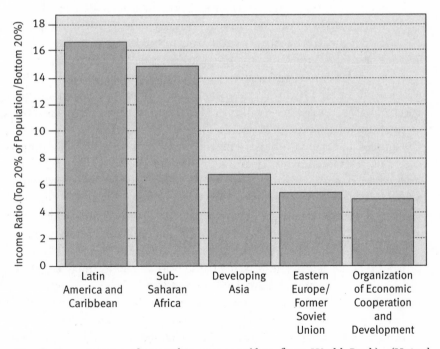

Fig. 3. Income inequality within regions (data from World Bank). (United Nations, *Global Challenge, Global Opportunity*, 7.)

These include life expectancy, low infant mortality rates, universal access to health care and education, political stability, low crime rates, access to work, gender equality, and clean air and water. In the last decade, not only has the gap between affluent and poor countries widened, but even in most industrial countries income inequality has risen at frightening rates. Worst of all, among wealthy nations, is the United States, in which, in 2000, over 30 percent of all income went to the top 10 percent, only 1.8 percent to the bottom 10 percent. This has worsened since 2000. Such income inequality is one reason why, in most attempts to measure overall welfare, the United States ranks below most western European countries.

The PPP can also miss some economic bases of a good life. Most services performed by homemakers and mothers do not make it into these accounts. Local barter transactions and black market sales (huge in some countries) are not counted. Thus, particularly in the poorest countries, even the PPP may somewhat underestimate the actual level of consumption.

In one critical way, national accounting indices almost always overstate the actual level of material welfare. This is what most concerns environmentalists. No such official estimates now include natural capital, and thus the environmental costs of production and consumption. Because of this, the present levels of income are not sustainable over the long term in most poor countries, and not even in wealthy countries without major substitutions of new types of energy and more drastic controls over pollution. Already, increasing amounts of capital and labor have to be devoted to environmental repair work, or the product of past, often reckless use of resources and the pollution of air and water. In some underdeveloped countries, if one deducted the annual loss of soil, of forest cover, and of endangered species, then the sustainable PPP might move toward zero. In highly developed and wealthy countries, such as the United States, the loss of natural capital might be only a small percentage of the total. But the lack of more specificity about such costs simply reflects the enormous difficulty of measuring the monetary value of natural capital. For example, if one assumes that global temperatures rise by $5\,^{\circ}C$ in the next century, then what will be the cost to the world economy? It could be vast, but we will not soon know enough to even come close to a firm estimate. And what should the United States, which contributes almost one-fourth of the greenhouse gases that are helping produce such warming, deduct from its present GDP in order to more realistically document its real annual income in sustainability terms? No one knows.

The United Nations maintains a System of National Accounts as part of its accounting division. In 1993, as a direct response to policies adopted at the Earth Summit in Rio in 1992, the United Nations tried to find a way to incorporate environmental costs into national accounting. This would have meant a revision in such categories as GNI or GDP. The problem was staggering in its complexity, and no revision resulted, but it did lead to a recommendation that the United Nations at least work toward such a goal and add supplemental or satellite accounts to address the environmental issue.[3] Since then, economists have developed various strategies to gain a new Sustainable National Income index.[4] In September 2005, the World Bank suggested that national accounts include certain natural resources, which often make up the largest share of wealth in poor countries. Unfortunately, it is these countries that are most rapidly exporting, or using up, their natural assets.

Few would deny that the present national accounting is outdated and misleading, but so far the problem has remained a very complex, highly technical, academic enterprise, with various contenting factions. The most limited addition would involve only natural resources that already have market prices attached to them, such as minerals, oil, and even soil. China, facing enormous environmental challenges, is the first country that is now planning a type of national accounting that includes environmental assets. The larger problem is accounting for life-supporting resources that are still part of the commons, such as oceans, streams, lakes, or the atmosphere. Also, how could a system of national accounts include global environmental costs. How could the United States calculate, and how should it pay for, its contribution to the depletion of the ozone layer, to ocean pollution, even to the acid rain that falls on Canadian forests and lakes? How could wealthy importing countries account for the environmental degradation they cause in the underdeveloped producing country? What is to keep wealthy countries from importing products that create environmental hazards abroad or exporting their own toxic wastes? Such issues implicate a system of international accounts that would, in proportionate ways, have to be incorporated into national accounts, and one can sense the level of international conflict that might ensue if the United Nations or regional agencies tried to implement such a system.

Equally difficult is any way of pricing the esthetic benefits of pristine forests and lakes, the opportunity to visit wilderness areas, the ability to enjoy threatened species of birds. One might poll citizens and find out how much they would be willing to pay in taxes each year to preserve such amenities, and on this basis give a monetary value to them. Or one might assume that present governmental resource regulations and reserves, and the costs that go with them, roughly indicate the value its citizens place on such amenities. But such measurements are meaningless in poor countries that cannot afford such taxes or cannot enforce environmental regulations. To the extent that the people of one country value habitats and biodiversity in other areas of the world, particularly poor areas, they should be willing to contribute to the foreign aid needed for their preservation.[5]

THE SPECIAL ENVIRONMENTAL CHALLENGES FACED BY POOR COUNTRIES

For the vast majority of humans, who live at a near subsistence level, such issues as sustainability must seem remote. Their great imperative has to be higher rates of productivity and increased consumption, whatever the long-term environmental costs. Given the large and usually still growing population in poor countries, this is an intimidating goal. Already, the assaults on local environments have too often reached crisis proportions, so much so that any sustained growth in incomes seems almost impossible. Yet, the assets available, in human capital, in sources of financing, in available tools of production, are meager at best, save for India and China, both of which have a large, university-trained workforce. Although most poor countries have tried to deal with environmental problems, and in some cases have had to do so, they have lacked the resources, or the political legitimacy, to enforce environmental legislation.

It is difficult to see how poor countries can alleviate most of these problems in the near, or even the distant, future. These run the gamut of environmental pressures: depleted fuels, eroded land, disappearing forest cover, threatened or already extinct species, uncontrolled urban growth, polluted air and water, and a scarcity of potable water or water for irrigation. Such poor countries have few tools to cope with such problems. Burdened by debts, by low market prices for exportable commodities, by political instability, they are all but helpless without major subsidies from wealthy countries. In part because of the highly subsidized and protected agriculture in the wealthy countries, they cannot even sell most food products on the world market. To make the situation even more cruel, they simply will not be able to retrace the paths of economic growth followed by Europe, America, and Japan. Not enough easily available or inexpensive resources remain for them to do so. And even if they try, environmental constraints will soon halt such growth—often not by any fault of their own, but because of the legacy left by rapid growth elsewhere.[6]

Since 1850, and at an accelerating pace since 1950, the industrialized nations have attained a level of production of goods and services undreamed of in the human past. In 2000, a census year, the United States illustrated this consumptive largesse. It enjoyed a GNI of nearly $10 trillion (1996 dollars). In the previous year, its citizens had a disposable (after depreciation of capital and taxes) income of close to $6 trillion. Its agriculture was so productive that Americans had to spend just over 8 percent of this income for food used at home, or what costs over 50 percent of income in some poor countries. It spent over twice this amount for housing and household operation and on medical care, a third more on its automobiles, and an eighth more for recreation. Americans even spent over $80 billion on jewelry and personal care products, such as cosmetics. Each American spent, on average, about $2,300 on recreation, or almost as much as the PPP of India.

One key to this increased productivity has been the replacement of muscle power by other forms of energy, mainly from the controlled burning of fossil fuels. Another necessary condition has been the development of new tools and techniques of production, and thus ever greater efficiency. This has paid off most of all in agriculture, by far the most efficient sector in affluent countries today (the smallest input of labor for the output). Increasingly, the sources of fuels, timber, minerals, and tropical foods to sustain this rapid growth have been the less developed areas of the world. For example, Americans have not only drawn down their resources, such as oil and gas, but those of the world as a whole. Wealthy countries less favored by natural resources, such as Japan and Britain, have been almost completely dependent on such foreign resources. Poor countries have not been in a position to resist the out-shipment of precious resources, the loss of their natural capital. They have depended on the income for growing populations. Without a market for unprocessed goods, few underdeveloped countries could begin to support their existing population. They are dependent either on trade or aid. One can only wonder what Nigeria will do when its oil runs out, given its engorged population and underdeveloped agriculture.

Almost all poor countries have tried to follow development patterns that succeeded in the wealthy countries, but only a few have done enough to improve agricultural production. Most have tried to introduce labor-intensive forms of manufacturing, with textiles often in the lead. And, indeed, as measured by present national income indices, most former colonial nations have enjoyed at least low levels of economic growth. Foreign aid and the green revolution have kept such economies growing. At least a minority of the population has benefitted, with a degree of affluence easily visible in favored areas of growing cities. Whether overall human welfare has improved is impossible to measure, but one can harbor doubts that it has.

What can poor nations do to move toward Western living standards? They cannot emulate the past history of the most industrialized nations. Few have the needed resources at home, and they cannot afford to import them, particularly energy. Population pressures have already decimated forests, eroded land, and exhausted local supplies of fuel even for cooking. Hungry peasants encroach upon parks and wildlife preserves, desperate for land, wood, or game. Others have overfished increasingly polluted streams, even as industrialized nations have joined in overfishing half the world's oceans. Agricultural reform might improve food production, but only by displacing most near-subsistence farmers. Few poor countries have the money or credit or needed skills to develop profitable manufacturing, and thus have to depend on foreign capital. Cheap labor is often their lure for foreign investment. Tropical countries have to export a few commercially important foodstuffs, or their dwindling reserves of timber, oil, gas, or minerals. Increasingly, sub-Saharan Africa depends upon imported foods. Such countries cannot afford to attend to developing environmental problems.

In the last two decades, the dominant environmental concerns in the wealthy nations have shifted toward global issues. This largely involves the past role of industrialized societies in creating the problems that are now manifest in the underdeveloped world, and their responsibility in mitigating such global problems as atmospheric warming and, with it, climate change; tropical deforestation and, with it, a loss of biodiversity; and the likelihood of increased famines because of degraded soils and scarcities of water and energy. In a sense, the great overarching problem for poor countries is continued rapid population growth, a problem that wealthy countries, with stable or declining populations, can do little to influence from a distance.

ENVIRONMENTAL MITIGATION IN WEALTHY COUNTRIES

In most respects, the citizens of the twenty most wealthy countries now enjoy the fruits of a century of environmental mitigation. As they look at their immediate surroundings, they see problems aplenty, but nothing to compare to the even recent past. Only forty years ago, people everywhere had to fear the effects of nuclear fallout from the testing of over two thousand bombs by cold war antagonists. No more, although some still fear accidents at nuclear reactors. In the early twentieth century, European and American cities, in the winter, suffered horrible smog and soot from the almost universal heating by coal. No more, although the continued use of coal for electrical generation contributes to smog, acid rain, and global warming. A century ago almost all human and industrial waste was dumped, untreated, in rivers and oceans. No more in wealthy countries, although problems of waste disposal still haunt them.

In the early twentieth century, farmers in the United States were still clearing forests and increasing the land cultivated, while erosion, by wind and water, was rife (think of the dust bowl or the red hillsides of the Southeast). No more. Despite a tripling of population in the United States since 1900, and a fourfold increase in agricultural production, the amount of cultivated land has declined by a third, and the forest cover is now more extensive than in 1900. Few now remember the ugliness of factory towns, or the tenements of large cities, or the unpainted shacks of share croppers, or when city streets ran with the manure and urine of horses. Epidemics of water-borne diseases (typhoid, cholera) were still present in 1900. Whales were becoming endangered species because of overhunting, while the last passenger pigeon died in a Cincinnati zoo in 1914. Americans came close to killing their last bison. Lead was a basic ingredient of paints, and soon also of gasoline. I could go on and on, if needed, to prove that for wealthy countries, from many environmental perspectives, the past was far worse than the present. But who doubts that fact?

The people of the underdeveloped world rightly envy the prosperity of the industrialized world, which is beyond their reach. They also value its ability to cope with environmental problems, which is even more beyond their reach. In so many areas, environmental regulations and new technologies of production have mitigated environmental problems in spite of increases in population and an even more rapid increase in per capita consumption. Not completely, of course, as present American realities testify.

Americans use energy more efficiently than in the past. They have reduced the carbon intensity of fuel as they moved from wood, to coal, to oil, and to gas (the generation of electricity by natural gas emits 50 times less carbon dioxide, per unit of heat, than a wood-burning stove). Yet, they still emit more carbon than ever before. This is a function of increases in population and, even more, consumption. Americans have reduced the emission of sulfur compounds, and in a very limited way nitrous oxides, but they still suffer from air pollution and acid rain. They have reduced most of the risks of waste disposal, but they are overwhelmed with its volume. By great effort, they have saved many endangered species from extinction, but some habitat losses have effectively ended any but isolated enclaves. They have increased, at a rate much higher than population growth, the amount of land preserved in parks and wilderness areas, national and state forests, and wildlife sanctuaries, but nothing can relieve the pressure of more and more visitors to such sites, a function of numbers, affluence, cheap transportation, and a much more widespread public appreciation of the outdoors. At great effort and great cost, they have improved air quality in most areas of the country, and water quality in some areas, but again the sheer numbers and a growing use have imperiled precious aquifers and threatened overused streams. Because of a thousand new chemicals, and new products, they have pushed at least trace amounts of new compounds into the atmosphere, often with unknown risks. But as a whole, environmentally caused human mortality seems to be at the lowest level in human history in developed countries, no mean achievement (at the same time, mortality rates for many other species have gone up).

Behind the achievement was a transformation in human values. In the United States, every poll reveals broad public support for environmental legislation, although not for radical or sacrificial legislation. In much of western Europe, the public support is even higher. People take extra effort to recycle waste products, fight new urban developments in order to save forests, and are deeply concerned about threatened species. Of course, it is easier to be concerned when the problem is at a distance or when local costs are low. But the gap in understanding, in attitudes, between present Europeans and Americans and those of a century ago is deep. It is difficult to understand people who shot bison for the fun of it, who killed songbirds en masse, who gained a bounty for every wolf killed, who almost reflexively killed any snake observed, who saw trees as obstacles to progress, or who casually dumped wastes into the nearest stream.

But the high-consumption countries, in a global perspective, have incurred a high cost for their income and even their environmental repairs. They have used up a large share of the easily procured fossil fuels, threatened the protective ozone layer by their emission of ozone-depleting gases, risked a rapid rise in global temperatures because of greenhouse gas emissions, pushed the level of pollution in oceans to dangerous levels, inundated themselves with waste, used enormous quantities of water, exploited the most easily mined of the world's mineral resources, and, in earlier centuries, in both Europe and America, stripped away a large share of forest cover. By their excess, they have created an earth that can no longer support the type of development, in poor countries, that has led to their consumptive excesses. They got there first, and took the best.[7]

PART TWO

Vital Resources

Soaring populations and growing per capita consumption have already created regional scarcities in basic resources. Such scarcities will, almost inevitably, grow much worse during the course of this century. In chapter 3, I offer a brief survey of the related problems of soil preservation and food production. In chapter 4, I turn to the present or impending scarcities of water and energy in much of the world. It is all but certain that the earth's supplies of productive soils, fresh water, and fossil fuels will not be able to support all, or even most, of the projected 9 billion people in 2050 with anything close to the present living standards of those who live in the twenty wealthiest countries. Regional shortages of water for irrigation and inescapably higher prices for petroleum may even require a reduction in living standards in some presently wealthy countries.

Soil, Vegetation, and Food

Humans largely live on the surface of the earth. They draw their sustenance from living organisms that dwell on, or near, the surface. Without food and water, life cannot survive. Without productive soil (and the plant life supported by soil), the world could not support half of its present organisms, or even a tenth of its human population. At present, in many parts of the world soil is degraded, water is scarce, and food supplies are declining. In 2005 more than 840 million people lacked an adequate diet, and each year thousands starve to death, while millions more die because of malnutrition and the diseases fed by it. Despite heroic efforts by the United Nations, the food crisis in the underdeveloped world has not improved in the last decade. In parts of Africa, it has grown worse.

SOIL

For humans, the most important part of the earth's crust is the surface of continental plates, or the areas of the earth largely covered by soil. A few people could survive if all soils disappeared. They could gain protein from fish or crustaceans, and needed vitamins from hydroponically grown vegetables or ocean vegetation. Today, the fastest growing source of protein for humans is fish, with 30 percent of these fish coming from fish farms, or aquaculture. But much of the food from aquaculture comes indirectly from the grain that is fed to fish. Thus, most people would die without the plants that grow in soil, and without the animal life that is directly or indirectly dependent upon continental plant life for survival.

What is soil? Any definition is arbitrary. Only the starting point is clear. Soil, by almost any definition, begins with the weathering of rocks. Water, glacial movement, freezing and thawing, chemicals (in air, water, and soil), the roots of plants, and even gravity itself help break rocks into smaller and smaller particles. Even hard, almost impermeable metamorphic rock (produced when igneous or sedimentary rocks are transformed by intense pressure and heat) eventually breaks down. The threshold between rock and soil is somewhere between small pebbles and sand. Most soils have particles much smaller than those in sand, the finest of all being clay, with silt in between. It is these particles of rock that contain the original nutrients needed for plant growth. Much of the weathering that led to such particles involved life itself (the weathering rate is up to one hundred times faster where abundant life is present).

But soil, as both scientists and farmers understand it, is more than particles of rock. It also includes the air and water that mix with rock particles, and without which plants cannot grow. It includes decayed vegetation, or organic matter. Soil is the home to a rich array of life, most microscopic but also fungi, worms, and insect larvae. These help break down cellulose, aerate soil, and liberate needed nutrients. Any rock particles porous enough for crop production will contain air (or gases), but some desert soils may contain almost no water. Farmers supply this by irrigation. Some arid soils, or new volcanic soils, may have almost no organic matter. Farmers can supply this through manure and other organic waste, and in time dying plants will add more.

Soil lends itself to many types of classification—by texture, by regional location, by agricultural uses, by formative processes, or by appearance. The system used today by the U.S. Department of Agriculture—the Comprehensive Soil Classification System (CSCS)—is tied to observable features of soil, or the layers or horizons visible at different depths. The system begins with only twelve orders, each with a Latinized name, but complicates this with suborders, great groups, subgroups, families, and series (over twenty thousand series are now recognized by the Department of Agriculture). Even the most skilled soil scientists cannot identify all families or series, or always agree on the proper classification. Most orders reflect formation criteria, but two involve alluvial soils either with no clear layers or the very beginnings of such. In this case, the orders reveal little about the chemical composition of the soil or its agricultural potential, although some alluvial soils are among the richest of all.

Among older soils, under the CSCS system, the orders that are most important for growing crops are subtropical soils with relatively thin layers of humus and nutrients but which are very productive with the use of manure or fertilizers; mid-latitude soils with more nutrients and less leaching; and, most productive of all, the humus-rich soils of grasslands or former grasslands. But even these major orders can vary widely in such agricultural factors as nutrients, organic matter, and acidity.[1]

Soils are fragile in many ways. Wind can blow away particles of soil and deposit them elsewhere, creating easily erodible loess soils. Water easily erodes barren topsoil, moving it into streams, or ultimately into the ocean, or depositing it along river valleys or in ever growing deltas. Mineral salts contained in water from streams can so accumulate in irrigated soils as to render them unproductive. The natural acids in rainwater, augmented at times by emissions from steam plants, factories, or automobile exhausts, can so increase the acidity of soils as to make them inhospitable to most food crops. The acidity reflects the displacement, at the molecular level, of nutrient ions by hydrogen ions. Some plants have adapted to naturally acid soils (blueberries for example), but most have not. Also, acid soils reduce the absorption of phosphorus from the soil or from fertilizers. Finally, the constant cropping of land, particularly with high-foliage plants, continuously drains away nutrients, leading eventually to soils too poor to grow almost any vegetation.

These hazards—erosion, salinization, acidification, and exhaustion—vary in their seriousness according to climate and soil types. Modern farmers are able to compensate for most of these hazards. Contours and no-till methods reduce water and wind erosion. Extra irrigation water, well beyond the needs of a growing crop, leach away much (but not all) of the accumulating salts, though at some hazard of creating waterlogged soil. The concentrated, often toxic minerals drained away from such dousing often end up in very polluted streams or lakes. It is relatively easy to "sweeten" sour or acid soils by the application of calcium carbonate (lime), or overly alkaline soils by applying sulfur compounds. And, of course, in highly efficient modern agriculture farmers annually provide most needed nutrients through chemical fertilizers.

In the past, farmers had to battle soil depletion with crop rotation (wheat, for example, was grown only every second or third year). Fallow fields, in time, produce enough decaying vegetation, either grass or weeds, to replenish both the organic content of soils and their nutrient levels. Thunderstorms add nitrogen to rainfall, and thus help restock fallow soils with that most variable, and most easily leached, soil nutrient (nitrogen, in the form of usable nitrates, is also the most expensive nutrient to produce in fertilizers, for only high temperatures and thus high-energy methods can extract these nitrates from the air). A larger source of natural nitrogen is nitrogen-fixing bacteria that cluster in oxygen-free nodules on the roots of legumes. Until twentieth-century processes made possible the manufacture of artificial nitrates, the only large source of nitrogen for fertilizer, beyond that of barnyard manure or other organic wastes, was guano deposits in such arid areas as Chile—nitrates accumulated over centuries in solidified bird droppings. By the eighteenth century, informed farmers also knew the value of nitrogen-fixing legumes, with clovers often planted as part of a rotation pattern, with the advantage that the clover could be harvested as hay or used for pasture. By the mid-nineteenth century, chemical fertilizers, most with little nitrogen, offered farmers a relatively cheap source of phosphorus and potassium (the other two major nutrients utilized by plants), which came from easily accessible natural deposits or from wood ash.

Climate and the vegetative cover have as much enduring impact on soil type and quality as the original rock content. Except in extremely arid areas, soil supports vegetation (with forests the most conspicuous) and, in turn, is continuously modified by the decaying remnants of dead vegetation. In cold northern areas, where conifer forests dominate, the soil is usually acidic, which, joined with short growing seasons, means little crop agriculture. Pasture and hay dominate. In humid tropical climates, rain forests dominate. Growth is very rapid, the number of species almost unbelievably large, and the roots, seeds, and fruit of the vegetation rich in food for animals and humans. But because of the continuous leaching of nutrients, the soil has only a thin layer of humus. Without extensive use of fertilizers, when cleared it can support crops for only a few years. In some areas, such as the huge Amazon watershed, even the sustained and profitable grazing of cattle requires fertilizer. In more arid tropical soils, with less leaching of soil nutrients, the usually open savannahs can often yield abundant crops when irrigated, particularly when they have been enriched over long periods of time by the decay of native grasses.

The great soils of the world are mostly in the mid-latitudes. There, at the northern extreme, the amount of soil leaching is retarded by closed winters (where the mean temperature is below freezing in at least one month, and where the ground remains frozen for at least part of each winter). This is the situation in much of northern China, in Scandinavia and most of Russia, and in Canada and the northern United States. These areas include some of the major grain belts of the world (predominantly wheat and maize), and with such grains also the greatest areas of meat production. Of all these mid-latitude soils, the best are in areas long dominated by largely treeless savannahs, such as those in the central United States. Here, not because of aridity but through frequent burning, often by human choice, only low areas or streambanks were forested when Europeans arrived. Here were the high grassland prairies of such states as Iowa. Each year the high grasses, even after grazing by bison, deposited a new layer of duff, which soon decayed into rich, black soil. In parts of the Midwest this prairie loam was up to fifty feet deep. This was one of the few soils in the world that had enough stored nutrients to sustain grain production for half a century without the use of fertilizers. No more. Even here, heavy cropping of maize eventually depleted even these best of soils, and today few farmers anywhere can dispense with fertilizer.

Some of the most productive cropland is in humid but warmer middle latitudes, the subtropical climates (frosty but open winters, with a mean temperature above freezing). This includes much of central China, the eastern United States south of the Ohio River, plus areas in southern South America and Africa, and in Australia and New Zealand. There soils suffer more leaching than in colder areas, and outside alluvial valleys have a thinner organic horizon. But the warmer summers and the longer growing season insure more rapid plant growth and provide a home for long-season crops, such as cotton, rice, and tobacco. But in only a few years, if continually cultivated without fertilizer, such soils will no longer support high crop yields, and in hilly areas they are subject to rapid erosion. The remedy for this relative infertility has been chemical fertilizers. It is not surprising that the cotton states of the American Southeast provided the first sustained market for commercial fertilizers.

A special humid agricultural zone involves a marine west coast climate, as in much of western Europe and the Pacific Northwest. Here open winters allow soil leaching, but the cool summers preclude long-season crops such as cotton. The crop varieties are similar to the cooler mid-latitude climates, with small grains, hay, sheep, and dairy cows dominating.

SOIL MANAGEMENT AND CONSERVATION

Soil is a precious resource, since almost all terrestrial life is dependent on it. Given its value, how have humans treated their soils? This is a very complex story. It has so many regional variations as to defy any generalizations. Often, humans have done what they had to do to survive, given the level of knowledge and skills, or given a lack of developed tools or available credit. Until after World War II, humans in almost all areas of the world had worked out reasonably stable forms of agriculture. They had to in order to survive generation after generation. Such agricultural regimes could, and often did, involve a very gradual withdrawal of stored soil nutrients (the great bank of nature) that they inherited from the past, with dire implications for the future. But, over time, even with slowly rising populations, the more advanced countries took needed action to insure a sustainable food supply. This meant efforts at soil conservation, restoration of eroded soils, and a gradual introduction from the outside of the needed nutrients. In fact, in both western Europe and the United States, such has been the increase in agricultural productivity that the amount of cultivated land steadily declined throughout the twentieth century even when, as in the United States, the population tripled. In the United States, the greatest abuses of the soil occurred before 1930, not since.

This does not mean that the draw down on soil resources has ended. Even in the United States, soil erosion each year still exceeds the very gradual buildup of new soil. In some underdeveloped countries, exploding populations and a very inefficient agriculture have so degraded the land as to lead to widespread famine. No quick answers are possible in such areas as the Sahel of Africa. Deserts have replaced over-grazed savannahs. Rainfall has declined. Rivers have dried up. Marginal croplands have disappeared. And the forest cover is all but gone. Even with the best of care, it could take centuries to restore what has been lost.

The oldest object of environmental concern has been soil. Since the development of cultivation, humans have always worried (so much was at stake) about the depletion or erosion of soils, even as they noted some of the unwanted effects of deforestation. Such concerns were widely aired in colonial America, and reached a crescendo of concern and warnings by the early nineteenth century. But only a few agricultural reformers, such as John Taylor or Edmund Ruffian, were able to implement a wide range of proposed changes, in the use of lime, in careful rotation patterns, in the use of legumes. They were wealthy, had large numbers of slaves, and could afford to introduce what they called scientific agriculture. Affluent farmers throughout America formed agricultural clubs or societies, in part for social reasons, but also to publish periodicals advocating the newest agricultural methods. After the Civil War, the federal government led the reform movement, through the new agricultural colleges funded by land grands, then by experiment stations, and in the early twentieth century by extension agents to work with individual farmers. In effect, the government assumed the cost of most research and development for this economic sector, and with spectacular results. Yet, until the 1930s depression, such efforts had only limited impact. In poorer areas, such as the Southeast, a range of economic and social problems—poverty, a lack of credit, few tools, low human skills, and small, share-cropped units— led to pervasive soil erosion and depleted fertility. The extension of crop agriculture into marginal rainfall areas on the great plains, joined in some areas by overgrazing, led during cycles of drought not only to crop failures but also to horrible wind erosion (the dust bowl).

The United States, much more than the countries of western Europe, was uniquely situated to absorb such a plundering of its soil simply because it had so much agricultural land of the highest quality in ratio to its population. Access to land remained cheap (the value of farms largely reflected labor-produced improvements or locational advantages, not a scarcity of useful soils). In such a low-rent context, incentives for maintaining the productivity of farmland were often low. The high cost factor was labor, not access to land. Land mining was often more profitable than paying the costs of maintaining fertility, whether by longer rotations, manuring or fertilizing, or choosing less depleting crops. This explains some nineteenth-century patterns. One was the large acreage owned by many farmers, much more land than they could cultivate with existing tools and in the absence of cheap hired labor. This led to something closely patterned after eastern woodland Indian agriculture—clear, farm for as long as the soil was fertile, and then move on to new clearings. The Indians allowed the used up land to revert to forest. Europeans in America turned it into pasture or hay until the twentieth century, when large areas of former farmland in the eastern United States reverted to forests. When farmers needed better soil, they cleared new fields on their own land. Later, when they exhausted forestland fit for cropping, they could sell their depleted farms and move farther west, where they could acquire excellent cropland at low cost.

Despite the pleadings of agricultural reformers, maintaining existing land was not always economically rational. In the same sense, it was not rational for farmers to harvest forest resources selectively. Of course, in a sense, farmers were making decisions on a short-term basis. Future generations, and society as a whole, would later have to pay for such degraded resources. But at the time, only governmental regulations could have prevented such choices. And, had there been such controls, the society as a whole would have had to pay for it at the time, because of higher costs for food and fiber. More intensive and socially responsible local development would also have delayed the settlement of the West, and the eagerly sought economic development that sparsely populated western areas so fervently desired.

By the Great Depression, an agricultural revolution was just beginning, one that would climax in the three decades after World War II in the United States, western Europe, Japan, and Australia and New Zealand. Its effect would be delayed in many third-world countries, but with no diminished impact. In brief, production per acre of land doubled in as little as one generation; the productivity of labor often quadrupled. In the United States, the size of farm units more than doubled, while the number of farms shrunk from nearly 7 million to 2 million (or about 800,000 that account for most production), even as the amount of land devoted to crops declined. The doubling of the world's population from 1960 to 2000 would have been impossible, even inconceivable, without this agricultural revolution, with all its human and environmental costs.

In the United States, the agricultural policies that made possible the explosion of productivity first came to maturity in the depression years—production controls, price supports, marketing incentives, and, often overlooked, a whole range of new federal programs that supported soil improvement and conservation. By the 1930s, a major conservation movement, which involved largely forestry and mineral conservation at the beginning of the century, peaked, and by then land had the highest priority (the dust bowl years, unprecedented summer heat and drought, and a spotlight on Southern economic maladies all helped create broad popular support for soil-related reforms). These came quickly. The federal government, in the New Deal years, purchased submarginal farmlands and helped states convert many of these into state parks, set up a new Soil Conservation Service with offices in every rural county, by 1936 tied farm price supports to soil conservation practices implemented by farmers, used the TVA for new and very successful experiments in fertilizer production and use, expanded exponentially research and development programs in the Department of Agriculture and in regional experiment stations, and, above all, offered a wide range of subsidies to help farmers initiate soil-saving strategies. For example, if one flies over almost any part of the United States today, they will observe thousands of farm ponds, literally dotting the landscape, almost all paid for in large part by federal funds. These not only help to control runoff, but also have important roles in wildlife management (most Midwestern farms are, in effect, small waterfowl refuges). The flyer will also observe, in all hilly areas, a mosaic of contoured fields, with their terraces almost always subsidized in their original development by federal funds.[2]

With all the attention, today, on air and water pollution, on toxic waste sites, on ozone layer depletion, or on greenhouse gases and their probable effect on global warming, it is easy to overlook the one most successful environmental program in most industrialized countries—soil conservation. In the United States, federal programs have worked beyond all expectations. This is most dramatically revealed in a comparison of air photographs of the Southeast in 1933 and today. Red, eroded fields, which were everywhere, are gone today. Most of them are now in grass, a few in new forests. Conservation policies, and in time self-interest, led farmers to make the needed repairs. The dramatic increase in farm productivity allowed farmers to withdraw crops from marginal lands. This process began in New England by the late nineteenth century, as cheaply transported grain and meat from the Midwest made hilly farms unprofitable. Owners deserted them, with most reverting to forests. Most Americans are surprised to find that forestland, some of inferior quality, increased throughout the twentieth century, although old growth forests have continued to decline. After World War II, with a pattern of continued surpluses, farmers throughout the country withdrew cultivation from marginal land, or, when subsidized by the federal government, from very good but erodible land that is now in a Conservation Reserve program. The marginal land reverted to forests or continued as pasture. The subsidized reserves of productive land, by the requirements set by federal agencies, are idle (annual or biannual mowing prevents reforestation). These reserved plots have a major role in wildlife preservation, and could, if needed, augment food production in the future. At present, it is hard to see any eventuality that will require their use in the near future, as agricultural gluts are a major problem in all the developed world.

GLOBAL FOOD PROSPECTS

Fears of global food shortages, at least in the near future, are misplaced. But local food shortages will probably increase, and with them starvation and death. One can even work out quite plausible scenarios that, with no increase in the land cultivated worldwide, will allow the earth to support a population double what it is today, and easily support the 9 billion people predicted by the middle of this century. I am not sure such scenarios are worth much. But if farmers around the world were as productive as Iowa corn farmers, they could feed more than 9 billion. They might have to stop growing nonfood crops (tobacco, cotton), and in time most people might have to become vegetarians (routing grain through cows and hogs wastes calories, but grazing adds to the world's supply of protein). Of course, most farmers around the world do not have soil as productive as that in Iowa, and, much more important, they do not have the machines, the pesticides, the fertilizers, the political stability, and the knowledge that makes such production possible. Yet, the advanced agricultural countries, those with the latest farming techniques, joined with the existing level of agricultural production in China and India, could grow enough foodstuffs to sustain the world's total population today and into the indefinite future. It is hard to calculate how much food Americans alone could grow if they utilized all presently reserved cropland, substituted food crops for cotton and tobacco, replaced suitable pastures with crops, utilized the gardening potential of roadsides and backyards and even golf courses, and moved back onto reasonably productive marginal land or began clearing forestland, thus utilizing soils that would delight any farmer in the Sahel of Africa.

The problem is, American farmers will never do this. They cannot sell, at a profit, much that they now produce on our declining number of farms. Also, the most calorie-intensive vegetables are not easily shipped to distant consumers. Food relief is bound to grow, for humanitarian reasons, and governments in advanced countries will continue to pay for such food. But it is simply inconceivable that such governments will spend a large share of their budgets for food relief, or what will be necessary if world populations expand to 9 billion without matching agricultural reforms in those largely poor countries that now have the highest birthrates. And even with the most generous outside support, political instability often prevents the delivery of food aid.

When one speaks of food, or of the soils that furnish it, one has to attend to enormous regional differences. People in some parts of the world have always faced food shortages. Famines have been a part of life. The Malthusian warning—that vice and misery are the ultimate means of controlling population growth—was not a prediction about the future but an observation of what prevailed in most of the world in 1796. Scarcity is a part of life, although humans through foresight and planning can escape the hard regime of scarcity. The one most important secret of such an escape are policies affecting the soil and farming practices. Hunger has proved a very intractable problem, with United Nations Food

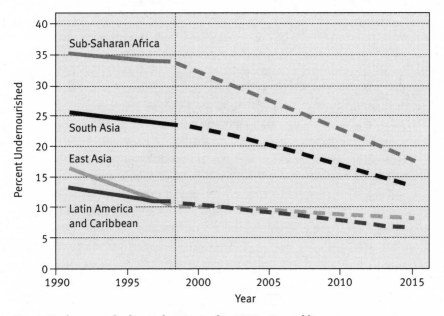

Fig. 4. Undernourished populations in the 1990s. Dotted lines represent progress required to meet 2015 goals to alleviate hunger. (Data from FAO.) (United Nations, *Global Challenge, Global Opportunity*, 6.)

and Agricultural Organization targets for hunger reduction so far unmet. Each annual World Food Day (October 16) reveals roughly the same 800 million hungry people, although as a percentage of the total world population this stable number represented a slight annual improvement (see figure 4), with even this percentage gain reversed in 2004. In 2000, the United Nations agreed upon a set of millennium goals that included the reduction, by half, of world hunger by 2015. In 2006 nothing suggests that it will even come close to meeting that goal. Note that hunger is only the extreme example of food problems. Almost 30 percent of the world's population suffer from some form of malnutrition, while 60 percent of children who die before the age of six have suffered from malnutrition. Most babies with low birth weight (23.8 percent worldwide) reflect malnourished mothers.[3]

The Green Revolution

At the time of the American Revolution, nearly 90 percent of the population was directly involved in agriculture. City artisans grew gardens and kept a cow. Even the most efficient farm family could grow enough food for only one more family. Today, around 700,000 family-owned farms, plus 40,000 corporate farms, provide over 90 percent of the foodstuffs, plus cotton and tobacco, needed by 260 million Americans, with a large surplus for export. This is produced on less land than in 1900, when farmers still made up almost 40 percent of our workforce (full-time farm operators today make up less than 1 percent of our workforce). And, by most criteria, this near miracle in productivity has paralleled a vast improvement in the condition of our soils. How did American farmers do it?

As the above facts make clear, the revolution most of all involved the amount of labor needed in agriculture. Given the cost of labor in America, the drive for efficiency has usually involved labor-saving strategies. In some cases, such as western wheat, the average production per acre, on semi-arid land, is often only half that in Pennsylvania or in Ireland. But the size of the fields and the highly mechanized custom planting and combining minimize the labor costs and make such wheat more than competitive on world markets. In all major crops, the gains have involved the replacement of draft animals and human labor by machines, the carefully calculated application of fertilizers, the use of insecticides, fungicides, and herbicides to control insects, diseases, and weeds, water management that involves not only routine irrigation but supplemental irrigation even in humid areas, and dramatic improvements in varieties grown, a gain almost fully realized through past methods of plant breeding and hybridizing, but one that may now face a new revolution through direct genetic manipulation. Equal but different efficiencies have transformed poultry and hog production, and the fattening of beef cattle.

The costs have mostly involved other aspects of the environment and not soil. American farmers still lose soil to wind and water erosion. Even forested land suffers some erosion. This is part of nature. But land, as now managed in America, is not an endangered resource. Techniques are available to improve depleted soil, although such can be costly (turning under legumes year after year to restore heavily eroded hillsides). Although the texture and native nutrients (especially trace elements) of soil remain important, the soil for a farmer is now not so much the source of nutrients as a container for the nutrients applied annually to fields. Unlike in the past, good corn land can be cropped indefinitely. Heavily irrigated soils cannot sustain agriculture indefinitely, although salinated soils can recover over time if not cropped. But the big problem in irrigated agriculture worldwide is not so much soil conditions, but the continued availability of water to feed crops and to leach away salts.

The costs of such efficient agriculture are many. Behind all the changes is the substitution of the energy created by burning hydrocarbons for the muscle power of people and draft animals. When humans first began cultivating land (an industrial revolution of transcending importance), they used their hands and simple tools. The total energy used, reflected in the calories burned by the worker, was less than the calories present in the harvested crops. The net gain came from the fecundity of the earth. In primitive agriculture, the using up of soil nutrients soon depleted the soil, but when a low population density prevailed over an extended landscape, it was less than the annual accumulation of new organic matter and nutrients. Thus, people simply moved to new land. This was true, for example, for the Native Americans in eastern North America at the time of European contact. Such an agriculture could provide a sustained yield forever. ·

When humans learned to use draft animals to pull plows and wagons (another great industrial revolution), they had to grow more calories to feed their livestock. This meant a much heavier demand on soils and, with exploding populations, the need to take into account the long-term

needs of the land. When early civilizations failed to find a sustained accommodation with the soil, they suffered, faced starvation, declined, and
even in some cases expired (the Mississippian culture in North America
may be such a dire case). The learning involved rotation patterns, the use
of manure or other waste products, and more benign forms of plowing
and cultivation. Early modern agriculture, or the type Europeans brought
to America, reflected this accommodation. But the sparse population in
America and the enormous wealth of fertility that had accumulated over
the centuries allowed early Europeans to break free of the traditional patterns and gain wealth from the draw down of soil nutrients that seemed all
but inexhaustible. This was, obviously, a pattern that could not continue indefinitely, and thus the nineteenth-century reforms in American agriculture
that prepared the way for the twentieth-century agricultural revolution.

If soils were the only critical resource, the United States could secure
an abundance of food into the distant future. In fact, given its unused
soil or soil committed to nonfood crops, it could easily double food production over the next two decades. If world markets create a high price
for foods, it might in fact do just that. But in spite of this fact, it would
be mistaken to refer to present American (or western European, Canadian, Australian) agriculture as sustainable. It involves a small, still easily
compensated for, draw down of soil nutrients, but a much more serious
using up of fossil fuels and of easily accessible phosphates and potassium. Of course, farms use only a small percentage of fossil energy (in
the form not only of machines but the energy used to produce nitrates
for fertilizer), when compared to electrical generation, automobiles, and
manufacturing. In this sense, it joins other areas of human production or
transportation tied to a depletable resource. If one could give a precise
meaning to the idea of sustained production, over an indefinite future,
then highly capitalized agriculture would have to absorb the long-term
costs made inevitable by future substitutions of new sources of energy.
These costs are impossible to estimate, but might be very high. Unlike in
the past, an efficient farmer uses a thousand times more calories than is
contained in the food produced.

The other side of environmental costs involves what agriculture re-
leases into the environment. Properly used, some of its waste products
are valuable, recyclable assets, as in the traditional uses of manure by
farmers. That is no longer true of the enormous lagoons of manure
accumulated by modern hog and poultry factories, or created by

huge beef cattle feeding lots. These can, and occasionally do, seep into groundwaters, with devastating effects, while the methane given off by such manure increases greenhouse gases, and in a few cases the sulphur dioxide endangers nearby residents. At the same time, the phosphates and nitrates that derive from chemical fertilizers are, in most areas of the country, the primary sources of stream and lake pollution. Joining these are the residues of pesticides, with their potential effect on human health or on fish, birds, and animals. Even the shift in insect ecologies have had unpredicted and damaging consequences (the killing off of beneficial insects, and the need for more and more chemical controls). Tractors and combines lack most of the pollution controls required on automobiles, and thus contribute more than numbers would indicate to air pollution. These costs, at present, are borne by the larger public, not by farmers. Many of the costs will not be clear until well into the future.

Today, the degradation of soils, rampant deforestation, and developing food shortages are regional problems. In a sense, this has always been true. These problems have worsened in much of the underdeveloped world during the last two decades, with the immediate future looking very bleak. Only in sub-Saharan Africa has land degradation advanced so far as to insure a continued decrease in per capita food production, and thus an indefinite dependence upon food imports. Political instability, huge governmental debts, low world commodity prices (for oil, other minerals, and tropical foods), rapidly growing populations (still over 3 percent a year in many African countries, even as birthrates are declining in most of Latin America and in India), disastrous governmental polices keyed to manufacturing development rather than agricultural reform, and finally the barrier to foreign sales because of heavily subsidized or price protected agriculture in industrialized countries—all have helped create the problem. The problem has two aspects: deforestation and low agricultural output.

DEFORESTATION AND INEFFICIENT FOOD PRODUCTION

Forests are the most visible and dramatic product of the soil. Trees grow on over half the land area of the earth. Only very dry soils, or very cold temperatures, preclude tree growth. Dense forests are limited to humid areas, but note that rainfall requirements vary according to temperatures. In northern Canada and Siberia, where winters are long and frozen, where evaporation rates are low, less than 10 inches of annual rainfall can support forest cover. In the tropics, even 30 inches may support only scattered, savannah-type trees. Rainfall patterns are also critical. Areas with wet and dry seasons, such as Mediterranean climates, nourish special types of deep-rooted trees, but these never make up a dense cover. In arid areas, trees grow only along streams. In the most general sense, the three great areas of full forest cover include tropical rain forests (the Amazon basin and scattered areas of Central America, much of central Africa, and a large area of Southeast Asia); mid-latitude deciduous or mixed forests (originally most of western Europe and parts of Russia, the humid areas of the eastern United States and southern Canada, a marine west coast belt from northern California to Alaska, and much of Japan and China); and cool-climate, mostly conifer forests (Alaska and northern Canada, across northern Eurasia, and at higher altitudes in mountain ranges around the world).

Thick forests are such a dominant form of vegetation that they not only depend on a favorable climate, but do much to shape the climate. Tree roots and the ground cover of decaying leaves slow the absorption of rainfall and thus prevent erosion, and so slow runoff as to retard flooding. By transpiration, trees add to the humidity of the air, and thus tend to increase rainfall. Trees, like all vegetation, absorb atmospheric carbon dioxide, and therefore are critical in slowing the buildup of greenhouse gases, although most of this carbon is eventually released back into the atmosphere. In mid-latitudes, forests lessen temperature extremes, moderate high and low cycles in stream flow, increase precipitation, and prevent most wind and soil erosion.

Of all species, humans have had the greatest impact on forests. Insects attack and sometimes kill trees, and today these most often are invasive species introduced through travel or trade. Beavers fell a few trees. Deer may over-browse trees, or kill all new tree growth. But only humans have deforested large areas of the earth, not only by cutting and burning, but also by the effects of acid rain, harmful pesticides, and imported diseases and fungi. In parts of western Europe, it is impossible to have any clear idea of what the forest cover was like in the distant past, before human occupation.

Human interactions with forests take many forms. One, so evident in early America, is getting rid of trees that are an impediment to agriculture. Another is the using up of trees as fuel or timber. Humans also harvest the products of trees without destroying them, as in gathering the fruits, nuts, or sap (for rubber, tar, turpentine, or maple syrup). Finally, humans often select and plant trees in behalf of a harvest (orange groves, apple orchards, rubber plantations). Throughout human history the greatest use of trees has been for fuel; this is still true in much of the third world. And it is this use that has led to the most critical environmental problems, problems based on rapid population growth and traditional patterns of heating homes or cooking food or, in India, cremating the dead. Even in tropical areas, fuel is a necessity for cooking. Most foods, particularly tropical foods, are not palatable or in some cases even safe without cooking. Cultural patterns help shape the type and amount of cooking; in India the traditional cuisine often requires elaborate and extended preparation.

The cumulative use of wood as a fuel in the South Asian subcontinent, by a population now over one and a third billion, is enormous, and approaching a crisis. Other fuels are not available, or are too expensive, as is also true in much of central Africa, where per capita incomes remain at around $300–$400 a year. In the Sahel of Africa, the wood is all but gone (see figure 5). Women, and they are the victims in this case, often travel ten miles to gather any organic materials they can find. The burden has become excessive; the future is all but hopeless without heavily subsidized outside relief (this could involve shipments of coal or wood).[4]

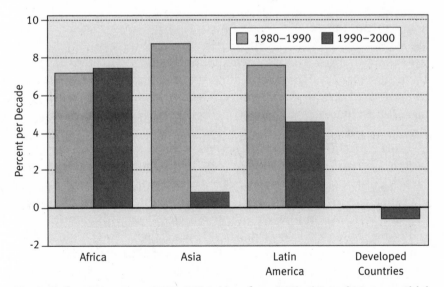

Fig. 5. Deforestation rate, 1980–2000 (data from FAQ). (United Nations, *Global Challenge, Global Opportunity,* 12.)

Equally critical in the underdeveloped world is the increased demand for tillable land. Here, again, an explosive growth of population, joined with agricultural inefficiency, has created the scarcity. This scarcity blocks efforts to preserve wildlife sanctuaries, to prevent overgrazing, or to limit the erosive effects of farming unsuited land. Most of all, it makes forest preservation an unaffordable luxury. With each generation, plots become smaller and less efficient. Water for irrigation cannot be expanded, or in the Sahel is actually declining with the desertification created by overuse. Desperately poor people cannot afford new tools or buy fertilizer. In most third-world areas, the potential for more food production, which in most regions remains large, simply cannot be realized. To gain more efficiency would require knowledge, capital, more extensive plots, and political stability. And even if agricultural reforms were possible, despite all these impediments, it would mean the expulsion of most existing farmers from the land. They would join the millions of third-world people flocking to urban areas, with small prospects for jobs, only the most primitive housing, and no water or sewer services. Thus, in much of Africa and South Asia, the remaining forests are endangered and reforestation almost impossible. The resulting climate changes are presently irreversible.

In countries with per capita income under $1,000, it may not make sense to try to introduce the capital-intensive agriculture that is now dominant in Europe and North America. In India, particularly in rice and wheat culture, Western techniques were very successful in the Punjab. But tractors and extensive fields are not an answer for the thousands of villages that contain most of India's population. Labor is too cheap to make machines profitable. And not enough jobs exist in services or manufacturing to absorb displaced village farm workers. India is cursed, already, by the millions of former peasants flocking to the outskirts of its major cities. The same is true in much of Africa. In these areas, productivity increases since World War II have usually involved improved varieties of rice and other food crops, not reductions in labor costs. But the benefits of the Green Revolution simply accompanied a rapid growth of population, and in time almost impossible pressures on forests, soils, and water resources. If the population could stabilize (even replacement birthrates will not accomplish this for the next thirty years because of the huge bulge of children and youth), then the goal for agricultural reform would have to be productivity increases on existing, often small plots, and only a gradual introduction of tractors, larger farms, and a cumulatively drastic reduction in the agricultural labor force. For many countries, this may be an impossible goal, for it requires a concomitant increase in manufacturing and services, in a context in which about the only inducement for growth in these areas is low wages. Outside investment, subsidized by richer countries, might work, if only the political environment was conducive (a big if), and if outside corporations were willing to support local development goals and not seek ways to exploit resources and make short-term profits (a huge if).

Even for underdeveloped countries, the situation is not all bleak. Food production per capita and per capita food consumption have risen rather steadily since the 1960s, or by 450 calories per day in the world as a whole, and 600 calories in developing countries. Much of this gain occurred in China (an increase of 1,000 calories). But at present agricultural production is stagnant or declining in sub-Saharan Africa. At the same time, people worldwide have moved to more balanced or nutritious diets. The percentage of total calories from cereals has declined, fat consumption has risen (to the 15 percent minimum for a healthy diet in most developing countries, except in Africa, and above the maximum of 45 percent for good health in industrialized countries and parts of Latin America). The consumption of fruits and vegetables remain much too low in most of the world, including even some industrialized countries. The consumption of meat, dairy products, and fish has grown worldwide, with fish consumption doubling since 1960 (the major source of protein for 1 billion people worldwide).

But these gains are now imperiled in much of the underdeveloped world, and particularly in Africa. In most cases it is not because of a shortage of land, or a shortage of water for irrigation. Expensive improvements in the transport of water could expand irrigation, while expensive fertilizer could expand production on existing land. The problems all involve other disabilities—most of all poverty, but also political instability, warfare and the resulting refugee populations, natural calamities (floods, droughts). Clearly, resource limitations will have a major impact in the future. The United Nations estimates that over the next thirty years the present inability of much of Africa to meet existing demands for cereals and meat will grow, meaning an ever greater dependence on food imports. The food exists, but poor countries cannot afford to buy it. The decline in subsistence agriculture, and the massive movement of peasants into cities, will only exacerbate the problem.[5]

No second green revolution seems imminent. The one most realistic hope is that genetic engineering can lead to large increases in yields. Even here the risks are high. However much plant breeders are able to create insect- or disease-resistant or more nutritious varieties, through time mutated insects or fungi may overcome the resistance. Already, in the major agricultural countries, it is hard to keep ahead of the game. And to an extent not yet fully measured, the shift in all parts of the world to a few new, very productive varieties has lowered the genetic diversity present in the past, with a much higher risk that disastrous new diseases could, in one or two years, almost destroy a given, highly bred crop, such as wheat, rice, or maize. Beyond all this, it is impossible, as yet, to estimate all the possible but unanticipated side effects of genetically modified plants and animals. These already include high seed costs and corporate monopolies.

FOOD PROSPECTS IN THE NEAR FUTURE

Such problems as soil loss, deforestation, and even widespread hunger are critical in some parts of the earth, but not in others. In high-income parts of the world, populations are already stable or declining and an ever more efficient agriculture has lessened, not increased, the land needed for food production. In these areas, it will be possible to convert more and more land to parks and wildlife preserves. Forestlands will, if anything, increase, and with careful management almost all present species can survive. In fact, in some areas biodiversity may increase. But such an irenic future will probably depend on new sources of energy, consumption changes in nonfood areas, less waste and pollution of air and water, and possibly very difficult strategies to slow global warming. In this sense, the major challenges for advanced economies will involve other economic sectors than agriculture, which, in many ways, was the great success story of the last century.

In a middle range of countries, measured by incomes and productivity (parts of Latin America, much of the Middle East and Southwest Asia, and the former communist bloc), the recent trends are mixed. In Latin America, population growth seems to have very recently turned rapidly downward, suggesting possible stability when the present bulge of youth have completed childbearing. These countries may duplicate a path taken by western Europe and the United States, but a century later. Yet, in much of Latin America the agricultural sector remains backward and inefficient, and environmental problems more acute with each passing year. Venezuela, with plenty of good land, has to import foodstuffs. Rain forests, and the biodiversity they support, are everywhere threatened. In the Middle East, oil has enabled Islamic countries to import foods, but this resource will not last. A population explosion in Egypt has swamped its traditional agriculture, as has population growth in Indonesia.

The former communist bloc has its own special problems. Populations are stable or declining in Russia and eastern Europe, but these countries are almost overwhelmed by environmental problems, and few have the resources at present to do the needed repairs. In Russia, agriculture is still a disaster despite some recent evidence of recovery. After the breakup of the Soviet system, in many years it did not feed its population, despite the soil and climate needed to sustain agricultural surpluses.

India and China, with over a third of the world's population, are low-income countries (part of the third world based on per capita incomes), but both have much of the infrastructure of highly developed nations (a large class of educated people, excellent universities, high-technology industries, and in some areas a very efficient agriculture). China may have stabilized its population; India may follow in thirty to forty years. China feeds itself (a great achievement), and in most areas with the caloric intake of Western societies. India, after enormous efforts, feeds its population, with grain surpluses in some years, but the caloric intake is much smaller than in the West, and a large share of the population is undernourished by Western standards. It has no margin of safety, but at least it has the human capital to try to cope with its overwhelming economic problems. It will be almost impossible for all the countries of South Asia to retain the remaining forest cover, to cope with soil erosion and increasingly disastrous floods, and to find the needed fuel for villagers. The problems in Pakistan match those in India; in Bangladesh, they are far worse. The present rate of global warming, if it continues, will exacerbate all these problems.

As is clear from what came before, sub-Saharan Africa, excluding the Republic of South Africa, faces the most intractable problems, not only in food production but in all economic and political areas. Political instability and unchecked birthrates only add to the problems. The area cannot meet its challenges without large and continuous outside help, not just in the forms of investment that may be profitable, but in types of education and infrastructure improvements that will enable these peoples to help themselves.

It may seem surprising to some, but for the United States the environmental problems attendant upon modern agriculture least involve the soil. We have plenty for our needs, and for any realistic projection of what we can do to help feed other parts of the world. Nothing is more misplaced than lamentations about how new housing developments, industrial parks, or shopping centers are taking over good farmland. Often, they do just this, but we have no scarcity of such land. We have a surplus. One may regret the displacement of farmers from high-priced, developable land near urban centers, deplore the esthetic horrors that replace such farms, lament the environmental costs of strip development, bemoan the loss of habitat for plants and animals, but soil scarcity is not a valid concern, not at present or in the foreseeable future. Of course, if our population grew at 3 percent a year, as in much of Africa, we might eventually regret such land-hungry development, but unless we open our doors to a flood of new immigrants each year, the population of the United States could soon stabilize at around 320 million (existing birthrates are at a replacement level, but no more).

Even without continued improvements in agricultural productivity, the United States has more land than it will soon need to feed and even clothe its population. Likewise, it has a sustainable supply of trees for timber and pulp. Such is the availability of good land that the United States has the capacity to grow much of its fuel for motor vehicles. Scientists are steadily developing more economical ways of converting vegetation directly into energy (ethanol or biomass diesel fuel), thus lessening the dependence on fossil fuels. Yet, the United States and other developed nations cannot isolate themselves from the problems of hunger, deforestation, and land degradation in other parts of the world. Ironically, today the very problems of food production in other parts of the world have helped, in a small way, to maintain a market for our agricultural largesse. But unless food-deficient countries can produce goods to exchange for food, or find ways of improving their own agriculture, the future will be bleak. Charity is only a temporarily stopgap. Thus, for the United States the problem is one of helping other parts of the world increase agricultural efficiency, conserve existing forests or reforest vulnerable watersheds, preserve threatened species, conserve and improve soils, and enforce what is often already quite idealistic environmental legislation. This will not be easy.

Water and Energy:
Will There Be Enough?

All of the most basic natural resources needed for human life are now either growing scarce or are frequently polluted. For the most part, the reason for this is a twofold development in the twentieth century—unprecedented population increases in underdeveloped countries, where per capita consumption has grown only slowly at best; and unprecedented increases of per capita consumption in industrialized countries, where populations are now stable or declining. Thus the squeeze comes from two directions, and in neither case is there any likelihood of any early relief. In Asia, Africa, and Latin America populations continue to grow, although at a slower pace than in the late twentieth century. In the wealthy parts of the world, consumption continues to grow at an increasing rate. And the 80 percent who lag behind in consumption aspire to the living standards of the wealthy. The earth, it seems, does not have the resources to support their dreams, and may not have the resources to accommodate a 50 percent increase in population among the poor, even at present levels of consumption, or a 50 percent increase of consumption among the wealthy. The vice is tightening already, and it will get tighter still in the coming decades.

The Squeeze

In the past, sparse populations in primitive parts of the earth could live on hunting, fishing, and gathering, and on water from springs or streams. In a cold climate, they needed protective clothing, usually gained from furs, and some form of shelter, such as a cave or a dugout or a wooden cabin. Without thought, they breathed the ever plentiful air. They used fire to cook food and warm their shelters. They used hand tools made from bones, stones, or wood to aid in the hunt, in food preparation, and in making clothing. The needed resources lay all about them. But even primitive humans could overhunt the game or take too many fish from streams. They also faced droughts, when the berries and nuts did not grow and springs and streams dried up. Even they could face a scarcity of basic resources, and perish from thirst and hunger.

In time, as humans gained more and more mastery over natural resources, populations could grow. People learned to cultivate crops, domesticate animals for food and their labor, smelt copper and iron to gain better tools, irrigate desert soils, and, finally, in the greatest revolution of all, use falling water or blowing wind or the burning of organic fuels in engines to do most of the productive work formerly done by hand tools or by their domesticated animals. In this long process, they gradually gained a near complete dominance over their natural environment, and literally transformed the earth for the benefit of humans. Without this transformation, the earth could not support even a billion people, let alone the present 6.5 billion. The most basic resources for the support of the large number of humans today are food, air, soil, water, and sources of energy. Since food is critical, and soil so foundational, I have treated them in an earlier chapter. Air remains plentiful, and thus the problems of clean air are part of the chapter on pollution. This leaves two resources that are, in some places, already scarce—water and energy. They are bound to become scarcer still in this new century.

WATER

Water is the most abundant substance on the face of the earth. In some sense, it will never be scarce. The supply, in the form of vapor, fluids, and solids, is almost constant (photosynthesis involves a chemical breaking of the hydrogen and oxygen bond, or a loss of some water, but other photochemical processes create water, such as the merging of oxygen and methane in the stratosphere or combustion of hydrocarbons, while small amounts of water enter our atmosphere on meteors or comets). Animals and plants use water, but do not destroy it. This is also true of most industrial uses of water, which may involve the heating or the pollution of water. Yet, for many plants and animals, including the human animal, water may be scarce. It is a problem of where, and in what form, water is present. Over 97 percent of the earth's water is in the oceans and has too much salt for the use of most land plants or animals. Of the 2.5 percent that is fresh water, about two-thirds is locked up in glaciers. This means that slightly less than 1 percent of the earth's water is fresh and in liquid form. Most of this fresh water is in aquifers, some all but inaccessible. But this still leaves a lot of accessible water, up to two thousand cubic meters for each person each year. This water can be used over and over again if it remains fresh (without salt) and clean (without pollutants). In a case of extreme need, humans can desalinize seawater, or melt glaciers, but only in each case by the expenditure of that other basic resource—energy.

The oceans are the source of most of our fresh water. Heat from the sun evaporates water at the ocean's surface, leaving behind most mineral content (salts). The water vapor remains in the atmosphere only a few days, on average, for it condenses into droplets and falls as rain or snow. Over two-thirds of the rain falls back into the oceans, but the rest falls on land, and thus provides the ever-present source of water for human consumption. This water from precipitation takes many paths, but it eventually flows back into the oceans—mostly via rivers, but small amounts return as rainfall that began as moisture from vegetative transpiration or evaporated fresh water and then moved over oceans. The journey back to the oceans can be long for some water, particularly that stored for centuries in deep aquifers. By one United Nations estimate, about 8 percent of water involved in this hydrological cycle is used each year by humans, while they use over half of the stream flow, mostly for irrigation, with the next highest use being for hydroelectric power or the cooling of steam and nuclear plants. Note that in each case the water is arrested in its cycle, but not diminished. Water used for irrigation will either evaporate on its way to crops, move down into groundwater (which feeds springs), or spend some time in the tissues of plants. But irrigation, although not destructive of water, does reduce stream flow, often to the extent of drying up the deltas of such major rivers as the Indus, Nile, and Colorado.

For all animals, the most important use of water is for drinking. Only in very rare cases are humans, anywhere, without access to some fresh

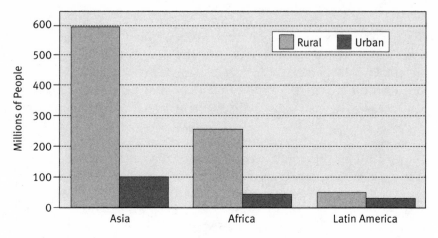

Fig. 6. People without safe drinking water (data from WHO/UNICEF). (United Nations, *Global Challenge, Global Opportunity*, 18.)

water. They rarely die from thirst. But many die from polluted water. In fact, around 1.2 billion of the world's population drink water that is unsafe (see figure 6). Over 1 billion lack access to any public water system, even to the extent of a hydrant along a street. Today, roughly half the world's population, or over 3 billion people, live in cities. In Africa, less than half of city dwellers have any access to a municipal water supply, and less than a fourth have access to sanitary sewers or even sanitary privies. Thus, in the world as a whole, the problem is not access to drinking water, but to safe water. In the last two decades, the world has made progress toward safer water, in both urban and rural areas. In part, this has resulted from education, and from inexpensive, local tactics, such as chlorine capsules to purify drinking water. In part, it also has resulted from better water treatment and delivery systems in cities. But anyone who has traveled to almost any underdeveloped country can testify to the continuing problem of unsafe water, not only for drinking but for personal hygiene (teeth brushing, bathing, food preparation).

The World Health Organization has set a minimum goal for water availability for personal use—just over five gallons of treated water a day per person, available within one kilometer of one's home. The United Nations World Water Assessment Programme has set a higher goal—to reduce, by half, all people without safe water and sanitary facilities by

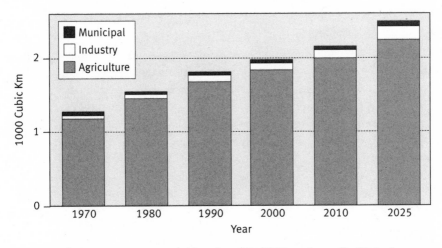

Fig. 7. Global water consumption (data from World Water Council). (United Nations, *Global Challenge, Global Opportunity,* 10.)

2015 (they are on target for water, not so for sanitation), and to provide both safe water and sanitary facilities to all people (an estimated 8 billion) by 2025, a laudable but surely impossible goal. It defines as its goal the availability of thirteen gallons of safe water a day, within a few hundred meters of each family. Compared to the amount used in most developed countries, even this may seem small, plenty to drink but barely enough for a daily bath, not enough to flush a commode more than two or three times, to say nothing of washing clothes or water used in cooking. Yet, few of the urban poor in underdeveloped countries receive this much, even when they have access to treated and safe water. Most of the poor people in the world have no access to sewers; they flush no toilets. Most bathe in polluted streams, if they bathe at all, and it is in such streams that they wash clothes. Polluted water is thus one of the major health problems worldwide. By United Nations estimates, it kills 4 million people a year, more than half of them children, with diarrhea being the leading cause. But in this chapter I do not want to focus on human-caused pollution (for that, see chapter 6), but on the availability of fresh water. Almost 90 percent of this fresh water is used in irrigation (see figure 7).[1] However, some of the same water used for downstream irrigation has earlier been used in households or industries.

IRRIGATION AND DAMS

Until humans began moving water to plants, almost all land vegetation depended on precipitation, with the exceptions being stream bank seepage or, in rare cases, coastal fogs. Irrigation seems to have begun with the earliest civilizations, which in most cases arose in arid regions (Egypt, Mesopotamia, India). One theory is that the need for irrigation helped stimulate the type of coordination and social order that marked the first civilizations. If one had been able to view the earth from an orbiting satellite five thousand years ago, the most telling proof of human occupation would have been irrigation canals and ditches. Human control over the water needed for crops has remained of vital importance. Without it, the earth could not support its present population.

Although only about 16 percent of cultivated land is now irrigated, this same acreage produces approximately 40 percent of all food. In many poor countries, irrigation accounts for up to two-thirds of all crops, and in almost every country the level of farm income is much higher in irrigated areas (reflecting the higher capital committed to such farming). One of the three main grains—rice—is, in many areas of cultivation, dependent on field flooding, even in humid climates. Although irrigation produces its own problems (most often the build up of salts or water-logged soils), in most cases the secure water supply of irrigation insures higher yields. Today, in underdeveloped areas of the world, those which face imminent food shortages, almost no soils remain unexploited in humid areas, meaning that the future expansion of farming will be in arid or semi-arid areas. This will increase the demand for irrigation, placing more pressure on streams or underground water supplies. In addition to this expansion, even in humid areas farmers in developed countries are increasingly using supplemental irrigation to increase yields or to protect against extended droughts.

The water for irrigation comes from two main sources—groundwater and streams. One dramatic exception is the use of expensive desalinated seawater in oil-rich countries such as Saudi Arabia. Early irrigation was from stream flow. Wells tapped groundwater for human uses, or for livestock, but until the invention of wind- and motor-driven pumps they were not a practical, or dependable, source of water for any extensive irrigation (groundwater finds an outlet in springs or artesian wells, and thus joins surface runoff in feeding streams). Depending on the type of underlying rock and soil, at a certain depth the soil or porous rock becomes saturated with water. This level, or table, which undulates with the contours of the terrain, can vary seasonally, and drop extensively in drought years. In the past, hand-dug wells had to penetrate this table to assure a steady flow of water. In arid climates, only deep wells, which require modern well-digging equipment, can reach the water table. This groundwater flows, exiting most often in springs, which mark the location at which the water table is at or close to the surface. But if humans draw too much of this water from wells, the table drops, springs dry up, and the base flow of creeks and rivers shrinks. Thus most shallow groundwater is a very limited and fragile source of irrigation water.

Not so in deep and often closed aquifers. These are large volumes of water that accumulate in porous rock over centuries, but underneath a layer of rocks almost impervious to water. This means a very gradual charging of an aquifer, and at times an equally slow exit of the nearly trapped water. Some aquifers are huge, extending over hundreds of miles and containing what may seem unlimited amounts of water. Deep wells that penetrate the rock barrier and reach such aquifers seem to provide plenty of water for irrigation, and indeed the flow may continue for decades or even centuries, or indefinitely if the pumping of water only matches the annual seepage that replenishes the aquifer. If the well taps an aquifer at the low point of a sloping pool, the water pressure may force the water to the surface (an artesian well), like a gusher in an oil field.

In both northern India and China, up to half of irrigation water now comes from private wells that tap into groundwater or easily accessible aquifers. But in time, if the outflow exceeds the slow rate of charging, even the largest aquifers will shrink, requiring ever deeper wells. Eventually, they can dry up. In the United States, over the past half century about one-fifth of all irrigation water has come from the huge Ogallala aquifer under the great plains (South Dakota to Texas). By 1970, farmers were using its water at ten times the rate of inflow. The shrinking Ogallala may last only another twenty years. The well depth required to tap it has already so increased as to lead farmers to give up on this source, and in North Texas the annual take is declining. The affected states have negotiated agreements limiting its use. Because of the slow charging, almost all modern irrigation based on either shallow or deeper and closed aquifers is nonsustainable. The ultimate limit is annual precipitation.

The same is true for flowing streams. Rainwater either feeds them directly, in runoff, or indirectly, by way of groundwater or aquifers that find an outlet in springs. The problem with streams is uneven flow. In many rivers, the base flow (from springs, some fed by deep aquifers) is only a tenth of that of peak flows, after winter snow melt or heavy spring rains. In dry periods, as the water table sinks, streams lose more and more water by seepage. In hot weather, they lose water by evaporation. Often the lowered flow coincides with the time crops need the most water for irrigation. Even ancient civilizations tried to cope with this problem by building low earthen dams, creating reservoirs to save at least some of the spring runoff. But to save most of the total annual runoff requires numerous high dams, and technologies of dam building that only matured in the late nineteenth and early twentieth centuries. High dams could also serve other purposes—reserves of water for urban water systems, hydroelectric production (dams not only create the falling water for turbines but so store water as to maintain an even flow over the year), flood control (to capture flood waters, but note that the timing for this may not be consistent with maximum energy production), and water sports. Although not the most economical way to improve navigation, and thus the transport of goods, high dams could, with large locks, serve this purpose also. Today, except in some Arctic areas, most rivers are to some extent under human control (this includes levy systems as well as dams), and up to two-thirds of the water reaching the oceans has passed over or through dams.

Dams are now a necessity. As the population surges to 9 billion, irrigation will become even more important. Here is the main avenue for increased food output in many parts of the world. The increase does not have to require more water. At present, most irrigation systems are very inefficient (as low as 25 percent of source water reaches the roots of plants). When water is moved by open, unlined canals, seepage and evaporation can steal up to half the original water. When the water reaches the crops by flooding of ditches or by spray, more of the water is wasted by evaporation or by absorption by soil that does not contain crop roots. If moved to crops by concrete-lined canals with some type of cover, and fed to plants by a drip system, as in Israel, irrigation can reach maximum efficiency (up to 60 percent or more). Such a system could expand production in now fully exploited river systems (Indus, Colorado, Niger) by up to 50 percent. But few countries can afford such capital costs, which are up to three times greater than in ditch irrigation. Note that irrigation water lost to evaporation or seepage is not necessarily a complete loss, for it may increase rainfall or leave more water for downstream users.

Drip systems also slow the process of salinization. Because of evaporation, minerals in river water can slowly accumulate in irrigated soils in arid areas, eventually curtailing and even ending production. The present means of postponing this disaster is the use of extra water, water not needed by plants, to flush as many salts as possible deeper into the subsoil, from this subsoil into drainage pipes and ditches, and then into heavily polluted holding ponds or lakes. Without proper drainage, this extra flushing water can lead to waterlogged soil, with some of the salt backing up to the roots of plants. Ultimately, no final answer exists for salinization in certain soils or climates. Only long periods of noncropping allows limited rainfall to lower the salt content of soil, with the recovery time determined by the amount of annual rainfall. Supplemental irrigation in humid areas largely avoids this problem, because of the flushing effect of normal rainfall. Despite all these costs, irrigation normally pays for itself in increased and secure production. But in most areas of the world, the future of irrigation is clouded. That based on aquifers is nonsustaining. Riverine irrigation leads to salinization, waterlogging, and dangerous drainage. Most critical, in areas of greatest need the river water is already fully used. The problems are regional in nature and have to be solved locally (it is almost impossible to import large quantities of water). In fully used drainage areas, only expensive drip systems can increase food production. Without these high capital costs, many countries have no recourse but increased importation of food. By one estimate, in 2025 around 1.8 billion people will live in countries without enough water to maintain present food production, and 350 million more will be able to maintain present production only by large and very expensive water projects.[2]

A growing scarcity of water for irrigation is regional in nature. Plenty of unused, or underused, agricultural land remains in humid, developed countries, such as the United States. But it is central Africa and much of Asia that already suffer from food shortages, and in the very areas where irrigation is necessary. Food habits have something to do with water. By an oft-stated rule, it takes one thousand pounds of water to produce one pound of food. But this depends on the food. It is roughly correct for corn and wheat (worldwide, grain is the leading food), but it understates the water needed for rice. It easily takes four times as much water for each pound of grain-fattened beef. Thus, poor countries with stable or declining agricultural production and developing water shortages cannot afford much beef, or even hogs or chickens.

The demands of irrigation can clash with other water needs, and in many river basins already do so, including the Colorado basin in the United States. Fortunately, most industrial uses of water, as in hydro-electric generation, or cooling in thermal plants, do not use up water and need not so pollute it as to render it unfit for irrigation. Waste water from household use, if treated, can also irrigate crops. Since a majority of urban areas are close to the ocean, well downstream from the site of irri-gated farms, the use of their treated waste water on farms requires costly infrastructure and pumping. However, the treated waste water from in-land cities is routinely reused in downstream water systems, factories, or farms. In underdeveloped countries, much untreated waste water, or water from severely polluted streams, ends up in irrigation canals, result-ing in numerous health hazards.

Another problem is that the use of practically all water from streams can have devastating environmental effects. Depleted rivers no longer feed vital wetlands and deltas, or sustain fish and other organisms. Thus, most countries will face increased pressure to maintain some minimal level of river flow all year round, which can severely limit the amount available for irrigation. In much of Asia and arid areas of Africa, the overuse of runoff water has already had devastating effects on ecosystems.

Even more than strip-mining, dams and their often huge human-made lakes have changed the face of the earth. The original, and now most often primary, reason for dams is irrigation, and still is in some of the world's great river basins (Nile, Niger, Indus, Volga, Tigris and Eu-phrates, Ganges, Columbia, Po, Yellow, Colorado, Missouri). However, all but the lowest dams now serve multiple purposes. In the most controlled river system in the world, the Tennessee, the numerous high dams are in one of the highest rainfall sections of the world. Little water is needed for irrigation there, and the dams primarily provide electricity and flood control. From about 1880 until 1970, the creation of more and more dams seemed to be a wondrous human achievement, with great popular support. The Tennessee Valley Authority became a symbol of multipur-pose river development. Imitations seemed to offer a major pathway to progress in underdeveloped countries, where the enthusiasm for dams remains. But in the industrialized world, and where strong environmental movements have emerged, the earlier enthusiasm has turned to doubt, to a new critical evaluation, and in some cases to efforts to dismantle older dams.

It is futile to bemoan most past dam construction. Without the water management they allow, the world simply could not support its present population. Yet, the cost of dams is high, much higher than realized in the heyday of great river basin projects. How one balances advantages against costs seems to depend on the perspective of the observers. High dams inundate good farmland or forests, displace people, disrupt fish migrations, and endanger the habitat of animals. Yet they supply a more environmentally friendly form of electricity than steam plants, support vast irrigation projects, reduce or suppress floods, often expand navigational channels, and offer many recreational opportunities. When all the water of a river is contained and used, the effects can be disastrous for the delta. Neither the Indus nor the Colorado now flow to the sea in most years, and the flow of the Nile is drastically reduced. This has reduced delta wetlands, allowed seawater to penetrate inland, stopped the growth of deltas, in some cases led to a retrenchment of land, and destroyed the habitat of both marine and land species. In Kazakhstan and Uzbekistan, large, Soviet-inaugurated irrigation projects have all but eliminated the limited annual flow of water into the huge but shallow Arial Sea, which has shrunk to less than a third of its original expanse and now seems doomed to end up as a salt flat, with huge costs to local populations, including a loss of fish and many bird and mammal species. Even levies to constrict or deepen the flow of streams can have adverse environmental effects, as proved by the Mississippi, which has concentrated a damaging amount of silt in a growing delta. The modern Mississippi has also drained valuable wetlands and marshes which were formerly replenished by a less controlled river.

In the last three decades, dam building has reached a new threshold in sheer size and scope. Four projects have dwarfed the size of former world record-setting dams, such as Hoover and Grand Coulee in the United States. Each of the four have been very controversial, and will be more so in the future. Two of these dams are on the Paraná River, which rises in central Brazil and later marks the boundary between Brazil and Paraguay, and then Argentina and Paraguay. Both are primarily hydroelectric projects, and thus not major sources of irrigation and food production. The first of these, at least in conception and early construction, but not completion, was the lower of the two, the Yacyretá Project between Argentina and Paraguay, a dam not yet fully completed, and one marked by corruption and international controversy. The other is the Itaipu Dam, between Brazil and Paraguay, but largely a Brazilian project. Over 600 feet high, and five miles wide, it was at completion the largest hydro-electric project in the world (12.6 million kilowatts from 18 turbines), and would remain so until the near completion of Three Gorges Dam in China in 2006. This Chinese dam is 594 feet high, with an expected reservoir 370 miles long, 632 square kilometers in area, holding 28.9 billion cubic yards of water. Its 26 generators will produce 18.2 million kilowatts of electricity (one-ninth of the present use in China), probably a record for all time. According to critics, it is an ecological disaster. But it is in a humid area of China, and primarily a power dam, not an irrigation dam.

Not so the Aswan Dam in Egypt, the most important irrigation dam in the world. It is not the largest or highest. Its hydro output is relatively modest, not only because the flow of the Nile is only that of a mid-sized river, but also because in most years the reservoir (Lake Nasser) is not full. But, at least until the completion of the Three Gorges Dam, Aswan was by far the dam that was most central, and critical, to a single country. Without the dam, Egypt today would not be able to support its growing population (up from 21 million in 1950 to 77 million in 2005). To understand the present Egyptian economy, one must grasp the role of this one dam.

The Nile is the lifeblood of Egypt. No other country is so dependent on a single river. Egypt is a desert. Only irrigation water from the Nile makes extensive human habitation possible. Almost all Egyptians live in a narrow strip on both sides of the river. Historically, the Nile provided water for irrigating early summer crops, but in the fall it flooded the low-lying lands along its banks. The floods were a vital aspect of Egyptian agriculture. They deposited a layer of silt each year, which continuously restored the fertility of the soil, allowing continuous cropping year after year. Also, the floods flushed out any salts accumulated from irrigation, solving the problem of salinization faced in most irrigated areas of the world. But like all rivers, the Nile was not always benign. In cyclical droughts, it floods diminished and crops suffered. As often as every decade, huge floods threatened the cities and villages.

Even before 1900, the need for a secure water supply led to small dams and in 1901 a then large dam at Aswan. As later enlarged, it could capture up to one-tenth of the waters from the average annual flood, and provided water for irrigation projects just below Aswan. By World War II it was clear that a high dam at Aswan, given the topography, could capture more than the annual flood waters, and thus allow a controlled use of all the Nile waters for irrigation. It could end the annual floods, and with this almost all the damages they could cause. But it would also end the annual siltation. A high dam could thus bring one of the great rivers of the world under full human control, or in a sense turn the Nile below Aswan into the world's largest irrigation canal. Humans could manage all the annual flow of the Nile, in what would be the largest and most secure irrigation system in the world. The older, lower dam remained, and other levies and control mechanisms supplemented Aswan.

The Aswan Dam came to fruition out of cold war conflict. The nationalist aspirations of Egypt's leader, Gamel Abdel Nasser, led to conflict with Britain, and to the Suez crisis of 1956. By then Britain and the United States had reneged on promised funding for the Aswan Dam, so instead Nasser used Suez revenues and support from the Soviet Union to build the 11,811-foot-long, 364-foot-high dam from 1960 to 1971. The dam, when full, would have a 288-mile-long reservoir, extending into the Sudan, or what was then the largest human-made lake in the world. It was so large that it could easily absorb even the greatest of Nile floods, and it even had a diversionary tunnel to a low area in the desert in case it needed to divert water from the dam. In fact, the lake has never been full. The dry tropical air causes a high evaporation rate (20 percent or so), meaning that it is difficult to fill. But it does provide perfect flood control. So far, it has offered complete protection against drought, but in the mid-1980s, after several dry years, Egypt was close to having to limit the water needed for irrigation. In the drought years it produced less electricity. At full flow, it could produce over 2 million kilowatts of electricity, or approximately one-half of the Egyptian demand at completion (it is now less than 15 percent).

Aswan gave a tremendous boost to Egyptian agriculture, more than doubling its potential yield. With no flooding, farmers could grow two or three crops a year, with an assured supply of water. This has enabled Egypt to feed its now inflated population. Of course, it suffered the problems that haunt irrigation everywhere—waterlogged soils when drainage systems were inadequate, salinization, and the need to replace the earlier flood-borne silt with fertilizer, which, along with pesticides, created the usual environmental problems. The lake absorbs a large input of silt each year, and eventually this will reduce the volume of water for flood control and irrigation (such is its size that a serious silting problem is more than a century away). The Nile delta has stopped expanding, and is now withdrawing as seawater moves farther inland. Delta fishing has declined, even as the mix of fish in the eastern Mediterranean has shifted because of the dearth of fresh water inflow. Thousands of Egyptians had to move out of the lower delta, while most coastal resorts were stranded or destroyed. The resettlement of peasants, particularly Nubians in the Sudan, led to numerous injustices, not by necessity but for political reasons. Despite all the problems, the dam gave Egypt at least a thirty-year reprieve on a looming demographic crisis, but that may be all. More efficiency in the movement and use of irrigation water, and in industrial and household uses of water, plus further improvements in agricultural yields, may postpone a food crisis for a few decades more, but not indefinitely if the population does not stabilize. A continuation of global warming, and more droughts in the central African headwaters of the Nile, could hasten the crisis.

Like so many other problems confronting the contemporary world, looming water scarcities and water pollution generally afflict countries least able to afford corrective strategies. In the next century, water shortages may become the most critical of environmental concerns. Global warming may adversely affect water supplies in many countries, although no one at present can predict the exact regional impact of warming on local precipitation and rates of evaporation. Like soil, clean water is not easily moved from areas of plenty to areas of scarcity. This is true even of drinking water, where packaging and transport costs can make water too expensive for poor people in underdeveloped countries. Thus, the challenge of providing safe water for household use and for irrigation is a regional problem, at least so far. It is as of yet a relatively minor problem in a water-blessed United States, except for the Colorado River Basin. Fortunately, here, Americans can afford conservation strategies. They will not suffer overly much if the citizens of Los Angeles or Phoenix have to play golf on brown fairways, close down their swimming pools, stop washing cars or watering grass except from their own waste water, and even bathe every other day rather than once or twice a day. They will suffer only slightly higher food costs if farmers in the great valley of California have to line and cover their irrigation canals, or even adopt a drip system for orchards and vegetable crops. But these precautions may not be enough if the population of the Southwest continues to rise and if a cycle of low precipitation (the present one began in 1999) continues to afflict the Rockies that feed the Colorado.

ENERGY

Most techniques that could help alleviate regional shortages of water, and often also food shortages tied to a lack of irrigation water, involve large inputs of energy, most of all the desalinization of seawater. Thus, energy and water are intimately linked resources, even apart from flowing or falling water's being used as a major source of energy. I here use the word energy for whatever does work, whatever directs and channels changes in the physical world. For humans, food is the fuel for such work, nerves and muscles the mechanisms that use up the energy provided by food.

Primitive humans had only muscle power for work. But because, alone among mammals, they had developed languages and were self-conscious, they were very adept at tool building. Tools, best symbolized by a hoe and a bow, leveraged tremendously the work of their muscles. But however complex the tools, food, as metabolized, remained the main source of energy to accomplish human goals. The one great exception was fire. In a sense, one might refer to fire as a tool. But in this case, humans only captured and controlled, or deliberately initiated, a complex chemical interaction, and let the radiated energy provide warmth in winter and palatable foods year round. Controlled fires could cluster animals for a kill, or could clear away trees or tangled grasses to make tillable fields. Even today, with the thousands of chemical processes under human control, combustion remains the largest source of productive energy worldwide. Controlled burning propels most of our ships, airplanes, trains, and automobiles, and in the United States it generates most of our electricity.

But for thousands of years, domesticated animals rivaled controlled burning as an energy source for humans. Muscle power dominated, but in this case it was the muscles of horses, oxen, or camels. To pay for this energy, humans had to procure food for their animals, at times by simply letting them forage, at times by collecting hay or grain for their use. But a man with a horse could raise ten times as much corn as one with only a hoe. The dominance of animal power only ended in the nineteenth and early twentieth centuries, and in some areas of the world it is still dominant.

Two other sources of power—falling water and blowing wind—have ancient origins. Simple sails to supplement oars date back to early Egypt. By the seventh century B.C.E., the Persians had developed mounted sails, or early windmills, to power grain mills. Because the wind blows only intermittently, the windmill was best adapted to water pumps, for drainage or for stored water in reservoirs, but in low-lying countries like Holland, with little water power, large windmills turned the millstones in flour mills. The earliest record of a waterwheel is in Greece in about 65 B.C.E. It was used to turn a millstone. Such waterwheels were widely used in the Roman Empire and in Medieval Europe. They were the main source of power for flour mills, later sawmills, and for some types of water pumps. By the eighteenth century, falling water, some tied to dams, became the main source of power for textile mills and other early factories, such as rolling mills for steel. The boom in textile mills in early nineteenth-century New England was dependent upon water power along the fall lines of rivers. Only in the late nineteenth century did steam engines slowly displace water power in most factories. Throughout America, until well into the twentieth century, most flour and meal was still ground by millstones turned by waterwheels, while in arid areas windmills pumped most water until electrification in the last half of the twentieth century. With electrification, falling water assumed a new importance, and worldwide about 20 percent of all generation is by water, with some mountainous countries almost completely dependent on hydro power. Wind, almost eclipsed by other sources of energy, is making a comeback for the generation of supplemental electricity.

From an environmental perspective, the development of steam power was momentous in its implications. Heated water turns to steam, and when confined the steam can build up a high pressure. The problem is how to use this pressure to do work for humans. At the end of the seventeenth century, in England, inventors found a way to use steam to create a vacuum to draw water. Soon thereafter they developed a piston for such pumps. Only after 1765 did James Watt and others perfect connecting rods and rotation mechanisms to use steam to turn shafts and pulleys. By 1800 several steam engines, with increasingly higher pressure in boilers, had begun to replace falling water in textile mills and soon afterward in rolling mills. This enabled factories to move from along rivers, even though the efficiency of such engines was low by modern standards. In 1803 an English inventor first used a steam engine to turn wheels, or the prototype of the locomotive. By 1830 the great railroad boom was under way in England, and soon in the rest of Europe and in the United States. As early as 1805, a steam engine was used on a barge, and gradually they became the main sources of power for ships. Thus, in less than a century, steam had revolutionized both factory production and transportation. Today, steam is still important in both industries, but in each case largely through the intermediary of electricity. Steam plants still produce over half of the electricity used in the United States.

With steam power, the oldest source of nonmuscle energy for humans, fire, came once again to the forefront. Fire is now the slave of humans, doing most of their work and expanding the potential output of muscle power by the hundreds or even thousands. It is quite true, in purely physical terms, that the average automobile engine can do the work of 150 horses (horsepower). The fuel for this work is hydrocarbons, which burn in the presence of sufficient oxygen. Most of these are the residue of past life (thus fossil energy), although in much of the underdeveloped world the hydrocarbons largely come from biomass (wood, dead grass, dried dung) and do not burn in engines but heat homes and cook food. Today, the only large competitors to the power of fire are hydro and nuclear power. Alternative sources of energy, such as geothermal, wind, chemical (as in batteries or fuel cells), and solar collectors, are all minor sources, but they may grow in importance. Except for transportation, an increasing share of energy reaches users in the form of electricity. Pure hydrogen, as a secondary source of energy, may have an important future. If so, it will resemble electricity, for it requires a primary fuel in its production. At present, the only economical way of producing pure hydrogen is from hydrocarbons, such as natural gas. A second and more costly source, electrolysis, requires large inputs of electricity. Note that in normal combustion, what really burns is the hydrogen, not the carbon. In fact, carbon is the problem, for in combustion most of it escapes as carbon dioxide, the rest as smoke particles (soot) or residual ash. Hydrogen, when burned alone, combines with the atmospheric oxygen that makes combustion possible to create water vapor, an environmentally benign emission.

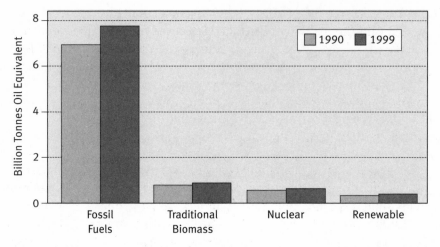

Fig. 8. Global energy supply (data from IEA). (United Nations, *Global Challenge, Global Opportunity*, 14.)

ENERGY SCARCITIES

Two critical issues attend all our burning. One is pollution, a subject addressed in chapter 6. The other is the availability of fuel. Will humans have enough energy to maintain present levels of consumption in wealthy countries, plus enough to raise incomes in the rest of the world to something close to those in Europe and the United States? Will they have the energy needed to supply the needs of the extra 3 billion people who will be on earth in less than fifty years? At present, the annual consumption of all types of energy has been rising at a rate of 1.5 percent to 2.0 percent a year, with most of this reflecting a steady increase in consumption in wealthy countries or rapid industrialization in China and India. Fossil fuels supply most of this energy (see figure 8). The future energy burden will be doubled if wealthy nations continue to increase their already high energy use and the other 80 percent of humans in poorer countries try to gain the needed energy to close the present large gap in incomes, a very difficult task since this is where almost all the 3 billion extra people will be born. If, for example, all humans could attain the present per capita incomes of Americans, who consume five times as much energy as the world average, and over fifteen times as much as countries with a per capita income of under $1,000, the energy needs of 2050 would be staggering (easily ten times the present use). And this ignores the expected gains in income in the United States and other wealthy countries. On the other hand, to keep energy demands at present levels would seem to doom the majority of humans to perpetual poverty, unless we can find ways to use existing energy sources much more efficiently, or find magical new and inexpensive sources of energy.

Energy demands are rising most rapidly in the world's two most populous countries, India and China (37 percent of the world's total). In China, 70 percent of electrical generation comes from coal, with its damaging pollution. China will continue to depend on coal for most of its electricity despite the energy produced by the Three Gorges Dam. Even more ominous is the rapid shift from bicycles and public transportation to automobiles in both countries, but particularly in China. The future possibilities here are staggering. If both India and China had as many automobiles, per capita, as the United States (almost 0.8 motor vehicles for each man, woman, and child), they would have close to 2 billion cars and trucks. They will never have so many. But this number does indicate the scope of the possible market for motor vehicles in these two most populous countries.

In 2005, China was just beginning to move toward a widespread private ownership of automobiles and light trucks (over 20 million and sure to double by 2010). With economic growth of over 8 percent a year, and a rapidly growing number of affluent citizens, the demand for automobiles is soaring (5 million a year, or almost a third that of the United States). At a slower pace, India also has been experiencing a boom in automobile use. Until recently, automobiles in these countries did not have to meet the stringent environmental standards of western Europe and the United States, but in 2006 China introduced tougher emission standards than those in the United States. This automobile boom is in areas where air pollution is already deadly for people with respiratory illnesses. It also insures that China, within the next two decades, will come close to matching the United States in its emissions of greenhouse gases. Above all, motor vehicles now require petroleum, with neither country possessing nearly enough local reserves. Neither nation will be quick to choose more expensive alternatives to the present gasoline engine. One shudders to think about the effect on oil demand caused by the almost certain explosion in automobile use in India and China in the next two decades, particularly if joined by the present annual increase of oil use in the United States (which consumes almost one-fourth of world production).

We have one relatively new source of energy, with almost unlimited possibilities of expansion. This is nuclear fission. Its fuel is either plutonium or an isotope of uranium. Plutonium is the product of one type of nuclear reactor. The major concerns involve safety, what to do with nuclear waste, and how to prevent a spreading military use of atomic energy. Increasing safety concerns and higher safety standards have made nuclear reactors uncompetitive given the present cost of fossil fuels. In 2005, nuclear reactors produced just over 6 percent of all electricity worldwide. Only three or four countries are now constructing new reactors, while a large share of existing reactors are old and close to a necessary closing. But increasing concerns about pollution and global warming are almost certain to spur new, and safer, nuclear plants in the next two decades. A possible future source of energy, again with almost unlimited sources of fuel (an isotope of hydrogen found in water), is nuclear fusion, or an imitation of the energy produced by the sun. The technological challenge is great, and the development of controlled fusion, at least with significant energy potential at competitive prices, is decades away at best.

What about other sources of energy beyond the present big three: fossil fuels, hydro, and nuclear? It may be possible, in the rather distant future, to imitate volcanoes—that is, to tap the enormous heat in the mantle and use it to fuel steam plants. So far, humans have not developed efficient ways of using the dry heat of the mantle, only thermally heated water, and even that usage is minuscule, with the largest amount of geothermal production being in California. It also poses its own environmental problems.

What we need are new renewable energy sources. At present, the most promising for electrical generation are windmills, which are growing rapidly as a supplemental source of electricity. Wind is already competitive in cost in many areas. Its theoretical potential is very large, but it suffers from the intermittent nature of wind. We have no way to store any large quantity of electricity. But wind farms, if part of a geographically large electrical grid, could in part mitigate this problem (the wind would be blowing somewhere at any one time). Also, wind power, like any source with a periodic excess generating capacity, could be used to produce hydrogen (through electrolysis), which could be used in fuel cells. At least in the near future, wind power will remain a tiny part of the total need for electricity, except possibly in Denmark. Opposition to noise and concern over bird kill have made it difficult to find sites for large windmill farms in the United States.

Solar energy is not competitive at present. We have the means of collecting and focusing solar energy to heat water on rooftop collectors, but this will remain a minor source. Thus, in the near future almost all solar energy will come from photovoltaic cells. Their cost is still many times higher than conventional sources of electricity, but they are already a valuable source of electricity in remote areas. The use of solar cells will remain decentralized, with most cells on the roofs of homes or commercial building. If incorporated in new construction, such cells may be cost effective. But given the growing electrical needs of the next fifty years, only nuclear energy would seem to offer a likely alternative to power generated by dams or the burning of fossil fuels.

In the transportation sector, the most promising present alternative to petroleum is ethanol derived from biomass. Both hybrid technology and the use of diesel engines can increase the efficiency of fossil fuels, but neither involves a renewable energy source. One exception is biodiesel fuel made from used cooking oil or other vegetative sources, but its potential is severely limited by its availability. Ethanol is a renewable fuel, and much less polluting than oil (no sulfur and up to 80 percent less carbon dioxide). Unlike such revolutionary new fuels as hydrogen, it requires no new infrastructure. It is already a major source of fuel for automobiles in Brazil (40 percent of all fuel), where a mix of 85 percent ethanol and 15 percent gasoline (called E85) is the standard. So far, in the United States, most ethanol is used as an additive to gasoline, at a usual concentration of 10 percent. Brazil produces most of its ethanol from the richest source, sugar cane. Corn (maize) is the source for most ethanol in the United States. Other small grains can also be used. Even in the United States, automobile manufacturers, particularly General Motors and Ford, are increasingly building flex engines, capable of using either E85 or gasoline, but few outlets sell the richer ethanol mixture. Midwestern farmers and agribusinesses love the federal subsidies that support a new market for corn, and the tariffs that prevent the importation of cheaper ethanol from Brazil. Clearly ethanol has much to recommend it, despite lower miles per gallon and more engine corrosion.

But some reservations are in order. At present, the only developed source for ethanol is agriculture, or hydrocarbon-rich plants. In the case of American corn (maize), the production of ethanol may involve almost as much use of fossil fuels, and as much pollution, as is saved by the reduced use of gasoline in automobiles. The amount of these costs is at present a controversial issue, but they involve the petroleum used in tractors and in shipping and in the production of chemical fertilizers and pesticides, plus the natural gas or other fossil fuels used in fermenting the corn and distilling the alcohol (the process is similar to the production of corn whiskey). Thus, for most of the world, the great promise of ethanol lies in new, still somewhat experimental, processes of gaining ethanol not from easily harvested sugars or starches in cane or grain, but from cellulose in coarse grasses, bamboo, corn stalks, even the bark of trees. Such cellulosic ethanol may be the magical solution to gasoline shortages in the future, particularly in India and China, but it will involve often unacknowledged costs. Dead grasses and weeds, for example, are the sources of organic matter in soil (a type of manure). If used up to produce ethanol, the fertility of soils will soon decline without the use of chemical fertilizers. Finally, the required amount of such fibrous fuels, if they are to replace most gasoline, is staggering.

How long will our fossil fuels last? This is a complicated question, one that involves quite varied estimates and engenders political controversy. What is clear, in all estimates, is that, relative to the present demand, oil is now the scarcest of the three fossil fuels, gas second, and coal the most abundant. World oil production is still growing at about 2 percent a year, and may continue to grow for the next two decades before beginning a necessary decline. It makes little sense to ask when the oil supply will run out. It never will in any absolute sense. If they are willing to pay very high prices, humans will always have access to some oil. Each year natural processes create new oil. Much more important, supplies of some non-conventional sources of oil (tar sands, albumin, heavy oil, or oil in shale) will remain indefinitely, since the cost of procuring much of this oil, or the environmental effects of producing it, are so high. Older oil wells never extracted more than 25 percent of the underlying oil, and even today the maximum return is at best 50 percent. At high costs, some of this remaining oil in abandoned wells can now be extracted. Finally, some of the present oil supply comes from the chemical conversion of the hydrocarbons in coal and natural gas. In other words, we can now make some of the valued distillates that we used to get only from petroleum. What is of great concern today is future natural limits on oil production that

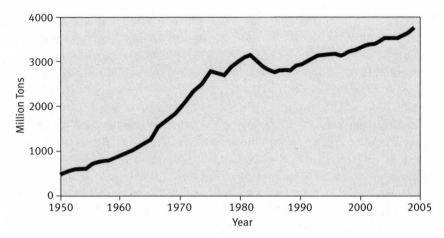

Fig. 9. World oil consumption, 1950–2004. (Worldwatch, *Vital Signs* 2005, 31.)

will force one of two outcomes: conservation in energy use and a shift to alternate fuels (this is the least disruptive alternative), or huge increases in oil prices and one energy crisis after another.

When most people think about an energy crisis today, they think about oil. For good reasons. Oil supplies 40 percent of all energy used worldwide (natural gas only 25 percent), it is the fuel for over 90 percent of transportation, and it is the largest commodity in world commerce. Petroleum is also a vital source of home heating, and a base product for thousands of manufactured items, particularly organic chemicals. To a large extent, the economic growth of the twentieth century rested on the availability of cheap oil, while the automobile was the most transforming innovation. For most people, it is almost impossible to imagine a world without access to affordable oil distillates. It will not be easy to curtail consumption, which is now rising at an average rate of about 2 percent a year. This surged to a frightening 3.4 percent in 2004, a possible omen of the future. Half of the increase was in China and the United States. World consumption is now above 82 million barrels a day, with almost one fourth of this in the United States (see figure 9).

How much oil have humans already consumed, and how much oil is still available for human use? Answers vary on the critical issue of remaining reserves, but not on prior use. In 2004, most experts agreed that humans had so far consumed around 1 trillion barrels of oil (usually stated as 1,000 billion barrels). From 1995 to 2000, the U.S. Geological Survey carried out the most extensive survey of oil and gas reserves ever conducted. Many experts contested its findings, but its survey has informed many United Nations agencies, and often is cited as authoritative, as it is by the International Energy Agency. It is among the most optimistic of forecasts, and politically has had the effect of lowering concerns about early shortages of oil reserves (what Americans, and the American government, want to hear). The USGS estimates that the total original amount of oil on earth that was recoverable by conventional methods (this does not include an even larger amount of oil that is unrecoverable by existing technologies, or oil whose recovery would be prohibitively expensive) was 3 trillion barrels, and along with this over 300 billion barrels of liquified gas that is a product of oil extraction. Humans have already used less than one-third of this total, leaving over 2 trillion more to be exploited. This is almost double the amount of proven reserves as of 2000, or 1.1 trillion barrels (enough for thirty-five years at the level of use in 2000), for it includes estimates of undiscovered reserves and of the expected growth in the amount of recoverable oil in existing reserves. It based this on extrapolations from past experience, which has revealed a growth in reserves that more than matched actual production (through exploration, the amount of known reserves grew as rapidly as did use), and on new technologies that have increased the recovery rate in existing wells. By these additions, it hopes to avoid what has been true for almost all past predictions of oil resources—estimates that soon proved much too low.

On the basis of its estimates, the USGS predicted that world oil production would not peak until after 2020 (the International Energy Agency agrees, but foresees a critical growth in unconventional production before then) and that any major supply problem would not develop until after 2036 (and for natural gas not until after 2050). This means that humans have time to find substitutes for oil and gas. But note that even this most optimistic scenario still means that the era of plentiful and cheap oil and gas will end long before the deaths of many people alive today.[3]

The leading critic of the USGS report is Colin J. Campbell of Britain, a well-known and respected expert on oil supplies. His view is among the most pessimistic. He believes that we have already used approximately half of the recoverable oil on earth, and that at best we will be able to recover only another 1 trillion barrels. He believes that most estimates of proven reserves are inflated (not so for the United States), particularly among OPEC nations, and for political reasons, since annual production quotas are based on percentages of "proven" reserves. He believes that in the first decade of the new century we have reached peak production, and that soon the annual world production of oil will begin a decline of over 2 percent a year. This will create the same type of oil crisis as suffered in the 1970s (one based on cartel control over production), with sharply increased prices for oil worldwide, or the soaring oil prices of 2004–2006 (based on political instability in the Near East, refining bottlenecks, a near speculative mania in oil markets, and the temporary disruptions of hurricanes Katrina and Rita).[4] The speculative increase did reflect realistic concerns over the shrinking of excess productive capacity to something close to zero. Any major disruption of production anywhere in the world today will lead to scarcity and high enough prices to curtail oil use (this might, in one sense, be a desirable outcome).

The politics of oil is critical to future scenarios. Oil production in the United States peaked in 1970 and has declined ever since. It has already peaked in Britain, Canada, and Venezuela, and will soon peak for Norway. It is now declining in thirty-three of the forty-eight largest oil-producing countries. The annual rate of new discoveries is now only one-fourth the annual use of oil. Up to 60 percent of proven reserves are in five Middle Eastern Islamic countries, with about one-fourth in Saudi Arabia (next in order are Iraq, Kuwait, Iran, and the United Arab Emirates). Already, the percentage of the total world production in OPEC countries is rising once again, and will continue to do so. Increased levels of production in these five countries may, indeed, postpone any decline in world production beyond 2020 (a cooperative Saudi Arabia has played the thermostat role recently). But in 2006 they had no more than 1 million barrels a day of spare productive capacity. In time even these countries will not be able to fill the gap between supply and demand, and the more they pump in the present the sooner their own production will have to begin a gradual decline because of natural limits. It is foolish for these countries to pump oil at maximum rates, for this lowers world prices, depletes their most valuable resource, and threatens their future. And if they do come to the rescue of an oil-thirsty world for the next two decades, this would only mean that, once the decline sets in, the decline curve would be much sharper and prices much higher. Such is the present dependence on the politically unstable Persian Gulf region that any major disruption of production there would lead to an immediate oil crisis. The rest of the world does not have the reserves needed to replace this one regional source.

Natural gas and coal do not pose the same supply problems as oil. The USGS estimate of the original gas supplies was slightly smaller than that for oil (the equivalent of 2.8 trillion barrels of oil), but so far humans have used only 18 percent of this, leaving a larger reserve than for oil. The problem with natural gas supplies, in the near future, will involve not natural scarcities but the cost of developing gas wells and transporting the gas to consumers. These costs are very high. This means regional scarcities that will endure for years. By most estimates, coal supplies will last for over two hundred years at existing levels of use. Coal reserves are based on the type of thick veins presently mined, not on the almost inestimable amount of coal in thin or impure veins. In addition to coal, the ocean floor has sequestered an enormous volume of hydrocarbons in the form of frozen methane. Thus, so far, humans have scarcely touched the total amount of energy resources. But most hydrocarbons are not presently accessible, or not economical to exploit (as is true of shale and of the methane on the ocean floor). One engineer has estimated that the total reserves of hydrocarbons amount to thirty thousand times the present annual rate of consumption. Such estimates are based on the amount of past photosynthesis needed to produce the present amount of atmospheric oxygen. If the world consumed fossil fuels at the American rate, this would last six thousand years.[5] What is clear is that only a small percentage of this total reserve would ever be usable by humans. And when, and if, unconventional exploitation becomes competitive, as it is now for Canadian tar sands, the environmental costs could be enormous.

The present trend, worldwide, is toward less-carbon-intensive fossil fuels. This means a steady increase in the use of natural gas, largely methane, with its four hydrogen atoms to one of carbon. Petroleum has two of hydrogen to one of carbon, coal one to one, and most wood ten atoms of carbon to one of hydrogen. Wood creates the most ash, the most aerosol-laden smoke, and by far the most carbon dioxide. Its continued heavy use in underdeveloped countries in part nullifies the pollution benefits of very low energy use. Natural gas, unlike most coal, has few impurities, burns cleanly, and primarily emits water vapor. Yet, it adds carbon dioxide to the atmosphere, and if one is concerned about greenhouse gases, even its continued use poses dangers. From this perspective, nuclear and hydro power are preferable. Already, the most accessible fossil fuels have been exploited. This means that in the future consumers will have to devote a larger share of income to energy unless more efficient technologies accompany the shift to deeper, more scattered, or less pure reserves of coal, oil, and gas. So far, invention has stayed ahead of the game, with fuel prices stable or even lower over the last half century. But, in time, higher costs for fossil fuels are inevitable, and this will encourage a more rapid shift to alternative fuels, probably safer forms of nuclear energy. However, the shift will have to be gradual, or else the human costs will be very high. Whatever the ultimate reserve of fossil fuels, the draw down of this nonsustainable resource will accelerate in at least the near future.

It is all but certain that fossil fuels will remain the dominant source of energy for at least the next thirty years. But if one has a fervent belief in invention and new technologies, then certain predictions are in order. Natural gas will largely displace the present use of coal in electrical generation except in China and possibly the United States, and the use of wood, coal, and oil in home heating except in the most impoverished countries. The construction of nuclear fission plants will gradually resume and account for almost 50 percent of total electrical generation worldwide by 2050. Hydro power will expand largely in developing countries like China, where opposition to high dams is muted and more rivers are as yet untamed. Except for air travel and most shipping, transportation (trains, automobiles, trucks) will turn more and more to biomass (ethanol), electricity (at first in hybrid vehicles, with small gasoline engines matched with battery-powered electric motors), pure hydrogen (natural gas will be the primary source), or natural gas. Such shifts will postpone the exhaustion of accessible petroleum reserves, allow time for a further conversion away from any fossil fuels, and leave large unused reserves of coal and shale. But natural gas supplies may be tight by 2050, which will stimulate more research and development on nuclear fusion or, if fusion power is already a reality, a more rapid conversion to it.

Accompanying the gradual shift to nonfossil fuels will be a continuing effort to burn fuels more efficiently. It is presently impossible to harvest all the BTUs present in any fossil fuel. The conversion of most of this to electricity involves further losses of energy. In some cases, such as gasoline in automobile engines, we may already be close to the maximum possible efficiency. This is also true in some factories, where economic pressures have stimulated energy savings. Some experimental designs for

the use of coal and oil in electrical generation can improve efficiency by
50 percent. At the point of final use, better insulated homes, plus more
energy-efficient light bulbs, furnaces, air conditioners, and appliances,
can expand the usefulness of fuels by at least 30 percent over present patterns. The gains in efficiency in all these areas have been critical in the last
thirty years, but in each case the increase in consumption (larger homes,
air conditioning, new appliances, more and larger private automobiles,
more mobility, the new electronic revolution) in developed countries
since 1990 has kept the total use of energy growing, while population
increases and, in East Asia, rapid industrialization have had the same effect in developing countries. Over the long run, the energy game will be
almost impossible to win without a slowing of population growth and
changes in patterns of consumption. It is indeed true that, at present, year
by year, the use of energy per capita, for each unit of GNI, keeps going
down in all developed countries. The trouble is that the units of GNI keep
growing even faster.

Energy Use in the United States

The United States consumes more energy than any other country, both
in total and per capita. Canada and the United States consume one-fourth
of all oil, and an even higher percentage of natural gas. Only China may
soon catch up with the United States in total energy use, but it does
not use nearly as much on a per capita basis. Our energy use is heavily
weighted toward fossil fuels. This leads to much more air pollution than
either hydro or nuclear power, and also involves more emissions of carbon dioxide, the major greenhouse gas. By the estimates of the Intergovernmental Panel on Climate Change, the United States discharged about
1,463 billion metric tons of carbon or carbon equivalents into the atmosphere in 1994, with CO_2 making up 85 percent of this. Today, its rise in
annual emissions is over 1 percent. The largest sources of these emissions,
by EPA estimates, are electrical generation (35 percent), transportation
(31 percent, with over half of this from private automobiles or light
trucks), manufacturing (21 percent), residential (7 percent, primarily
for heating), and commercial (5 percent, largely in buildings). The United States gains 52 percent of its electricity from coal-fired steam plants,
and these account for 85 percent of the CO_2 emitted by such utilities. It
will be almost impossible to reverse the present annual rise in fossil fuel

use. One tool would be to persuade Americans to consume less electricity, by various conservation measures. However, no government effort is likely to persuade affluent Americans to lower the size of their houses or to cluster them in more compact urban enclaves.

The United States does not lead the world in energy use, or in CO_2 emissions, because it has neglected environmental issues or failed to pass effective environmental legislation. In fact, it leads the world in energy efficiency, per unit consumed. Its role almost entirely rests on its high level of overall consumption, its dependence on fossil fuels, and its housing and transportation preferences. Briefly, the United States, to a greater extent than most western European countries (particularly France, with its nearly 80 percent reliance on nuclear power), relies primarily on coal for electrical generation (52 percent), which accounts for 40 percent of all fuel burned in America. The mix of fuels is important, and works against any early reductions in this area (political and regional issues also complicate coal use, for coal state congresspeople will fight hard to protect its market and local jobs).

The method of generation is no more important than patterns of electrical consumption. This is a function of living standards, such as the number of appliances in homes, and of the detached, increasingly large houses preferred by Americans. Even as family size has decreased (from 3.4 in 1960 to 2.8 in 1990), the average size of new homes has more than doubled since 1950 (from less than one thousand to over twenty-four hundred square feet in 2005), and is still growing very rapidly. The electronic revolution has contributed to home energy use. Multiple television sets are now joined by computers (these alone have increased the home use of electricity by up to 10 percent). Home heating places a large demand on electricity, heating oil, and natural gas, while air conditioning drains summer electricity in the hot and humid Sun Belt. By greater efficiency in the use of coal, by its now stalled nuclear power program, and by a gradual conversion to fossil fuels that emit less carbon (particularly natural gas), the United States has halved its emission of carbon for each unit of energy in the last fifty years. But population growth and much higher levels of consumption have precluded any reduction in total emissions.

The location and dispersed placing of American houses help explain a second unique American consumer pattern—the exceptionally large use of energy in transportation, most in private automobiles and small trucks. Recent energy use has risen most rapidly in the transportation sector, worldwide. Americans travel twice as many miles in automobiles as do western Europeans, use over double the amount of gasoline to propel them, use automobiles for over 85 percent of their travel (80 percent and growing in Europe), and have less and poorer forms of public transportation. The increased percentage of women working has increased commuting volume. Lower income workers often live in far-out suburbs to reduce housing costs. The United States in 2005 had around 220 million motor vehicles, the highest in the world, or more than one vehicle for each licensed driver. Two-car families are giving way to three or four. Shopping centers, long shopping hours, parental transportation of children to schools, and the high ownership of automobiles by teens all help account for a resumed increase in gasoline consumption by automobiles in the 1990s.

Oil consumption for automobiles is now rising each year. The trend toward new levels of efficiency in automobile engines, which was mandated by energy and environmental legislation in the 1970s, slowed by the late 1990s, when the average miles per gallon of vehicles began to go down once again (40 percent of the increase in carbon emissions since 1990 have been in the transportation sector, with gasoline consumption by motor vehicles up 2.1 percent in 2001 despite a slow economy). This is not due to less efficient engines, but to a consumer preference for larger ones, in vans and sports utility vehicles. In 2003 the average weight of automobiles and small trucks in the United States exceeded 4,000 pounds for the first time since 1976 (the average was 3,202 in 1981), and rose to around 4,060 in 2004. The average miles per gallon of fuel has dropped from 22.1 in the late 1980s to 20.7 in 2003. In fact, never in American history did cultural and economic trends so favor the private use of energy as in the 1990s—high employment, rising incomes, low petroleum prices, long distances, large houses, multiple appliances, and gas-guzzling automobiles or vans (because of new efficiencies, industrial energy use apart from utilities stabilized or declined). Smug Europeans should note that their consumptive trends, including more detached housing and more automobiles, is rapidly following the American example. In some consumptive areas, such as second homes, Sweden is already ahead of the United States.

On the supply side, considerable reductions in energy use are possible through more efficient electrical generation. Very recent and promising new techniques of generation could make this possible, but the costs will allow replacement only as older plants wear out. The most dramatic reductions require a change in fuel (for example, to natural gas instead of coal, or to nuclear plants). Each change entails costs. Few utilities can afford to upgrade older but still functional generators, and in 2002 President George W. Bush, by executive order, allowed utilities to make significant changes in existing facilities without having to adopt mandated new emission targets (see chapter 5). Alternative energy sources have long tantalized Americans, and in the near future it seems that wind power has some potential in certain areas of the country. Solar power is still uncompetitive, while only a miraculous new battery technology can make periodic generation (wind, sun) widely practical. The use of natural gas will increase where it is competitive with coal (as in parts of the Southwest), but in 2004–2005 its supply was so short as to double its cost. Nuclear energy, the great hope of the 1960s, may revive, but at present no new plants are under way in the United States because of safety concerns. Fusion energy, if ever developed, is still decades away. But any of these shifts will cost someone. Government incentives (such as tax breaks) will cost the public. Tougher regulation will lead to higher rates.

In the United States, the second most effective reduction of energy use would be in the transportation sector. In some areas—airplanes, railroads, barges—the room for short-term savings is minimal. Not so for automobiles and trucks. The gasoline shortages and soaring prices of the 1970s revealed what Americans could do to save on energy. High gasoline prices, mandated mileage standards, a national speed limit, more efficient engines, and a turn to smaller automobiles all helped reverse the growth in both unit and total gasoline consumption, which only in the 1990s began to grow once again. These efficiencies helped balance off a continued growth in miles traveled and automobiles owned. These savings ended in the 1990s, when gasoline prices fell below that of bottled water. In principle, a few political choices could once again cut gasoline use sharply—a restored and enforced 55 miles per hour speed limit, a one dollar a gallon gasoline tax or a tax on carbon emissions, sharply progressive taxes on automobiles or trucks as their miles per gallon rise above the average for all vehicles, restrictions on parking in inner cities, major subsidies for public transportation, and more incentives for the development of alternative fuels (ethanol, natural gas, biodiesel, hydrogen).

Yet, the one area in which early change is most likely is in automobiles. The standard gasoline engine in automobiles may be closer to
extinction than people anticipate. Both fuel costs and air pollution have
driven the search for new alternatives. Fuel cells that burn hydrogen is an
alternative pushed by the Bush Administration, but it will take years to
perfect a production model, and its widespread use would require a new
and very expensive infrastructure. All-electric cars have been around for
over a hundred years, but existing battery technology limits them to short
distances. Engines that burn natural gas are already used on buses, while
diesel engines, widely used in Europe but not so much in the United
States, are more efficient than gasoline engines. But the most promising
alternatives, for the near future, are flex engines that burn E85, and the
type of hybrid vehicle that Honda and Toyota first developed in Japan and
soon marketed in the United States. By 2006, most automobile manufac-
tures had hybrid models for sale or under development.

It is now possible, with existing technologies and no major changes
in the existing infrastructure, to build an automobile that consumes less
than 10 percent of the gasoline used by a conventional gasoline engine.
What is required is a hybrid car with a flex engine, one that can use E85.
These will probably be on the market by 2007. If the United States, in
the next ten years, could convert all new automobiles and small trucks
to such flex hybrids, and require ethanol as the fuel, it would no longer
be dependent on any foreign oil and might even be able to meet its now
repudiated quota for greenhouse gases under the Kyoto Protocol. Magic!
Not quite. The problem is the needed supply of ethanol. We could not
grow a fourth of the corn needed to produce it, and Brazil would not
be able to export enough even if we lowered the tariff barriers. The only
possible source of so much ethanol would have to be the now experimental and expensive cellulosic process, which may or may not become
cost effective.

Another innovation could dramatically reduce the use of either gasoline or E85. By 2010, production models of "plug-in" hybrids should be
on the market. Toyota is now at work on a plug-in version of its Prius.
Several individual inventors have already added larger capacity batteries
and a home charging capacity to modified hybrid vehicles. The goal is a
plug-in battery pack that can propel a car, in the electric mode only, for
up to twenty or thirty miles on one charge. The likely solution will be
lithium batteries, which are lighter than the present lead-acid batteries.

Such a hybrid could, in short-distance and city driving, all but eliminate any need to use the gasoline engine, saving it for higher speed highway trips. Such a hybrid could, on average, attain up to one hundred miles per gallon of fuel. Burn only E85 and the gasoline use would be minuscule. The problem is the cost of the new type of batteries, and thus how soon production models can compete in the marketplace. The wave of the future, if political events should lead to a major oil crisis, may well be flex engine, plug-in hybrids that require less than one gallon of gasoline, plus six gallons of ethanol, for every five hundred miles traveled.

Major changes in types of energy use or in consumptive habits will affect most Americans, some adversely. The equity issues could be major. If we replace the standard gasoline engine in automobiles and trucks, the drastic reduction in the demand for oil will not only threaten the profits of major oil companies, but the jobs of thousands of workers, not to mention the effect on oil-producing countries. If we tax gasoline to spur a reduction in private consumption, the people most affected will be low-wage workers, who have been forced to live in mobile homes twenty miles from urban or suburban jobs. If we tax heating oil, it will be the poor who suffer most. If we should use taxes to curtail the production of large automobiles or SUVs, the middle class would revolt. And so it goes for all efforts to limit energy consumption, or to shift to nonfossil forms of energy, for the present level and types of energy use reflect the cheapest alternatives, calculated on a relatively short time scale.

As one faces the always uncertain future, one confronts starkly different forecasts. On one side are the technological optimists, who use past experience to bolster their belief that new techniques will enable humans to stay ahead of what seems to be looming scarcities. After all, fusion could take care of much of the energy problem. On the other are the environmental alarmists, who cite present trends to demonstrate the near certainty of early crises involving both energy and water. At the crux of the debate is the wide divergence between developed countries and those who are poor or only slowly overcoming low incomes. If, in the next fifty years, the present balance of wealth and income continues as it is today, if the present rate of growth in India and China comes to a halt, then a few technological innovations may prevent any severe world crisis involving either water or energy. It may be possible, with limited aid from the wealthy, to insure the continuation of at least present living standards for the additional 3 billion people who will almost all live in the low-income areas of the world. It may be possible to continue the present pace of growth in incomes among the slowly decreasing percentage of people (down from 20 percent to 15 percent) who will be privileged to live in developed, high-energy societies. One aspect of this growth will be continued gains in dealing with several environmental problems, although I doubt that such managed growth can take place without a reduction in biodiversity.

But I have profound doubts that any new technologies will solve the larger problem, one that is ultimately moral and political as well as economic. I simply cannot conceive of any scenarios that entail a continued growth of world population and a continued growth in levels of consumption in wealthy countries while providing the needed energy, and in some cases the necessary water, to close the gap in incomes between the few developed and the many underdeveloped countries—or that even come close to closing this gap. And note that energy and water are not the only required resources for such a narrowed gap, and thus something closer to worldwide equality. Ultimately, any hope of having the vital resources needed for all the people on earth rests on two very difficult shifts—away from high fertility rates in poor countries, and away from certain types and quantities of consumption in wealthy countries.

PART THREE

The Human Threat

Balancing the threat of scarcities in vital resources is the destructive impact of humans on their own living space. The rapid expansion of population in much of the world, new modes of production, and exploding consumption in industrialized countries have all led to an unprecedented pollution of air, soil, and water. Pollution has joined with the loss of habitat to create a major extinction crisis, and thus a loss of biodiversity. I devote chapter 5 to the overall problem of pollution, and to American responses to such pollution. In chapter 6, I explore the difficulties of preserving the present level of biodiversity.

Pollution, Waste, and the Ozone Layer

For most people, references to an environmental crisis suggests images of polluted soil, air, or water, or pollution on surfaces or in objects of consumption. Most dangerous ingredients in our environment have natural as well as human sources (a few, such as radon or pollen, are completely natural), but it is the part that is of human origin that we generally refer to as pollutants. In most industrial countries, the largest body of environmental regulations relate to pollution and the types of human production and waste disposal that cause it. The cost of avoiding, containing, or removing pollutants has absorbed an ever larger component of governmental budgets. The subject is enormously complex. It joins with a second problem—the availability of life-supporting resources, with soil, air, water, and energy the most important. For many people, these are already scarce, which suggests all the issues tied to conservation, efficient use, and recycling. Since polluted resources may not be safe for human use, the mitigation of pollution and its effects may increase the resources available for human survival.

POLLUTION: DEFINITION AND HISTORICAL BACKGROUND

Certain ingredients in the environment are harmful to humans, or indirectly pose a threat to humans because they endanger animals or plants or degrade or deface valued artifacts (such as buildings or art objects). But what is harmful in one setting, or at one time, may not be at another. Oxygen, for example, is necessary for animal life, yet free oxygen is toxic in many contexts, including the human body (in the form of free radicals). Ozone, a special atomic form of oxygen, is a major air pollutant. Yet ozone in the stratosphere screens out most of the dangerous ultraviolet light that can cause so much damage to life at the earth's surface. Carbon dioxide is necessary for photosynthesis, and thus for plant growth. Next to water vapor, it is the most plentiful greenhouse gas, and thus helps warm our planet. But in too large quantities in the atmosphere, it may help induce dangerous warming or so reduce oxygen as to threaten animal life. In some cases, certain chemicals are poisonous in large quantities (fluorine) but life-enhancing in small amounts (to prevent cavities in teeth). And what is toxic to humans is often food for bacteria. Throughout most of human history, the pollutants created by human production and consumption were rather quickly and safely absorbed back into the environment, largely through bacterial action in soil or water.

Simply defined, a pollutant is any material substance that poses any threat, direct or indirect, to human welfare, and which results from the direct or indirect effect of human action. This is, admittedly, a definition with a human bias. It ignores the perspective of other species. A pollutant, so defined, is dangerous, and thus a pollutant, not necessarily because of any inherent qualities, but because it is at the wrong place, at the wrong time, or in the wrong quantities. Here, "wrong" has a evaluative content. No object is a pollutant simply because it exists. Everything has a place in our world. Context is all important. The carbon monoxide emitted in a volcano is not different, chemically, from that emitted by an automobile tailpipe. Thus, it is impossible to escape a human perspective in determining what is dangerous and what is a pollutant, just as the human perspective turns some flowering plants into "weeds." Indeed, we deem many chemicals as pollutants because of their impact on nonhuman species, but in each case because these plants or animals have some perceived value for humans, even if the value is one of beauty appreciated. An escaped herbicide that kills not just the weeds in a nearby corn field but also my tomato plants is a pollutant. It is out of place. No farmer would classify an insecticide that kills unwanted bugs as a pollutant, yet the same insecticide that kills his cucumber beetles may blow into my yard and kill prized honey bees. Perspective thus makes all the difference. Pollutants may be gases, and thus without fixed shape or volume, or fluids, without fixed shape, or solids.

Even early Homo sapiens (language using, self-conscious human-oids) had a unique role in their environment. They could exert much more control over their surroundings than other animals. They could co-ordinate their activities, accumulate knowledge about how to cope with problems, invent ever more useful tools to extend their power over the physical world. Even at the hunting and gathering stage, they were re-shaping their world. They controlled fire, for cooking food, for keeping warm, and at times for burning woods or grassland (to corral game or just for the fun of it). Fire is dangerous, often in ways they did not recog-nize. In poorly ventilated caves, or in later huts, it could produce deadly levels of carbon monoxide. In all cases, it created smoke and soot and, to a limited extent, polluted nearby air. But hunting and gathering meant small and dispersed human populations, and thus less human impact than became possible with cultivation and herding, and with this much larger and more concentrated populations.

Environmentalists, with some justice, often attribute the first major threat to the environment to the development of agriculture. Indeed, the massive reshaping of the earth's land areas began with domestication and cultivation. Without agriculture, the human population would, of neces-sity, have remained very small, and the human environmental impact low in comparison to that of later, settled communities. In most areas, farming required the clearing of forests. With the conversion of large tracts of land, this led to less photosynthesis, a lowered absorption of CO_2, a slightly diminished amount of humidity and rainfall, higher temperatures, and more soil erosion, creating dust and major stream siltation. The open grazing of forests and savannahs, by cows, sheep, and above all hogs, further degraded land and vegetation. But early ag-riculture was not efficient by modern standards. Each family had only a small surplus for sale or exchange, after feeding themselves and their livestock. The density of population remained small, although farmers could, and usually did, cluster their now permanent homes in villages. Some of these, with favorable locations, would grow into commercial cities. Thus, cities were one product of cultivation and a settled form of life. But until farming became efficient, large cities were few, since most human energy still had to be devoted to agriculture, supportive arts, and homemaking.

City life led to new environmental problems, ones scarcely recog-nized on scattered farms or in small rural villages—air and water pollution and the accumulation of solid waste. The smoke from the inefficient burning of wood for cooking and heat could accumulate over cities, particularly in winter and during air inversions, leading to smog and dangerous levels of ozone, carbon monoxide, and various oxides of nitrogen and sulfur. The air inside houses was often even more polluted. Untreated human excreta polluted streams and spread infectious diseases. And often, carelessly disposed solid wastes accumulated in dumps, under houses, or in sink holes. In time, cities became mounds of layered debris, with each layer reflecting the clutter of past civilizations. For archaeologists, these mounds provide rich information about the human past. One mark of civilization was the effort to deal with these problems. In Greece and Rome, for example, we find aqueducts to import relatively pure water into cities, sewers to remove untreated waste to rivers or oceans, and planned dumps for solid waste. If the discharges were not too large, bacterial action could get rid of most pathogens in soil or in flowing streams, while heat-induced chemical reactions or falling rain could cleanse the air. The oceans were so large, in comparison to human-created pollutants, as to serve as a relatively safe universal dump. The pollution problem became acute only with much larger human populations, new forms of production, dramatically higher levels of consumption, and chemically based technologies.

One pattern has remained constant from the earliest humans. The greatest source of air pollution has been the burning of biomass or fossil fuels. What has changed is the amount burned, and the number of people doing the burning. In North America and Europe, over the last two hundred years, the growth of population and a presently stable population have accompanied a gradually accelerating growth in per capita consumption. With this, per capita use of energy and chemicals has soared. In the underdeveloped world, since World War II, the most dramatic growth has been in population, with a modest growth in per capita consumption. Population growth alone has increased energy use, particularly of wood and coal. In the two most populous low-income countries, India and China, the rapid growth of manufacturing and some highly efficient and mechanized agriculture have pushed their use of fossil fuels closer to the level of developed countries. If present trends continue, China will soon consume more fossil fuels than the United States (but not nearly as much per capita). It already consumes more coal.

IN AIR, WATER, AND SOIL

Few pollutants are restricted to any one location, such as air or water. For example, an insecticide is first of all a powder or in solution, then turned into vapor or droplets for spraying on vegetation. Since some of the spray remains on the surface of crops, small residues may be eaten by humans or animals, while other particles move into the soil and eventually pollute streams and the ocean. Air pollution takes precedence only in one sense—it can be more universal than pollution of soil or water, for air encircles the globe and some forms of pollution remain in the air long enough to gain a uniform density worldwide. This is true of the human-produced (and in many cases human-invented) chemicals that deplete stratospheric ozone (see below), and of most greenhouse gases (see chapter 8).

Almost any element or compound can become airborne. Technically, dust and liquid droplets are not part of the air, but only temporarily suspended in it. Even dangerous heavy metals, such as lead, arsenic, and mercury, can exist as airborne particles. In fact, lead was long one of the most dangerous air pollutants because of the widespread use of lead in gasoline. Small levels of mercury now pollute the oceans, leading to dangerous amounts in fish that are at the end of a food chain. Some trace gases in our atmosphere are so concentrated as to pose a danger to life. Oxides of sulphur and nitrogen are not stable, forming new compounds or dissolving in water. These aerosols, such as sulfate (SO_4), reflect light and help cool the earth and acidify rainwater, which creates acid rain. It is difficult to rank, in order of damage, the various trace gases or their chemical children and grandchildren. But today, by most evaluations, the big three are tropospheric ozone, oxides of sulphur, and oxides of nitrogen. Except for ozone, these are not among the most dangerous of gases, but their rank derives from the scope of their influence or the difficulty of controlling them. The major source of sulfur compounds is electrical generation with sulfur-containing coal. Automobile emissions are the leading source of tropospheric ozone. Most nitrogen compounds have a largely natural origin, but these are augmented by human burning and by nitrogen fertilizers. Fortunately for humans, ozone and most sulfur compounds either have a nasty odor or irritate the skin, and thus are detectable even at low concentrations.

In most cases the reduced (without oxygen and usually hydrogen-based) compounds of sulfur and nitrogen are less toxic than the oxides, and the proportion created by human activity is less. Ammonia (NH_3), a very pungent gas, is largely a product of biological decay in soils and swamps, a decay increased by excess nitrogen fertilizers, but it is also a product of oil refining and some waste burning. As housewives know, ammonia is a valued cleansing agent, and is used in the production of fertilizers, plastics, explosives, and dyes. When in contact with water, ammonia can convert to ammonium (NH_4), which is the form in which most plants absorb their needed nitrogen. At very low concentrations, ammonia is not toxic to humans, but always unpleasant because of its odor. The most dangerous reduced form of sulfur is hydrogen sulfide (H_2S), which is a very deadly gas in concentrations of 10 percent or more. It has a notorious "rotten egg" smell, and is highly flammable. It can be a product of organic decay, particularly in sewers. It is also a natural product of the leaves of plants, but rarely in high enough quantities to be dangerous. It can be a dangerous release from oil or natural gas, and is a byproduct of several forms of manufacturing, particularly paper, textiles, plastics, and dyes. Around some pulp mills, it is the leading cause of odor pollution.

An often overlooked type of pollution is that of pungent and nauseating odors or loud or unpleasant noises. To the extent that otherwise dangerous gases or aerosols cause discomfort from their smell, odors are a component of air pollution, and today are controlled by clean air legislation. Other odors are not easily controlled by legislation, such as that of manure spread on fields by farmers. Some unpleasant odors are useful, such as the stinking components placed in natural gas. Loud noises have become a part of modern civilization, and to an extent are inescapable. But most local governments have regulations to reduce the level of sound. Even in the absence of noise and sound pollution laws, odors and loud noises can become a public nuisance, and face civil action if not police action. But in this chapter I will focus upon the other forms of air pollution.

As everyone knows, both methane (or natural gas, which is largely made up of methane, or CH_4) and carbon monoxide are odorless and colorless killers in confined areas. But methane, when contained, is a valuable fuel, far more efficient and less polluting than any other fossil fuel. It is also a greenhouse gas. Methane is only the most abundant of over six hundred other hydrocarbon compounds in the modern atmosphere, most deriving from combustion. Any local supply of natural gas will contain several of these, along with the dominant methane. Carbon monoxide, the most abundant of all atmospheric pollutants, is now most often human-caused through the incomplete burning of hydrocarbons. Fortunately, it is rather quickly oxidized into carbon dioxide in the open air or consumed by soil microbes, meaning that, away from the immediate vicinity of CO output, the rather constant level in the atmosphere is not dangerous to humans. Today, most deaths from carbon monoxide are caused by confined automobile exhaust or misplaced or malfunctioning stoves, furnaces, or space heaters. A major source of nonfatal but unhealthy levels of CO is cigarette smoking.

Except for heavy metals, most pollutants involve the very elements that are necessary for life. This is most clear in the case of various hydrocarbons, plus the many compounds of sulphur and nitrogen that are on almost any regulated list of toxic chemicals (at the point of emission, these are sulfur dioxide and two oxides of nitrogen, but in the atmosphere they undergo chemical reactions that create dozens of other gases or aerosols). Today we live in an age of chemicals, many synthesized each year (not originally part of nature). Some estimate that over seventy thousand different chemical compounds are in use every year. Of these, over a thousand are probably toxic (that is, pose some threat to human health, with cancer the greatest concern), and each year in the United States the Environmental Protection Agency adds new chemicals to its list of proven, probable, or possible toxic substances. Each year farmers use millions of tons of pesticides, most now made up of synthesized organic compounds. In the wrong place, and in high concentrations, almost all of these are toxic for humans, and thus have to be used very carefully.[1]

Water is almost as important as air as a repository of toxic chemicals. In the past, water posed its greatest danger to humans through the pathogens within it. Such is still the case in many poor countries. Even a century ago the United States was cursed with epidemics of typhoid and cholera because of pathogens in water. Developed countries have eliminated most such threats through rigorous controls over the quality of drinking water, although it is impossible to eliminate all potentially dangerous trace elements in water. In some areas, the natural water supply contains dangerous levels of arsenic or fluorine, and these are difficult to screen out. In homes, antiquated lead pipes still pollute drinking water. In some rural areas, wells have become polluted by toxic chemicals that have invaded the groundwater or even deeper aquifers.

In developed countries, the problem is not primarily water for drink-ing, but water in streams and lakes. Until very recently, humans every-where used streams as a depository for all manner of wastes, including solid waste. Untreated sewage joined storm drainage and industrial dis-charges. Runoff from agriculture included nitrogen and phosphorous from fertilizer, which joined the phosphates in detergents used in laun-dering and dishwashing to cause a surfeit of nutrients and so much veg-etative growth as to strip water of the oxygen needed by fish and to hasten the gradual eutrophication of ponds and lakes. These joined rem-nants of pesticides and herbicides, toxic metals from mines, and heavy metals, such as selenium, from the leaching water used to remove salts from irrigated fields. In low concentrations, and over time, bacteria in water can digest most waste products, but not all, and not in huge quan-tities. Thus, throughout the world, most streams and lakes are polluted, in some cases to the extent that they no longer support any life at all. In others, dangerous chemicals so accumulate in fish, or in birds that eat fish, as to threaten life or as to render fish unfit for human consumption. These polluted waters then flow into the oceans, to the extent that even this huge volume of water is now threatened, particularly in relatively isolated gulfs or seas (such as the Mediterranean). This poses more long-term damage than such dramatic events as a major oil spill.

In developed countries, the most dangerous forms of water pollu-tion now face regulation. Water treatment and purification is possible but expensive for single-point sources of pollution, such as municipal or corporate discharges. Less effectively regulated are non-point sources, such as the runoff from pesticides and fertilizers used by farmers, or siltation from eroded land, or the long-term pollution caused by long-abandoned mines, or the bacteria deposited by grazing cattle in open streams. No good answer is available for the heating of water caused by power plants.

Soil is different from air and water. Humans do not consume it, but only emissions from it or plants grown in it. Most soils are teeming with life, from earthworms and nematodes down to all manner of mi-croscopic organisms. These live on decaying vegetation and help recycle vital gases back into the atmosphere. Most air pollutants eventually fall to the oceans or to earth. Acid rain increases the acidity of soil, and can be very harmful to trees or other vegetation. Heavy metals and many organic chemicals can remain in the soil for decades. Some plastics are so inert that they take centuries to break down. But a plastic bottle is not necessarily a pollutant, in the sense that it poses a threat to human life or to plant or animal life. Most plastic waste contaminates but does not pollute the soil. But even inert contaminants are not always benign, for strips of plastic may ensnare a bird or a mammal. Insecticides often kill beneficial bacteria or worms in the soil, and so long as the chemicals remain active in soil (usually not long), the ground is to that extent polluted. The same is true for lingering herbicides, if they inhibit the growth of desired plants. Chemical fertilizers in soils can feed the runoff of excessive nutrients into streams. But, as a whole, most soils are not significantly polluted except where they have become a dump for human waste products, and particularly very toxic wastes. Such wastes include the excreta of domesticated animals.

In the past, the major problem posed by polluted soils was the spread of disease pathogens. This remains true in underdeveloped countries. In developed countries, it is more often toxic chemicals that pose a direct threat to humans, while greenhouse gas emissions from landfills are an indirect threat because of global warming. Humans have always used land as a dump for unwanted items. This began with their own excreta. Such waste became dangerous only with the increase in the number of infectious diseases. But only a bit over a century ago did humans become aware of the sources of infection, and only then did they have a compelling reason to find safe ways of disposing of excreta, either in sanitary pits or privies, septic tanks and drainage fields, or in sewage systems. Bacteria will purify human wastes, as well as that of other animals, just as bacteria will consume dead bodies and most other organic materials. But it takes time for this, and too much organic waste can overwhelm natural scavengers.

The amount of waste produced by humans in high-income societies would have been unbelievable to our progenitors of even a century ago. In a sense, we are drowning in our own waste. Individuals in a farm family in 1840 would never have thought of waste as a problem. They produced so little. A privy took care of their own excreta. The manure from their livestock was a valued fertilizer for their fields. Any leftover food items went into slop for their hogs. Newspapers became their toilet paper, or kindling for their wood fires. Ashes from their stoves went onto the garden as a fertilizer or into an ash pit, where rainwater seeped through and provided the lye needed for soap or hominy. Worn-out clothes, and they had few of these, provided the scraps needed for a new quilt, while worn-out furniture was burned in a stove or in an outdoor trash fire. The main disposable items, as had been the case for centuries, were broken glassware, buttons, worn-out pots and pans, and worn-out stoves or farm tools. These they tossed into the nearest sinkhole. If careless, they created a growing dump in a secluded area near house or barn. Otherwise, they had no garbage problem. But cities did, and so did new factories, with some, such as tanneries, producing toxic wastes.

How different it is today. Americans now produce almost two thousand pounds of solid waste per capita per year. Much of this is household waste, the rest industrial and governmental. Disposal is a major national problem. About two-thirds of all this solid waste now ends up in landfills. The other third is recycled, incinerated, or composted (primarily leaves or tree limbs). A small proportion of this solid waste is highly toxic, and includes such specialized items as medical or hospital waste (now plentiful because almost all items used on patients are disposables), nuclear waste, and industrial chemicals. Two-thirds of this solid waste ends up on, or in, soil. In all cases, it contaminates the soil and almost always pollutes it, at least in the immediate area of a dump or landfill. The worst pollution is in dumping areas for industrial chemicals and at abandoned mines. Added to all this is another, not easily classified form of solid waste—the large masses of manure from large chicken and hog "factories" and large beef feeding lots. If not contained, this manure pollutes streams. It emits methane, a greenhouse gas, and at times a deadly amount of sulphur dioxide. If turned into a liquified soup in lagoons and spread on fields, it can pollute the nearby air and offend those who have to smell it.

Consumption patterns and the relatively low cost of consumer goods support our wasteful society. Some estimate that easily a third of all food served on American tables ends up in garbage bags. The inedible stems or peelings or cores that used to go to the hogs now go into the garbage can. Most Americans have dozens of changes of clothes and shoes. Containers of all sorts—bags, cans, bottles, boxes—accumulate every day, and most end up in the trash (this despite a growth in recycling). The amount of unrecycled waste paper continues to expand yearly. A stroll along almost any street on garbage or trash day reveals how much reasonably intact furniture or toys or pots and pans Americans throw away, or how many still functional appliances. The cost of replacements is so low, and labor costs so high, that repairs are rarely cost effective. Besides, Americans want new versions, and are willing to pay for the privilege. It is not true that manufacturers deliberately insure early obsolescence. As a whole, in almost every product area, quality has continued to go up and the normal life span of appliances has never been higher. Our largest household disposable is usually the automobile. Sooner or later too many of these end up in back yards or in junk yards, although most are now recycled for their steel. Cast off automobile and truck tires seem to be everywhere, and so far the recycling of such rubber is not profitable.

In the case of pollution, as for most issues of environmental concern, the wealthy and poor countries are moving ever farther apart. Despite still rising levels of energy use, the annual introduction of new chemicals, and the continued proliferation of waste, most wealthy countries have been able to develop a wide array of regulations to control all types of pollution. At the very least, air, water, and soil pollution have stabilized, despite the dramatic increase in per capita consumption. But poorer countries have not had the resources, or the political stability, needed to regulate pollution. If anything, it is worse year by year. In South and East Asia, stretching from the Arabian Sea to Japan, almost half the world's population now suffers annually increasing levels of air and water pollution. They are under a permanent haze created by suspended particles and aerosols, most of human origin, and most caused by the unregulated consumption of wood and coal. Both health and climate are at risk.

Two issues guide efforts at pollution control. First is the amount of risk posed by any type of pollution. This is a complex problem, one that has led to much scholarship. Almost always, the risk of greatest concern is human health. The knowledge needed to assess this is often missing, thus leading to major research efforts. Almost every science may be involved. The second issue is cost. It is impossible to protect people from all environmental risks. A certain number of people will die next year because of some type of pollution. Life expectancy in a population is reduced by pollution. It is relatively easy to estimate the number that will be affected by cigarette smoke, but how many will die of respiratory diseases caused, at least in part, by asbestos dust? Government regulators try to answer such questions, and often have erred by being overly cautious. But for dozens of chemicals, the risks are far from clear, and firm estimates are impossible. If a society could afford it, then it should always err on the side of extreme caution. But no society can afford all the regulations and controls that might save a few lives, not without sacrificing the quality of life enjoyed by almost everyone. Economists insist that environmental regulations must be cost effective. What this requires is often as difficult to determine as the degree of risk. Obviously, as economists point out, there are opportunity costs for enforcing any form of regulation. That is, the money spent cannot be used elsewhere, to meet other human needs. So tradeoffs are necessary. In some sense, a utilitarian calculus has to apply, which means support for policies which offer the most utility, or satisfactions, or happiness to the most people.[2]

LEGISLATION IN THE UNITED STATES TO CONTROL POLLUTION AND WASTE

Today, in most countries in western Europe and in the United States, hundreds of different laws regulate almost every imaginable form of pollution, including even noise pollution. Roughly similar laws exist in many developing countries, but enforcement has usually been lax. I will here survey only the major legislation in the United States that deals with air and water pollution and waste management.

Beginning as early as the 1950s, Congress passed a series of pollution control acts for both air and water. Each new law since then has been in the form of amendments to earlier legislation, meaning a complicated body of regulations. By convention, but not always by legislative name, these series of bills have become known as Clean Air and Clean Water Acts. The first tough acts came in 1970 (air) and 1972 (water). A series of revisions followed, with the most comprehensive for air in 1990, and for water in 1977. The Clean Air Act of 1990 is one of the most complicated laws ever enacted by Congress, with over eight hundred pages of regulations. In broad terms, the 1990 amendments simply updated controls over smog, acid rain, moving vehicle emissions, and hazardous or toxic pollutants contained in the 1970 act, and added new, very detailed regulations for ozone-depleting gases to honor international agreements.

In 1970 smog was the dominating issue. The 1970 act had detailed rules governing what the EPA would soon designate as three criteria air pollutants, ozone, carbon monoxide, and particulates (soot, dust, smoke). Its primary rules involved these pollutants as they affected human health, with secondary rules based on threats to other forms of life or to property. In the case of smog, or primarily ozone, the act specified five levels of nonattainment of stipulated goals, expressed in parts per million. The 1970 act set threshold levels for ozone at 0.12 ppm, but in 1990 the new amendments lowered this to 0.08 ppm measured over a one-hour period. All private persons (this includes corporations) had to have permits for all criteria pollutants released into the atmosphere. But the major problem with ozone involved motor vehicles (over half came from automobiles in urban areas), and here the states had to bring all geographical areas into compliance with the regulations by particular deadlines. Many cities did not meet these goals, and thus in 1990 Congress not only raised the ante, but at the same time set up more gradual and reasonable compliance deadlines. The Clinton Administration added even higher standards in 1997 (a maximum of 0.085 ppm of ozone measured over eight hours), but court challenges kept these from going into effect until 2001. Cities and counties that failed to comply with the new standards risked the loss of various federal grants, particularly for transportation, and permits for new businesses.

The EPA has not seemed very eager to enforce the higher standards for pollutants. Only by April 2004 did it determine which cities and counties were not in compliance with the new air quality standards. Ozone was the major concern, although new rules governed the emission of sulfur and nitrogen oxides by power plants. The level of noncompliance was no surprise, for municipalities knew that they had not met the new ozone standards. In fact, 474 counties were not in compliance. They made up a relatively small percentage of the total amount of land (eighteen states, largely in the West, were fully compliant), but they were concentrated in populous metropolitan areas. Over half the American population lived in noncompliant counties, with most in California and the eastern United States. All of four states—New Jersey, Delaware, Connecticut, and Massachusetts—were noncompliant, in part because of pollutants that blew in from states to the west and south. Because the violations were so widespread, the affected counties will not face as early, or as harsh, sanctions as environmentalists had wished. They have three years to develop plans to reduce the ozone and soot levels. Those close to compliance have to be fully compliant by 2007, those at the moderate level (most) have to comply by 2010, and those with the most severe problems have until 2021.

Motor vehicles are the major source of ozone and such other criteria pollutants as CO. A major precursor of ozone is nitrous oxides. Ironically, the lead-free gasoline and catalytic converters required by the 1970 act have actually increased these oxides. Automobile pollutants per vehicle were down by from 60 percent to 80 percent from 1970 to 1990, but air scarcely improved in many cities, simply because the number of automobiles and the miles traveled had increased so rapidly (from 1 trillion miles in the 1960s to 4 trillion by 2002). Thus, the act of 1990 had even more stringent antipollution regulations for moving vehicles, including locomotives and airplanes. Under the 1970 act, pollution control in engines had to last only fifty thousand miles; after 1990 they had to go for one hundred thousand miles (still very inadequate because so many cars now run for over two hundred thousand miles). Automobiles also had to have dashboard indicators of any failure in the pollution control system. New regulations governing gasoline went well beyond the abolition of lead, and for certain noncompliance areas included more expensive, reformulated gasoline, or gasoline-ethanol mixtures. An increased number of metropolitan areas had to begin automobile inspection programs. Truck engines had to meet the pollution requirements of automobiles, and new regulations reduced the emissions of diesel engines. Some regulations applied to small engines, such as those on lawn mowers. Cities received incentive payments for strategies to reduce driving (for public transportation, high-occupancy vehicle lanes, reductions in downtown parking spaces). To meet the 2004 standards, some counties may have to resort to very unpopular measures, even to the extent of prohibiting lawn mowing by gasoline mowers in periods of very hot weather.

The second largest source of air pollution are factories, with steam plants for electrical generation the single largest source of industrial air pollution. Both the 1970 and 1990 acts required permits for all polluting emissions, which are largely sulphur dioxide and two nitrous oxides, which cause most acid rain. Also, industrial emissions contain the largest number of hazardous pollutants. This is particularly true of chemical plants, pulp mills, and oil refineries. The 1970 act listed only seven toxic pollutants; the 1990 act listed 189 and gave the EPA the authority to add to this list (it does so every year). Any plant that can be identified as a source of toxic air pollutants has to meet the highest possible standard: the maximum available control technology. Producers face very high penalties if they violate this standard. For the acid-forming oxides, which are an unavoidable product of fossil fuel consumption, producers have to gain a permit for an allowable level of emissions. These levels will become more restrictive through time, and require new technologies in all new plants. For both sulphur and nitrogen oxides, the 1990 act provides for a market-based system. The EPA has established an emission release allowance system (for example, one ton of SO_2 equals one allowance). According to national goals, based on the target level of allowable pollution, each producer receives a certain number of allowances, and faces high penalties if it exceeds the number. But a producer can shift the array of pollution emissions among different plants, so long as all of them do not exceed the total quota. If they beat the standard, they have surplus allowances that they can retain to use against future violations, or to sell to other firms that face penalties. This market-based system adds some flexibility and provides a strong incentive for voluntary reductions.

In some cases, enforcement of clean air statutes has proved very difficult. The best example is emissions from steam power plants. In the Clean Air Act of 1970, Congress set tough, new emission standards to be met by 1975. In most cases, utilities met these standards for new plants, but could have met them in older plants only at great expense. Congress thus grandfathered in older plants. By 1977 it was clear that most utilities were patching and upgrading older plants, and thus legally evading the new standards. Thus Congress so amended the act as to require an upgrading to new standards when a utility made substantial repairs to older plants, or what the EPA called new source review. Very few utilities complied with this new regulation, and the EPA was lax in enforcing it. The utilities argued that it was unclear what amounted to routine maintenance and what counted as substantial upgrades. This noncompliance meant that overall air standards remained unmet. After 1993, the new Clinton Administration tried for years to work out some compromise with utilities to get voluntary compliance with new source review, but the utilities still sought ways to evade what, in some cases, would have been very costly updates. Thus, the EPA turned increasingly to legal action in order not only to change corporate behavior, but to force compliance for earlier failures to meet new source requirements. For the utilities, it seemed as if the EPA had changed the rules after years of nonenforcement. The utilities had a great deal at stake, and to some extent so did rate payers, who would have to pay for clean air.

The conflict came to a head in the new George W. Bush Administration after 2001. The utilities had contributed heavily to Bush's campaign, and they expected regulatory relief in several areas of environmental legislation. An energy shortage in California and a large blackout in the East offered an excuse for relaxed enforcement. A new and very controversial energy bill sponsored by the Bush Administration would have replaced new source review by a modified pollution trading system. But Congress never passed his energy legislation. Through executive action, the Administration still found a way to eviscerate new source review, just at the very time the EPA was finally achieving success in enforcing it. The trick was in the phrase "substantial modifications." Even the Bush Administration EPA had suggested that any repairs over 0.75 percent of the value of a generating unit was "substantial." If set much higher, utilities could completely upgrade units, by degrees, and evade the 1990 emission standards required for new or substantially modified plants.

In August 2003, a new EPA Administrator announced that utilities (plus factories, refineries, and chemical plants) could spend up to 20 percent of a generating unit's replacement cost without having to meet new pollution standards. This, in effect, killed new source review and meant that utilities could continue using old, heavily polluting plants indefinitely, so long as they upgraded them over five years. Fourteen state attorneys general brought a suit to block implementation of these new rules in late 2003. In June 2005 the Court of Appeals for the District of Columbia ruled that the EPA had the authority to issue new, more lenient rules for defining pollutants, but at the same time faulted the agency for its application of several rules. In general, this was a victory for the utilities and the Bush Administration, but with enough qualifications to meet some of the demands of environmentalists. In March 2006 the same Appeals Court ruled that, consistent with the actual wording of the Clean Air Act, the EPA could not implement the new 20 percent rule. This was a bitter defeat for the Bush Administration and energy companies. The case may end up in the Supreme Court.[3]

The Clean Water Act, as amended several times, shares many similarities with the Clean Air Act. The largest body of regulations date from the Federal Water Pollution Control Act of 1972, and from many revisions of this act in 1977, or what most now call the Clean Water Act. Incremental changes since then have not been as important as the Clean Air amendments of 1990. The Clean Water Act of 1977 has three explicit purposes: first, to reduce the direct discharge of pollutants into our lakes, streams, and nearby oceans; second, to encourage and help fund the development of municipal waste water treatment facilities; and, third, to contribute to the management of polluted runoff water (non-point pollution). The effect should be the protection of fish, shellfish, and other wildlife and the provision of healthy water-based recreation. The Clean Water Act does not encompass groundwaters, or in any way deal with the quality of water available for human uses. Other legislation directly controls the quality of drinking water, while pollution control for most federal water projects, such as those by the Corps of Engineers, involves the Environmental Impact Statements mandated by National Environmental Policy Act of 1970. Even more than under the Clean Air Act, the EPA works with the states in controlling water pollution. The federal government sets the standards, but it is usually the states that enforce them.

In effect, the Clean Water Act involves federally mandated permits for all persons (and thus corporations) that discharge pollutants into navigable waters, federal funds for state or municipal waste water systems, and guidelines and in some cases financial incentives for non-point pollution or runoff beach improvements. It has rather elaborate regulations, and heavy penalties, for offshore oil spills. Its definition of pollution includes sewage sludge and the effects of stream dredging. It has some exceptions. It does not require permits for the return water from irrigation, or the storm runoff from mining and oil drilling (other legislation controls much of this, particularly strip-mining). It includes a provision for cleaning up polluted lakes, carried out through state-based inventories and projects, and a joint Canada–United States program for the Great Lakes. But most of its detailed regulations and penalties involve its permit system for direct discharges, and thus its goal of maintaining or restoring water quality. Its greatest limitation is the control of non-point pollution, which above all else involves agricultural runoff. It does have some control over city runoff and storm sewers, but there is no easy way to measure the contribution of any one person or firm to the fertilizer, pesticides, or household detergents that contribute up to one-half of the pollution of our streams and lakes. Under other legislation, the EPA does closely regulate the use of pesticides. The EPA has worked to reduce non-point pollution by guidelines and voluntary action, and in cooperation with involved states it has helped develop some broad watershed protection projects (one involves the Susquehanna and the pollution of the Chesapeake Bay), and with them state regulation of certain farming practices.

A final major category of EPA regulation is solid waste. Here the legislative background is complex, as always, but by far the most important authorizing legislation is the Resource Conservation and Recovery Act (RCRA) of 1976. It offered the first detailed federal rules for the disposal of both solid and hazardous waste, and it empowered the EPA to use various tactics to encourage the recycling and recovery of materials, to encourage the reduction of waste at its source, and to help local governments clean up existing waste. This final responsibility took on major and very expensive implications with the Superfund legislation and program that began in 1980. Dozens of more specialized bills—involving such pollutants as medical waste, asbestos, used oil, mining waste, pesticides, radiation, and batteries—supplement the RCRA. The two largest sources of solid waste are corporations and municipalities. Both dispose of most nonhazardous solid waste in landfills, followed by incineration and composting. The federal government provides detailed guidelines for landfills, but the actual regulation of such legal dumps is by the states. Various rules govern the disposal of hazardous materials, including medical waste. Some has to be incinerated, some is chemically transformed, and some goes into special landfills.

Waste reduction, nationally, usually means recycling, since Americans are unwilling to lower consumption or give up the convenience, or safety, of the elaborate packaging used for almost all consumer products, or to repair and continue in use outdated appliances or automobiles. Older deposit and refund programs, as for milk and soft drink bottles, have all but ended. The EPA encourages recycling, monitors and instructs local governments, and publishes effective promotions to get citizens to recycle and to buy recycled products, but the actual programs are locally developed. Most municipalities now have either curbside (over nine thousand) or drop off (twelve thousand) recycling. Since 1990, recycling has doubled, and now joins composting to save 64 million tons that would otherwise end up in landfills or incinerators. That adds up to 28 percent of solid waste. Americans now recycle 42 percent of all paper, 55 percent of aluminum cans, 57 percent of steel cans, 40 percent of plastic bottles, and 52 percent of all appliances. Because of federal regulations, almost all automobile batteries are recycled. The major limit on recycling has been a market (or demand) for the products, with great volatility in prices for paper in particular. To a surprising extent, consumers have been willing to cooperate with recycling programs, even when this has required extra effort or expense. What is not clear is the potential for any drastic increase in recycling, given the market constraints. Organic waste can be incinerated, and has often provided profits for cities when used to generate electricity or to heat buildings, but here a method of waste management often runs aground on antipollution legislation. Composting will remain a useful disposal method for leaves and grass clippings, but probably not much else.

The final mandate of the RCRA—cleaning up existing waste—has become a major project for the EPA, but only for hazardous wastes. The experience of the citizens of Love Canal, a residential neighborhood near Niagara Falls, New York, became a cause célèbre by 1978. Around a thousand people had moved into homes constructed over or near the site of a former industrial dump, in an old canal, a site that by the 1970s contained buried and almost forgotten barrels of waste chemicals from a plant that had manufactured pesticides and petrochemicals. After a flood, the contents began seeping to the surface or into basements. Tests revealed toxic chemicals, although at low levels. But one child had birth defects and learning difficulties, which the parents attributed to the seeping chemicals. By the very nature of the handicap, no one could establish pollution as the cause. But EPA measurement of drainage from the area found a wide variety of toxic chemicals, some in low concentrations, despite cleanup efforts by the chemical company that owned the site (it was not the original polluter).

When EPA-funded tests found chromosomal damage in eleven of thirty-six residents, a type of near hysteria broke out in Love Canal, with protests and confrontations, plus nationwide media coverage. Because of the chromosome study, plus some statistical evidence of higher than normal incidence of miscarriages and birth defects, President Carter declared Love Canal a disaster area and used disaster funds to help in what became a complete relocation of the residents. Later studies somewhat lessened the degree of possible risk and suggested a degree of overreaction by authorities, but clearly, at the time, a series of often confusing or conflicting studies justified the fear on the part of residents. It also justified a broader national concern about other such toxic waste sites, for such worries were obviously not restricted to Love Canal.

This concern led Congress to enact the Comprehensive Response, Compensation, and Liability Act of 1980. Congress also authorized an original $1.6 billion trust fund to pay for the contemplated cleanup of waste sites, with the money coming from new taxes on crude oil and commercial chemicals (likely targets, because these were two primary sources of toxic wastes). By 1986, when this so-called Superfund was already almost depleted, Congress broadened the tax base and mandated that the fund be replenished from money recovered from those responsible for the pollution. The liability was retroactive (the polluters had not violated existing laws at the time of pollution), and it applied to present owners who had purchased such sites even if they did not know the sites were polluted. Even if several companies or individuals had shared in the original dumping, any one of them could be held fully responsible (important because so many people and companies who had contributed had died or gone out of business). This insured a continuous series of lawsuits over liability when parties who were identified as being responsible were not willing to fund the cleanup voluntarily. In many cases, the liability provisions seemed unfair, which caused the EPA no end of bad publicity.

From the beginning, the EPA tried to identify toxic waste sites, and to rank the most dangerous for early cleanup. The first sites were those, such as Love Canal, that had led to relocation, those that offered the greatest threat to human health if they leaked, and, even if these criteria did not apply, those that each state selected as the highest priority. By 1996 the EPA had identified thirteen hundred sites that threatened health or the environment, and had completed the cleanup of over two hundred (in 1990, families began to move back into Love Canal, and the Superfund effort there was completed by 2004). These successful cleanups tended to be at emergency sites, those that posed immediate dangers to people. In this respect the fund was an early success. But the larger, more costly sites, or those encumbered with endless lawsuits, caused the expenditures to soar, with much of the money going to lawyers and consultants. Administrative reforms in the Clinton Administration have speeded up a painfully slow and expensive process (over $60 billion spent so far). At first glance, the program's achievements seem impressive (assessment of over 44,000 sites, some remedial work on over 5,000 of them, 846 completed through construction or removal activity (many of these still contain some toxic materials and have to be reviewed every five years), and 649 with ongoing construction. But each completed project has taken over ten years and cost around $25 million, with almost one-third of the cost going to attorneys. Yet, despite intense congressional scrutiny and consistently unhappy administrations, the effort continues. The problems are real, and no other mechanism is available to alleviate them.[4]

The measure of impact from all this environmental legislation is not the present status of air, water, soil, or even toxic waste sites. Each has improved, at least in many areas, but rising consumption keeps upping the ante, particularly for air and water. The true measure is how much worse each would have been without the regulations and enforcement. Given the trends in the 1960s and early 1970s, this is difficult to imagine. At the policy level, the balance between tight and more relaxed regulation will continue. At present, under the Bush Administration, the opponents of tougher regulation have had the upper hand. Environmental advocates have never felt as beleaguered. But to a large extent the regulations are here to stay, and have broad public support. Despite the policy controversies, the momentum favors a continuation of existing programs, continuous policy reviews, and gradually higher standards in almost all areas.

STRATOSPHERIC OZONE DEPLETION

The United States has taken the lead in one area of international pollution control. Arguably, the most ominous pollution ever to confront humans, at least in its potential effects and universal scope, are a large number of gases, most produced by humans, that help reduce the amount of stratospheric ozone, and thus the major shield of the earth's surface against often deadly ultraviolet radiation. Because of its significance, I will end this chapter with the story of stratospheric ozone depletion and international efforts to mitigate the problem.

Early efforts to control ozone-depleting gases followed other international agreements involving pollution. In the 1950s and early 1960s, the most pressing international problem seemed to be the fallout from aboveground testing of atomic bombs. This led to the Test Ban Treaty of 1963 (only France and China continued tests beyond that date). By the 1970s, acid rain had become a major concern, particularly in Europe. In 1979 the United Nations established a Convention on Long Range Transboundary Air Pollution, a convention that never led to any binding protocols, but which did lead to a worldwide air pollution monitoring network. European countries also worked out binding protocols for sulfur and nitrous oxides. Several international agencies supported scientific cooperation involving almost all types of pollution. These included the World Health Organization, the World Meteorological Organization, and the World Climate Programme of the United Nations. But in scope, and effectiveness, none of these rivaled the effort to protect the ozone layer.

Ozone depletion reflects a very complex history, one full of irony. The story demonstrates how human inquiry, and what seem to be wonderful new products, can end up causing unanticipated and serious harm to the life-supporting mechanisms of our planet. The story began in the 1920s when a scientist working for the Frigidaire Division of General Motors synthesized a new refrigerant, a chlorofluorocarbon (CFC), to replace earlier toxic and corrosive chemicals. Soon scientists developed a family of six such gases, each with a slightly different molecular structure. In the 1930s the DuPont Corporation gained a trademark—Freon—for the CFCs used as refrigerants. The importance of the CFCs and their multiple uses did not become clear until about 1950 (which is also when the buildup of CFCs in the atmosphere first took off). CFCs had some wonderful attributes—flame resistant, inert in the troposphere, and thus noncorrosive, or qualities almost perfect for refrigerants, aerosol sprays, and various solvents. These new gases demonstrated that inquiry, in many cases, involves not discovery but the creation of new compounds not previously present in nature.

Most CFCs in commercial use eventually ended up in the earth's atmosphere, directly so in the case of aerosol sprays, and as a result of leaks in the case of refrigeration. At first, no one sensed any danger, and thus humans rather recklessly used CFCs. As we now know, the amount of chlorine in the atmosphere began to grow rapidly after 1950, reaching four times its earlier, natural level by the 1990s. By the 1970s, different measurements of the ozone layer in the stratosphere indicated a thinning. By 1973 the chemical interactions of chlorine and ozone were known. Then, in 1974, in a Nobel Prize–winning article, Sherwood Rowland and Mario Molina revealed the stratospheric role of CFCs and attributed much of the recent ozone thinning to such human causes. This implicates a complex story about the earth's atmosphere and its role in making surface life on earth possible. Soon after this alarm, global warming became a second major concern, with CFCs again implicated, for they are very powerful greenhouse gases.

Most early life on earth was under water or under land. Intense ultraviolet radiation precluded most forms of life at the surface. Only a very limited methane screen then impeded such radiation. But, in time, as ocean vegetation created more and more atmospheric oxygen, this changed for the better. Less and less ultraviolet radiation reached the earth's surface. This was because of the increased screening out of such radiation by ozone. Ozone is an atomic variant of oxygen. Oxygen normally exists in a molecular form with two atoms; in ozone it has three atoms. It forms naturally in thunderstorms, when intensely hot bolts of lighting create it from atmospheric oxygen. For commercial uses (such as disinfectants or bleaches), a controlled electrical discharge creates the needed ozone. It is also a byproduct of combustion, since nitrogen oxides react with hydrocarbons to produce small quantities of ozone. It is the most irritating ingredient in smog, for it is both noxious and toxic. Heavier than normal oxygen, surface ozone hangs about and does not usually rise into the stratosphere (though a small amount may reach the stratosphere in the tropics).

Ozone is one of the minor gases in our atmosphere, but the atmosphere is large. It holds about 3 billion metric tons of ozone, about 10 percent near the surface, where it is a major pollutant (bad ozone), and the rest in the stratosphere (good ozone), where it screens out enough ultraviolet light to make human surface life possible. Our present mode of stratifying the atmosphere directly reflects the role of ozone. The layer of air just about the earth's surface, or the troposphere, varies seasonally in height from as low as eight kilometers to about eighteen. In the troposphere, where weather phenomena take place, the air temperature cools with elevation, or with less pressure or compression and thus less molecular activity. This creates a temperature gradient of cooling up to the top of the troposphere, or to the tropopause. Here, the normal temperature gradient reverses, and the atmosphere warms as one moves higher. It is this zone of warming, or really of a huge air inversion, that we call the stratosphere. It varies in height from season to season and from area to area, but on average is a band from about fifteen to fifty kilometers. At its top, or stratopause, the now very thin air resumes its normal pattern of cooling. Since it is the process that creates upper level ozone that causes most of the warming, the stratosphere might be referred to as the ozonosphere. Stratospheric warming has many implications for climate, totally apart from the ozone formation, but these are not relevant to this chapter. For example, large cyclonic storms, with rapidly rising warm air, often push up to the tropopause, but the inversion, the increasingly warm air, stops the upward, convective spiral, thus setting a limit to the intensity of storms and acting like a lid to keep most water vapor and condensed droplets in the troposphere.

Fortunately for humans, and for all surface life, oxygen in the stratosphere absorbs some ultraviolet radiation from the highest frequency, or shortest wave portion of the ultraviolet spectrum, with wavelengths below 240 nanometers (nano means a billionth). This chemical interaction warms the surrounding air, and disassociates some normal oxygen molecules into single atoms (O_1). Some of these merge with normal oxygen to produce ozone, or O_3. The ozone created by this process is thinly spread through the stratosphere, but is most thick at about thirty-five kilometers. If compressed, the total amount of stratospheric ozone would make a layer of only three millimeters over the earth's surface. But this ozone layer, thin as it is, does a wonderful service for life. It absorbs most of the ultraviolet radiation with wavelengths above about 240 nanometers (closer to visible light) and up to 320 nanometers. It does not absorb all this ultraviolet radiation, and thus our sunburns, wrinkles, and skin cancers (one good effect—the creation of vitamin D by the body). But the more it blocks the safer we are. If the ozone layer thins, then we are more vulnerable, and such afflictions as skin cancer rise, as they have risen in the last two decades. For, quite clearly, the ozone layer has thinned.

What causes it to thin? Normally, stratospheric ozone breaks down through time. Single-atom oxygen molecules (O_1) occasionally merge with ozone (O_3) to create two normal oxygen molecules (O_2), a process called recombination. The process is slow, in part because the oxygen atom ion is so scarce, and in part because such single atoms continue to combine with O_2 to create more ozone. Various other gases act as catalysts to speed up this process of ozone decay. Without these, the amount of stratospheric ozone would be approximately double its present levels, with a range of possible effects, including more warming of our atmosphere. The major catalysts are nitrogen oxides, various hydrogen compounds, and, most important recently, three halogens (fluorine, chlorine, and bromine) and their compounds. Only a very thin mixture of chlorine exists naturally in the atmosphere, in the form of methyl chloride (only 75,000 tons). Thus, almost all the chlorine catalysts derive from human-produced CFCs or other closely related gases, such as hydrochlorofluorocarbons (HCFCs), or over 300,000 tons in total. Inert in the troposphere, in the stratosphere CFCs, as well as several other halogen-based gases, break down under ultraviolet bombardment. It is derivative forms, two steps removed from CFCs, such as pure chlorine or chlorine monoxide, that serve as catalysts to ozone depletion. The chemical processes are complex, but fully understood. Note that, as catalytic agents, the derivatives of CFCs do not merge, except briefly, with ozone, but keep on stimulating its breakdown as long as they remain in the stratosphere, and this can be for over one hundred years.

Chlorine derivatives of CFCs are not the only ozone-depleting gases, but just the largest of at least a hundred molecularly distinct gases attributable to human causes. Bromine compounds are actually more powerful catalysts than chlorine, but fortunately less plentiful. However, today, bromine compounds have become more significant because of more effective controls over chlorine. Despite restrictions, use of the two most important bromine compounds are still growing—halons, a family of gases used primarily in fire extinguishers, and methyl bromide, increasingly used in agriculture to sterilize soils and vegetables and fruit. At present, no comparable, inexpensive substitutes have been found for either.[5]

After 1974, all these atmospheric processes were well understood. The question that does not yet lend itself to a definitive answer is, what amount of ozone thinning is attributable to human-produced gases, and what to other natural processes? By 1985, satellite and ground observations in Antarctica revealed larger than normal wintertime thinning of the ozone layer over this frozen continent, or what some referred to, not quite accurately, as holes in the layer in late winter or early spring, after wind patterns had largely isolated Antarctica from any mixing from the middle latitudes. These "holes" had not existed before the 1950s. Few people, except some antienvironmental kooks, denied the influence of human-produced chlorine gases on polar thinning. Here the process involves other chemical reactions than those described above, reactions involving stratospheric clouds over Antarctica and an almost indisputable role for chlorine. In brief, the cold Antarctica air freezes the nitrogen in chlorine nitrate, freeing large quantities of chlorine, a catalyst for ozone recombination. The frozen nitrate creates a type of cirrus clouds. Note that these conditions—a pool of isolated air and nitrate freezing—are largely limited to Antarctica, although up to a fourth of such reactions occur in some years in the less isolated Arctic atmosphere. In recent years in Antarctica, the late winter loss of ozone has been as high as 60 to 70 percent, with the resulting increase in ultraviolet radiation being as high as 150 percent or even 300 percent locally. Even in the Arctic, radiation has increased by 25 percent in very cold winters.

The thinning elsewhere does raise some problems of causation and exact measurement. The thinning has been slight in the tropics but averaged an alarming 3 percent thinning each year below pre-1980 levels during the 1980s at mid-latitudes, or 4 percent each year from 1978 to 1992 (these are not cumulative amounts, but yearly departures from the 1980 base). The regional differences are great, and even in a few northern latitudes the thinning has been very limited. The rate of thinning, at first for no clear reason, jumped abruptly in 1992–1993, with up to an 11 percent decline in some areas. This caused great alarm. Then, just as suddenly, the thinning slowed after 1993, and has shown some volatility since then. The unusually rapid thinning, as we now know, was one result of the eruption of the huge Philippine volcano Pinatubo in 1991. It pushed aerosols into the stratosphere, which scattered light and slowed the production of ozone. From 1997 to 2003, the ozone layer has been stable in the tropics, but down by 3 percent on average in the mid- and higher latitudes of the Northern Hemisphere, and down 6 percent in the same latitudes in the Southern Hemisphere. This has meant an increase in ultraviolet radiation of from 5.2 to 7 percent. Because of such volatility, a few scientists still doubt that human causes have significantly influenced ozone thinning in the middle latitudes, and have suggested alternative theories, none, in the estimation of a majority of atmospheric scientists, fully persuasive or evidenced.

To the extent that CFCs and other human-produced gases have caused the thinning, then ozone depletion is, in almost all respects, an ideal problem for international alleviation. The role of human activity is almost beyond doubt. Since human health is at stake, the risks are very high, higher than for any other form of air pollution, although scientists disagree about the degree of risk so long as the degree of ozone thinning remains small. Soon comparable, but not always inexpensive, substitutes for CFCs and other halogen-based gases were available. The solution was clear, and in this rare case a solution that could work rather quickly—get rid of human-contributed CFCs and other ozone-depleting gases. Even before the extent of the problem was clear, in 1978 the EPA placed a ban on CFC aerosols except for medically critical inhalants. A few other countries followed. Then, as the dangers of CFCs became more clear, a group of nations, meeting in Vienna in 1985, signed a convention that required them each to take appropriate steps to reduce ozone-depleting gases.

Worldwide attention to the so-called ozone hole in Antarctica created a new urgency. Thus, ninety-three nations signed a 1987 protocol in Montreal on Substances that Deplete the Ozone Layer. The industrialized countries committed themselves to reducing the production of CFCs by 20 percent by 1993 and by 50 percent by 1999, with underdeveloped countries to follow within ten years. Meeting in London in 1990, with greater urgency, these same countries so amended the protocol as to require production of CFCs and certain other ozone-depleting gases to stop by 2000 in industrialized nations, and production of HCFCs (widely used, interim substitutes for CFCs in cooling) to stop by 2040, even though none of the HCFCs are even one-tenth as depleting as most CFCs and some only one one-hundredth as depleting. China and India, plus other developing countries, still had an extra ten years to meet these mandates through phased reductions. The richer nations committed funds to help underdeveloped countries reduce CFCs through a Multilateral Fund, which so far has spent over $1.5 billion in underdeveloped nations. In addition, the United Nations–sponsored Global Environmental Facility has contributed about a third as much. The United States exerted leadership in seeking global answers to the ozone problem, but faced charges of hypocrisy because it was largely American companies that developed patented substitutes for CFCs.

In 1992, at Copenhagen, these same nations moved up the targeted phase-out of CFCs and a few other gases to 1996, and of HCFCs to 2030. In further meetings of the parties to the Montreal Protocol, in Montreal in 1997 and Beijing in 1999, new amendments either added new substances to the list (now near one hundred in all) or set tighter timelines for compliance. As of 2003, all developed countries had already phased out almost all production of halons, CFCs, carbon tetrachloride, methyl chloroform, and a few other minor gases. As of 2005 they had phased out methyl bromide, and they have pledged to phase out almost all HCFCs by 2020, with interim targets along the way. Fortunately for the reduction effort, it was these wealthy countries that had produced most of these now proscribed gases. Underdeveloped countries are now in the process of phasing out the production of CFCs, methyl chloroform, and methyl bromide, with a scheduled reduction of 70 percent by 2010 and elimination by 2015 (all difficult goals). For HCFCs, which are now their main substitute for CFCs, they have until 2040 for final elimination.

To a large extent, the frequently amended Montreal protocols are working. Because the more developed countries had contributed up to

90 percent of ozone-depleting gases, their efforts alone assured that the concentration of such gases in the lower atmosphere would decline, as it has rather dramatically since the mid-1990s. By 2000 the stratospheric concentration of CFCs had stabilized, and by 2005 it was beginning a gradual decline. Because of the lag effect, the actual beginning recovery of the ozone layer may be ten or even twenty years away. But measurements in 2003 revealed that the rate of ozone thinning in the upper stratosphere has begun to slow, suggesting that in a few more years the turnaround will occur. By present projections of the Ozone Secretariat of the United Nations, stratospheric ozone should recover to pre-1980 levels by around 2050.

By 2000, the Montreal Protocol had already become the most successful international environmental effort in history. It has led to a reduction of around 87 percent of the production of all ozone-depleting gases. According to the "what if" estimates of the Ozone Secretariat, without the Montreal Protocol the stratospheric ozone would have declined to 50 percent of pre-1980 levels in northern mid-latitudes, 70 percent in southern, by 2050. By then, the level of ozone-depleting chemicals in the atmosphere would have risen by five times. According to its challengeable estimate, the number of melanoma cancers would have increased by 1.5 million annually, and eye cataracts by 150 million. Note that the people most affected by increased ultraviolet radiation are light skinned, and that the largest effect is in the higher latitudes. But the impact of ozone thinning involves much more than humans, since all surface life depends on the ozone barrier.

But the victory is not yet won. It depends on full compliance with the Montreal Protocol (in any given year, about twenty countries admit some degree of noncompliance). In both 2003 and 2004, the Bush Administration asked United Nations treaty administrators for large exemptions from the 2005 ban on further production of methyl bromide. The size of the requested exemption (23 million tons in 2005) exceeded the total of all exemptions requested by other countries. The Bush Administration acted in behalf of farmers, food processors, and even golf course owners. These groups use methyl bromide to sterilize soil, vegetables and fruit, and even meat. This exemption would set a dangerous precedent. Since the most important ozone-depleting gases remain in the atmosphere from 50 to 115 years, the quantity of these gases in the stratosphere is only now nearing an all-time peak. The ozone thinning over Antarctica reached a record level in 2000, and the ozone over the Arctic has declined in some years by up to 30 percent. Plenty of CFCs are still in use in refrigeration, and despite rigid rules for recapturing and recycling them, some will continue to escape into the atmosphere. The leading bromine compounds are still growing in use. Even developed countries still have a right to use small quantities of CFCs in medical inhalers, and to produce and sell CFCs to underdeveloped countries until 2015. Thus, even CFCs will stay around a good while. It is also important to note that the best replacement refrigerants, hydrofluorocarbons (HFCs), are among the most powerful greenhouse gases. Even as the Montreal parties were urging their use, those involved in global climate control efforts were trying to end their use. In poor countries, the cost of CFC replacement may be almost prohibitive. One dilemma involves American and European companies which will sell, at a price, new gases to underdeveloped countries, but will not surrender their corporate secrets.[6]

Finally, the reduction of ozone-depleting gases may not reverse the thinning of the ozone layer as much as predicted because of several feedback mechanisms. The recent rise in global temperatures, however explained, has helped increase heat absorption in the troposphere and cooled the lower stratosphere. This cooling will reduce the normal creation of stratospheric ozone, and thus retard the recovery of the ozone layer. But possibly compensating for this will be other effects, such as less warming as production of CFCs and other greenhouse halocarbons decline. Any increase of tropospheric ozone (air pollution), which also screens out ultraviolet radiation, will at least in part negate the impact of less stratospheric ozone on ultraviolet radiation at the earth's surface. But pollution controls, if effective, will reduce tropospheric ozone and thus reduce ozone screening. To further illustrate the complexity, a restoration of the ozone layer to pre-1980 levels will increase warming, but probably not as much as the elimination of CFCs will help cool it. If the present decline in the strength of the earth's major magnetic field continues, or moves to a reversal of poles, this will create extra nitrogen oxides (a product of unscreened protons in the solar wind) that will act as catalysts to ozone recombination, and thus could lead to major declines in the ozone layer. No one at present can predict exactly how all these interactions will affect future ozone levels or the amount of ultraviolet radiation at the surface.

The ozone layer makes clear the difficulty of predicting the effect of new chemicals. Most chlorine compounds are very dangerous to humans. Two families of compounds, dioxins (chlorinated dibenzodioxins) and PCBs (polychlorinated bipheyls), have already proven this. But CFCs seemed to be the exception, useful and benign gases. It took a half century to find out otherwise. Any number of new chemicals that now seem innocuous or even beneficial may turn out to be very dangerous, in ways we cannot at present predict. Think also of DDT. When they are clearly dangerous, they are at that point pollutants. Many greenhouse gases seem not only innocuous, but are even necessities for life itself, yet at present, in too large amounts, they pose such a threat to climate change that they are on the way to becoming critical pollutants.

The Extinction Crisis

Not all of the harmful effects of human activity involve pollution. Equally critical are the threats that humans pose to the welfare or even survival of other species in what is now a period of rapid extinctions. These include habitat loss, the spread of destructive alien species into new habitats, and the deliberate killing of nonhuman species. These and other challenges constitute what most naturalists view as a major extinction crisis.

The earth supports an enormous variety of organisms. How many species are on earth today is beyond any measurement. About 1.75 million are described species, although the exact boundaries among species, subspecies, and varieties are not always clear. Humans have probably observed, although not always classified, about 2.5 million species. Beyond that, the guesses vary widely. The United Nations Environmental Programme, in what amounts to a mean among all the guesses, usually estimates a total of 14 million species. Some scientists think the number of insect species alone is close to 30 million, and some estimates of the total number of species are as high as 100 million (some people include viruses among the total, while others do not, since a virus cannot reproduce except in a host cell). The total number of species shifts annually, as some become extinct, and as enough mutations begin to accumulate in some populations as eventually to justify the identification of a new species. Throughout the earth's history, most of the species that ever lived are now extinct. The profile of life is ever changing, and in what seem to have been five catastrophic periods in the past, over half of all species then living became extinct in relatively brief periods of time. Such mass extinctions were followed by periods of rapid evolutionary change, as mutations, most normally either of no import or harmful to individual organisms, now were more often favorable, allowing lucky organisms to adapt to unoccupied environmental niches.

THE PRESENT EXTINCTION CRISIS

The earth is now in a new period of massive extinctions. We simply do not know enough details about past extinction episodes to make quantitative comparisons, but it is possible that in this century the number of extinctions will exceed that in any past century. The one all-important necessary condition for most present extinctions is quite clear—the impact of humans. Never before has one species so dominated the earth, or so affected its surface and atmosphere. In the past, most human-caused extinctions involved human predation. Not so today. Humans are so numerous, use up so many resources, take up so much space, produce so much pollutants or waste, and contribute to such major changes in climate that more and more species will not have a safe place to live. Humans have taken away their life support and have so polluted the air, land, and water that they are no longer safe. Almost equally damaging is that mobile humans have introduced alien or invasive species in every corner of the earth, with often disastrous results in the host environment. As in past shifts in the climate, the warming now under way, if it continues, will in itself doom many species, particularly those that can survive within only a narrow range of temperatures and cannot migrate fast enough to keep up with temperature changes. The relatively slow pace of extinctions, over the last ten thousand years, is in large part explained by an unusually long period of climate stability.

How rapid is the present loss of species? No one knows, or can know with certainty. The most important loss may be among microorganisms, including bacteria and protozoa. Most of these are probably not yet identified, with many in the oceans, which are now vulnerable to pollution and warming. So are other marine organisms, including coral, which has created enormously bio-productive reefs, about one-fourth of which are already destroyed and most of the others endangered. Unfortunately, the largest proportion of species in danger are well below the level of public awareness and concern, which largely involves vertebrate animals and vascular plants. These are a tiny part of life as a whole. If one uses 14 million as a good guess, then all mammals combined (we do have a reasonably complete inventory of these) make up less than 0.002 percent of all species, all birds only 0.004 percent, and vascular plants less than 0.02 percent. Among identified species, almost 60 percent are insects, but everyone assumes that we have not begun to identify all microorganisms. Bacteria might well rival insects in numbers of species, since bacteria lurk unidentified in soil, deep in rocks, and at the bottom of oceans. In the United States, at the level of identification and concern, the largest number of extinct or endangered species involve plants, insects, freshwater fishes, and, in a special category, mussels, snails, and crayfish, which are uniquely frequent and varied in the streams of the United States. We lead the world in endemic species (those present nowhere else) of these invertebrates.

Extinction is a normal part of nature. Most organisms are highly specialized, for they fit a small and often localized niche. If the environment shifts, many formerly well-adapted species are helpless and die off. The environmental shift may involve climate (a period of warming or cooling, a shift in precipitation), a rare weather event (a flood or extended drought), a population surge among key predators, or such catastrophic events as a huge volcanic explosion or an asteroid collision. The die off of at least seventy large mammals (including the hairy mammoth, giant sloth, saber-toothed tiger, and horse) in North America at the end of the Wisconsin glacier (after 11,500 years ago) may have involved both climate change and human predation. Most present extinctions involve either habitat loss or competition from invasive species. More often than not, it is humans who have taken over or transformed a habitat (such as by deforesting land or polluting streams) or introduced exotic species. In the whole history of the United States, the most damaging alien species has been the imported chestnut blight (a fungus), which has killed all but a few American chestnut trees, in most respects the most valuable of all eastern hardwoods (valuable not only to humans but to numerous wildlife).

The American chestnut represents the present American situation— very few extinct species but hundreds of threatened ones. The chestnut has survived in areas of transplanted trees hundreds of miles from the moving edge of the spreading blight. A few sprouts still survive briefly in its former range. Plant breeders are close to a blight-resistant strain, but it would take centuries for the chestnut to regain its earlier preeminence in American woodlands. Because of awareness, and protective policies, relatively few extinctions will occur in the near future in affluent countries among plants and vertebrates. Even in poor countries, with few resources to protect threatened species, outside aid may help preserve at least a small population of threatened mammals and birds. A few will survive only in zoos or isolated preserves. They will then be visible souvenirs of what has been lost in the way of effective biodiversity. One might argue that what is important is not bare survival, but integrated populations in ecoregions, however one defines these. But lower in the chain of life, and in the tropics, the pace of extinction will undoubtedly accelerate, often among as yet unidentified species and among those that elicit little human concern. This will happen, if for no other reason, because there will not be enough living space for all species now on earth.

Why worry about extinctions? This is an important question, and an exceedingly complex one. If one's moral concerns embrace the welfare of other species, and involve a commitment to the right of all life to survive and flourish, then one will react to the human-caused death of all the individuals that make up a species much as one does to human genocide. Something precious, something of inherent value, has been lost. This is true even if the loss poses no material threat to humans, or in some cases might even improve human existence (disease pathogens, disease-carrying mosquitos or rodents). The implication of such solicitude for all life might seem to lead to a reluctance to take any life at all. But all animal life depends on plants. Thus, the logic of the position would have to be that humans harvest plants, and possibly also animals, but selectively, in such a way as to preserve the integrity of the species. Some extinctions would still occur, but humans would not be guilty of eliminating any form of life.

Most arguments for preserving life-forms involve esthetic loss or human material needs. Esthetic loss is a powerful but almost always selective motivator. When most Americans think of extinctions, they think of magnificent Siberian tigers or ivory-billed woodpeckers. They recall, with a sense of loss, the passenger pigeon and Carolina parakeet, and rejoice at the last minute recovery of the American bison or of the bald eagle. They hope against hope that, someday, we will find a surviving pair of Bachman's warblers or that the highly probable sighting of a male ivory-bill in Arkansas in 2005 means that breeding pairs have survived. Our experience is diminished by the loss of such species. But not so for invisible microscopic life, for most insects except butterflies, and for most mussels and snails (presently the most threatened in the United States). Human concern for these less visible species almost always involves utility, or what they contribute, directly or indirectly, to human welfare. What does it matter if fifteen endemic mussels in the Clinch River in Southwest Virginia die off? Who does it hurt? What possible, vital role do they serve for the river or even a wider ecological community? What would be lost if the last few Florida panthers die? They are merely a subspecies of a cat widely distributed throughout the Americas, and presently doing well in much of the western United States (there called mountain lion, and elsewhere either puma or cougar). In the past the Florida panther possibly was a major predator of deer or other wildlife, and thus helped maintain a balanced and sustainable ecology. But in their remnant, carefully monitored and protected status, they no longer serve such a larger role. For many people they have esthetic value. But in what sense do they have any other utility? No one really knows, but in all likelihood none at all.

In many cases, the survival of one species depends upon the survival of others. If the pollen-bearing plants that provide the only food for specialized insects die off, so do the insects. In the same sense, without pollinating insects some plants will be unable to reproduce. Without specific birds, many species of insects will soar in numbers. The linkages are often so complex that it is almost impossible to predict the effect of any extinction. It is also almost impossible to identify critical species in an ecosystem, or those whose survival is vital to the health of the whole.

For the United States, Hawaii is by far the most spectacular and unique ecosystem. Far from any other land, the Hawaiian Islands are of relatively recent volcanic origin, and before human contact half of their land-based flora and fauna was endemic to the islands (over eight thousand endemic species). The same is true for the Galapagos Islands, off Ecuador, but they have a more restricted array of organisms. In each case, human changes in land use and the introduction of alien species have been devastating for most endemics. In Hawaii, beginning with the original Polynesian settlers, endemic species have moved to or close to extinction in large numbers. Of Hawaii's fifty-two endemic birds at the time of the first European contact (the Polynesians had contributed to up to sixty extinctions already), eighteen are extinct, one probably extinct, and most others imperiled. For the rest of the United States, only three birds are clearly extinct, and one probably so.[1]

Then another question: what does it matter that human populations have introduced a new array of species, and slowly killed off the natives? Once again, one may love the diversity, or cherish the beauty of native species, or value their scientific revelations, but is there any economic loss? If so, what, and to whom? Why not import the flora and fauna that worked so well back home? To use a prominent American example, are streams worse off because the introduced eastern rainbow trout, in most of the country, has replaced native trout? Once again, no one can offer a confident answer. Here the issue is not just a loss of organic diversity, but how much can substitutions fulfill the same functional role as lost or threatened native species. For example, forests are critical, as photo-synthesizers, as carbon sinks, as modifiers of climate, but various mixes of tree species may serve these same critical roles. Yet, at a finer level, specific trees have irreplaceable roles in nourishing various forms of life that depend on their flowers and fruit, even as trees differ immensely in the quality of timber they provide for human use.

The most visible and valued forms of life, from the human perspective, are often not the most critical components of an ecological commu-nity. Much more important may be the multiple and often rarely noted organisms, from insects, worms, and fungi to bacteria that lurk in soil, water, lagoons, and decaying vegetation and flesh. And at this level, the main problem is not so much extinction, although this occurs, but a thinning of populations or their elimination from some locations. In the oceans, it is doubtful if many species of cyanobacteria or phytoplankton will become extinct, but a severe reduction in numbers could so lower the total output of photosynthesis as to dramatically raise levels of atmo-spheric carbon dioxide and, over a longer period of time, significantly lower the amount of oxygen in the atmosphere. Both pose dangers to animal life, and thus to human life. In the last two decades, a rapid warm-ing of the atmosphere and a very gradual warming of surface ocean wa-ters have already threatened many marine organisms that thrive on the nutrients in cooler water.

Concern over declining populations of wildlife or fish probably pre-dates human civilization. Words like biodiversity and ecosystem are new, but not the problems that led to their use. What is new is the nature of the human threat. With the "invention" of agriculture, humans radically changed the local habitats for certain forms of life, but until the mod-ern era this rarely caused any extinctions because of the low population density and the amount of forested land that remained. Thus, for most of human history the threat of human-caused extinctions or near extinctions usually involved overhunting or overfishing, with little awareness of what was at stake until it was too late. People killed animals for food, for bones needed as tools, for fur, and just for fun. Even as late as the nineteenth century, in both Europe and America, millions of people, if they had the opportunity, killed almost all types of wildlife at abandon, including songbirds. Today, except for a few large mammals in Africa and Asia, hunting is rarely a threat to species survival, and in many cases it has been hunters who have worked to protect or expand wildlife populations. They have bought into the idea of sustainable harvest. In the case of fish, which provide a primary food source for millions of people, the story is different. Overfishing remains a major problem worldwide. Human predation and pollution are the major threats to ocean fish populations, with living space less significant.

INTERNATIONAL EFFORTS TO PRESERVE BIODIVERSITY

Protecting endangered species is now an international crusade. In this effort, unlike for global warming, the United States has taken a leadership role. The story is also very complex. Compared to the United States and western Europe, the threat of extinctions, if not to ecological balance, is much greater in tropical countries and poor countries. Because of often very costly protective strategies, few species identified as being in danger of extinction will actually become extinct in wealthy countries, and, as in the United States, some species at the brink of extinction will be helped to recover. This is not true of poor countries, most in the species-rich tropics.

The largest public-private international organization devoted to biodiversity is the International Union for Conservation of Nature and Natural Resources (IUCN), or what most refer to as the World Conservation Union. It has compiled and maintains the most complete list of endangered species for the world as a whole, or the *Red Book of Threatened Species*. Table 1 records the Red Book list of threatened species up to 2006. For some groups, such as insects, this list cannot be even close to the likely total. Also, it does not contain microorganisms.

Post–World War II international efforts to protect biodiversity began in 1946 with the drafting and signing of the International Convention for the Regulation of Whaling. After enough ratifications, this went into

Table 1. The 2006 IUCN Red List of Threatened Species, summary statistics. (IUCN.)

	Number of described species	Number of species evaluated in 2006	Number of threatened species in 1996/98	Number of threatened species in 2000	Number of threatened species in 2002	Number of threatened species in 2003	Number of threatened species in 2004	Number of threatened species in 2006	Number threatened in 2006, as % species described
VERTEBRATES									
Mammals	5,416	4,856	1,096	1,130	1,137	1,130	1,101	1,093	23%
Birds	9,934	9,934	1,107	1,183	1,192	1,194	1,213	1,206	12%
Reptiles	8,240	664	253	296	293	293	304	341	51%
Amphibians	5,918	5,918	124	146	157	157	1,770	1,811	31%
Fishes	29,300	2,914	734	752	742	750	800	1,173	40%
Subtotal	**58,808**	**24,284**	**3,314**	**3,507**	**3,521**	**3,524**	**5,188**	**5,624**	**23%**
INVERTEBRATES									
Insects	950,000	1,192	537	555	557	553	559	623	52%
Molluscs	70,000	2,163	920	938	939	967	974	975	45%
Crustaceans	40,000	537	407	408	409	409	429	459	85%
Others	130,200	86	27	27	27	30	30	44	51%
Subtotal	**1,190,200**	**3,978**	**1,891**	**1,928**	**1,932**	**1,959**	**1,992**	**2,101**	**53%**

Table 1. (continued)	Number of described species	Number of species evaluated in 2006	Number of threatened species in 1996/98	Number of threatened species in 2000	Number of threatened species in 2002	Number of threatened species in 2003	Number of threatened species in 2004	Number of threatened species in 2006	Number threatened in 2006, as % species described
PLANTS									
Mosses	15,000	93	–	80	80	80	80	80	86%
Ferns and allies	13,025	212	–	–	–	111	140	139	66%
Gymnosperms	980	908	142	141	142	304	305	306	34%
Dicotyledons	199,350	9,538	4,929	5,099	5,202	5,768	7,025	7,086	74%
Monocotyledons	59,300	1,150	257	291	290	511	771	779	68%
Subtotal	**287,655**	**11,901**	**5,328**	**5,611**	**5,714**	**6,774**	**8,321**	**8,390**	**70%**
OTHERS									
Lichens	10,000	2	–	–	–	2	2	2	100%
Mushrooms	16,000	1	–	–	–	–	–	1	100%
Subtotal	**26,000**	**3**	**–**	**–**	**–**	**2**	**2**	**3**	**100%**
TOTAL	**1,562,663**	**40,168**	**10,533**	**11,046**	**11,167**	**12,259**	**15,503**	**16,118**	**40%**

effect in 1948, but it did not stop whaling for two decades. It did promise protection when given species became endangered. Because of building international concern, it finally gained a near-complete moratorium
on commercial whaling in 1986. To a large extent, this effort to protect
our largest mammals has worked, since most whale populations have stabilized and begun increasing. By the time of the moratorium, the largest
of all mammals, the blue whale, was very close to extinction, and it is still
threatened. A few nations, such as Japan and Iceland, have found ways to
circumvent the ban on commercial whaling, but as yet not to such an
extent as to threaten any species.

The IUCN began in 1948. It is, officially, a private organization with
its headquarters in Switzerland. It is funded by assessments of its members, which include governments, governmental departments, divisions
of the United Nations, most major nongovernmental environmental organizations, and even corporations. In 2003 it had 980 members, and an
annual budget of about $70 million. Its two central concerns today are
trying to deal with the extinction crisis and, closely related, maintaining the integrity of ecosystems. It does not have the funds to undertake
major projects on its own, but works closely, in a facilitative way, with
local or regional organizations, and in this sense depends very much
on voluntary labor. More than most environmental organizations, it emphasizes the economic benefits of biodiversity (food, lumber, traditional
medicines, genetic resources) and seeks the active support of multinational corporations. Because of its Red List of threatened species, and an
Internet-based and continuously updated body of information about species, it provides an invaluable service to governments and private environmental organizations. It has facilitated, and at times cooperated with,
several United Nations environmental organizations, and has sponsored
two widely publicized World Conservation Congresses, the last in 2000
in Amman, Jordan.[2]

The most important of official organizations is the United Nations
Environmental Programme (UNEP). UNEP was a product of the Stock-
holm Conference on the Human Environment in 1972. This conference
is now correctly recognized as a landmark in modern environmentalism,
unrivaled in significance until the 1992 Earth Summit in Rio. It came at
a propitious moment, or what turned out to be the high tide of contemporary environmentalism. In the same year, the Club of Rome published
its controversial book, The Limits of Growth. It followed by two years the first

Earth Day in the United States, and also the most comprehensive environmental bill ever enacted in the United States, the National Environmental Policy Act (see chapter 9).

UNEP is an umbrella division of the United Nations. Several conventions involved with environmental issues are under its jurisdiction. This includes those involved with global warming, where its impact has been greatest. It has coordinated various environmental programs, and has made sustainable development one of its priorities. In the area of biodiversity, it has sponsored two conventions, a so far somewhat limited Convention on Biodiversity and the critically important and successful Convention on International Trade in Endangered Species of Wild Fauna and Flora (usually referred to as CITES). UNEP has compiled and published what are, as of 2006, three major reports on the world's environment, the *Global Environmental Outlook* (GEO). The last, in 2002, is the most comprehensive survey available, and has informed much of the content of this book. In many ways, the 2002 GEO is the most pessimistic of the three. Almost all trends, beginning with population growth, unprecedented resource use and consumption in the developed world, and a widening gulf of wealth and income between wealthy and poor countries, has created almost irresistible pressures on the environment. If anyone wants to probe the depths of pessimism, then read the GEO evaluation of environmental conditions in Africa.[3]

The most recent major international effort to protect biodiversity began with the Earth Summit in Rio in 1992. At that time, 157 countries signed a new Convention (a name used for most United Nations environmental initiatives) on Biological Diversity (CBD). Subsequent to this organizational meeting, a few other countries, including the United States, signed the convention. But it went into effect only after thirty countries had ratified the convention. In 2003, a total of 187 nations had ratified and become parties to the convention. Among large countries, the United States alone was conspicuously absent, and so far it still has not ratified the CBD. At present there is little chance that it will, for reasons that will become clear in the following discussion. In some respects this is ironic, for the CBD is in many ways an endangered species act for the whole earth, and its original charter contains much language from the Endangered Species Act (ESA) of 1973 and the National Environmental Policy Act of 1970, including a provision that all parties to the convention must require some type of environmental impact statements.[4]

The original convention, in often very general or even a bit muddy language, committed the nations of the world to various strategies to protect biological diversity and, of course, to the sustained use of biological resources. In this purpose it parallels that of most nongovernmental environmental organizations and the American ESA. But from the beginning it has had a second agenda, one at times only loosely related to biodiversity—to provide binding rules for the diffusion of genetically altered organisms. The CBD has sponsored research on biological diversity, located environmental hot spots around the world, and encouraged member nations to enact legislation and establish refuges to protect endangered species. But all of its early advocacy stopped short of any binding and enforceable rules. The original convention made clear that rule-making and rule-enforcing would be through protocols adopted in subsequent meetings of its ruling body, the Conference of the Parties (or COPS, which is a type of legislative body made up of member nations).[5]

The convention suggested only one area for future protocols—that of genetically altered plants and animals. And here is where it has had enormous difficulty, first in maturing a protocol acceptable to its parties, and, subsequent to the approval of such in 2000, in gaining the required fifty ratifications for it to go into effect (it went into effect in September 2003). Clearly, this Protocol on Biosafety will be a major reason for the United States not to ratify either the convention or this, its first protocol. I fear that the controversies surrounding genetically altered life, or what the CBD calls living modified organisms (LMOs), will so dominate the CBD in the next few years as to diminish its role in other issues possibly more central to biodiversity.

The Protocol on Biosafety is at least courageous, for it involves a very sensitive issue around the world. It also, in an indirect sense, makes the United States a target of some very tough rules, for the United States has led the world in introducing new genes to alter plants, most in behalf of better resistance to diseases, cold, or insects, or in behalf of better nutrition. It has also altered animals, mostly for research or to produce needed medications. But genetically altered foods, particularly corn, soy beans, and rice, have aroused fears, and at times overt protests, in much of the world, including western Europe and even in underdeveloped countries that, despite a desperate need, have at times refused food aid involving altered crops. With little awareness, most American consumers have accepted such foods with little protest, and apparently with no adverse effects, although this is a controverted issue.

The language of the Protocol on Biosafety reflects some of the controversies that attended its maturation. Its language is often deliberately ambiguous, and so full of jargon as to be almost unreadable. Because of its charter, it has to key its proposed rules to the possible threat genetically altered organisms pose to biodiversity, but it always includes a reference to adverse effects on human health as well. It is not very clear what the precise threat to diversity is, unless altered varieties of crops or animals will lead to the extinction of existing species (for example, genetically altered salmon might escape into the ocean and eventually displace the native salmon or spread unwanted diseases into the wild). One might suppose that genetic engineering would increase diversity, for in time some alterations could lead to new species. What the protocol does is set up rules for the transfer of genetically altered organisms across national boundaries, particularly when the new organism will be released into the new environment. It carefully qualifies the rules so as to exempt certain medications, and, in most respects, it also exempts food or animal feed for consumption so long as it does not entail the release of the new genes into the host environment. But even in this case, the exporting country, if it ratifies the protocol, will have to identify the genetically altered food or feed and so label the boxes used to ship it. Thus, importing countries can make an informed decision about buying the product.

The protocol places a major burden on exporting countries, even those which do not ratify the protocol. Importing countries who have ratified are obligated to follow its rules for importing living modified organisms. Exporting countries have to notify any importing country of products containing genetically altered content. The importing country can accept, reject, or ask for more information. If it wishes, it can force the exporting country to submit to a scientific assessment, and pay for it. In any case, it has over half a year to make a decision, and no decision does not mean that the import takes place (it is possible for an importing country to use this device, in effect, as a barrier to trade or as a substitute for a tariff). If a country with such an altered organism unintentionally causes it to enter the international market, it must notify all the parties to the convention. The protocol does not clarify enforcement procedures, including penalties or the liability of exporters, but leaves this to future COPS (the first met in Malaysia in February 2004). The protocol does list the beneficial possibilities of biological engineering, and permits im-porting countries that have no concern about a product to import it im-mediately, without the waiting period. The United States, joined by a few other major exporters of biologically modified crops (Argentina, Canada, Chile), led the opposition to the protocol, and has so far refused to sign, let alone ratify, the final product, as have Australia and Brazil.

It is now clear that most countries will ratify the Protocol on Bio-safety. What is unclear is how it will be implemented, whether member countries will provide the needed funding, and whether it will have any real effect on world trade. In almost every sensitive area of the protocol, the critical decisions have been left to future COPS. A main support for its effective implementation is a permanent Bio-Safety Clearing House to supervise trade in such organisms. At present, it is not much more than a web-based data clearing house. From the beginning negotiations, underdeveloped countries were the most avid supporters of a strong pro-tocol, which promised them some protection in areas where they did not have the technical expertise to make informed decisions about imports. The countries of the European Union generally supported the proto-col, often responding to very strong public sentiment against genetically modified crops. At times, anti-American sentiments may have influenced this posture. In the background of the long, contentious fight to mature the protocol was a larger worldwide debate about the issue of modified organisms, which in turn was often joined with massive demonstrations against the World Trade Organization, which had generally resisted the new protocol.[6]

The United Nations Convention on International Trade in Endangered Species (CITES) has been much more influential than the CBD. Its ori-gins reflect early advocacy by the World Conservation Union (IUCN). In one of its conferences in 1960 it advocated some type of control over trade in endangered species. In 1963 the IUCN called for an international convention or treaty to control such trade. It began developing drafts in 1964, and presented a second draft to a conference in 1971. This was a propitious time. At the Conference on the Human Environment in 1972, eighty-eight nations discussed a draft proposal. In March 1973, at a con-ference in Washington, D.C., these countries signed the draft convention and, after ratification by the required ten nations, it went into effect in 1975. Soon thereafter the United Nations Environmental Programme as-sumed direction of this new convention, and the Earth Summit at Rio in

1992 gave added endorsement to CITES, which now includes all but a handful of the nations of the world.[7]

What CITES did was set up a demanding body of regulations governing all trade in endangered fauna or flora, dead or alive, or any parts derived from such animals and plants. In much of the underdeveloped world, poaching and smuggling of endangered species was driven by international trade. CITES placed a major responsibility on all countries that ratified the convention, for they had to develop polices to protect the ecosystems that supported endangered species, and work to so manage wildlife as to support sustainable incomes in each country. Each ratifying country had to appoint a managing agency to implement the new regulations. One half of the purpose of the Endangered Species Act in the United States in 1973 was to designate such a management agency, in this case the Fish and Wildlife Service.

To control trade in endangered species, the convention set up three lists of animals and plants, or what it denominated Appendices I, II, and III. By species, they include subspecies, and in some cases regionally endangered populations, and also in some cases list not just species but a whole genus. For all species in Appendix I, or those most clearly endangered, the convention in effect prohibits almost any trade at all, and in the rare exceptions requires a permit from both the exporting and importing country. For Appendix II, which involves threatened species that might soon become endangered, it mandates export but not import permits. Appendix III has been a bit more confusing. It allows member nations to list locally endangered species, those that normally do not involve international trade, and asks other members to respect and help such countries. Such countries require an export permit for trade, but importing countries have no clear duties under this Appendix. It is not clear that it has had much impact. Tropical countries have most used Appendix III. Over one thousand species are now in Appendix I, with some of these involving genuses and thus multiple species. Up to five thousand animals and twenty-five thousand plants have received some protection under all three Appendices.[8]

CITES works with a minimal budget of about $2.5 million a year, which derives from assessments paid by member countries. It is more like a treaty than an action agency, since it places the responsibility for enforcement on member nations. The members have to set very stiff penalties for those who violate the trading rules. Among the exports that have most involved CITES are coral, crocodile skins, caviar, ivory, black rhinoceros horns, sturgeons, sharks, and seahorses. The elephant went on Appendix II in 1977, moved up to Appendix I in 1989, and, for some nations with growing populations, went back to Appendix II in 1997 and 2000. CITES lists the Whaling Convention as an associated control measure. Listing in Appendix I and II is by the Conference of the Parties, with nominations from member nations, which are required to document requests with careful scientific data. For species, or parts, that move in international trade under Appendix II, CITES has clear rules for marking all shipments. Each year, both exporting and importing countries have to render detailed reports on all trade. CITES likes to boast that, since its first listings, no species has become extinct because of commerce.

THE DEVELOPING AMERICAN CONCERN FOR WILDLIFE PRESERVATION

In the United States, concern about deforestation, wildlife destruction, and even extinction developed in the early nineteenth century. Trained naturalists were, by then, beginning scientific studies of the environment. But, so far as I know, the most emphatic denunciation of the human impact on wildlife came in a book first published in 1864 by George P. Marsh, a then sixty-three-year-old son of Vermont, a two-time congressman, a friend of John Quincy Adams, a supporter of the early Smithsonian Institution, and in his last career our first minister to Italy. Marsh was not a trained naturalist, but he was a keen observer of the human impact on the natural world, with his long years in Italy and his observations of the Mediterranean world supplementing his New England perspective. His book was originally entitled *Man and Nature*, but he called later editions, including one published in Italy, *The Earth as Modified by Human Action*. It has become a deserved classic in environmental studies. Marsh anticipated almost every theme in contemporary environmental protest, and composed what amounted to a Puritan-type jeremiad about human irresponsibility. At times, he was apocalyptic in his predictions, often prescient in his often necessarily speculative judgments, but, as one would expect, often wrong in his understanding and a bit too severe in his prophecies about the future.

Although he did not use the term, Marsh was an eloquent advocate of biodiversity. His single greatest concern was the deforestation occasioned by agriculture, and with it changes in climate and even geography. He anticipated James Lovelock's Gaia theory in his emphasis upon how much both climate and geography were shaped by life, how the interaction of various organisms shaped what we would now call ecosystems, and how humans, by disrupting the balance of living systems, risked future calamities, not the least being the extinction of many species. He tried to gauge the degree to which different orders of life shape climate and geological evolution (he eulogized trees and birds, applauded the role of reptiles and insects), listed the higher species already extinct in Europe because of human action, and, most original, speculated that the greatest role of all might be performed by microscopic life. In his words: "It is highly probable that the reef-builders and other yet unstudied minute forms of vital existence have other functions in the economy of nature besides aiding in the architecture of the globe, and stand in important relations not only to man but the plants and the larger sentient creatures over which he has dominion. The diminution or multiplication of these unseen friends or foes may be attended with the gravest consequences to all his material interests, and he is dealing with dangerous weapons when he interferes with arrangements pre-established by a power higher than his own."[9]

At the time he wrote, Marsh was not aware of any species that had become extinct in America, and only one seal off its coasts. He noted the flocks of passenger pigeons, the herds of bison, but did not yet anticipate their extinction or near extinction. He noted the near extirpation of the beaver to feed the needs of European fashions, but saw it as recovering when silk hats replaced fur and felt. What he deplored was the reckless killing of birds and animals, often for no human use, and the imbalances in nature these actions could cause, with unknown effects on human welfare. However, none of these, in his view, would come close to the imbalances created by modern agriculture and the reckless assault on our forests. Yet, here again, he anticipated no extinction among trees, or other plants, but did emphasize the dangers, as well as at times the usefulness, of introduced species.

A conservation movement began to affect policy in the United States just after the Civil War. Wildlife preservation was one goal of this movement. From this concern came a series of actions and legislation that led eventually to the Endangered Species Act of 1973, which was, and still is, the most ambitious legislative effort to protect biodiversity in the world. By 1900, and particularly after World War II, this concern led to international treaties or conventions. To an extent not properly appreciated by most people, the ESA was as much a response to international agreements as to concern over domestic wildlife protection. The story is complex in each case.

The first federal effort in America to protect fish and wildlife dates from 1864, or the year that Marsh published the first edition of his now-famous book. The federal government transferred the Yosemite Valley to the State of California with a provision that the state had to protect its fish and game from "wanton destruction." Yosemite, largely through the efforts of John Muir, would later become a national park. In 1872 the federal government created its first national park, Yellowstone, largely to protect its thermal features, but with the same proviso about fish and game. Only after 1894 did it do much to enforce these provisions, but at least a small bison herd barely survived in the park (down to 92 in 1902)—one of the thin threads that saved the bison from extinction. This remains the only free-ranging herd in the United States. In 1908 the federal government set aside a national bison range in Montana, and in 1912 it started a national elk refuge (the first use of this term for any federally protected land). The fate of the bison was a great spur to conservation efforts. By 1890, less than one thousand bison had survived, and with this awareness the fate of what Americans mistakenly referred to as a "buffalo" became a much publicized national concern. Its wanton slaughter, for sport as often as for prime bits of its meat, and the policy of killing bison as a way of starving plains Indians into reservations, was a national scandal.

The U.S. Congress began a system of national forests in 1881 (at first this meant federally owned land set aside in the West), and in the same act it offered some protection for fish in Alaska. In 1871 it created a federal office, the Commissioner of Fisheries. In 1883, the new American Ornithologists' Union began agitating for a model law to prevent the killing of endangered birds, and helped gain in 1886 a Division of Economic Ornithology and Mammalogy in the Department of Agriculture. These were, at first, largely fact-finding and advocacy departments, but they were the genesis of the later Fish and Wildlife Service (FWS). The need for regulation and protection of various species of wildlife was soon apparent, with much of the early concern being for waterfowl devastated by overhunting and habitat loss. The government effort had strong support from conservation organizations, from elite hunting clubs, including the Boone and Crockett Club so loved by Theodore Roosevelt, and, for fish, the Izaak Walton League. Since all such early efforts had as a goal not the elimination of hunting and fishing, but a sustained supply of game, informed sportsmen gladly supported conservation. At the same time, farmers and ranchers accepted protection of valued birds and animals, since all the early governmental protection agencies helped lead the campaign to shoot or poison the "varmints," such as the wolves, coyotes, prairie dogs, and hawks that threatened sheep, cattle, chickens, and crops.

Ironically, women's hats had a vital role in American conservation. By 1900, many hats featured the feathers of such spectacular birds as the brown pelican and the snowy egret. The plume trade drove these species toward extinction, arousing a determined movement to save them. The modern Audubon Society, formed by the union of state Audubon societies in 1905, originated in efforts to save these species. In Florida, the local bird watching or Audubon societies were able to get state legislation to protect the egrets and other plumed birds. A sympathetic President Theodore Roosevelt, in 1903, placed the small, federally owned Pelican Island, off the eastern coast of Florida, off limits to feather hunters, who had brought the brown pelican close to extinction in Florida. An Audubon Society volunteer became the first wildlife warden, at a salary of one dollar a year. Thus began the American wildlife refuge system.

After 1900, most states began regulating hunting and fishing, with license fees to pay for game wardens to enforce rules or to support fish hatcheries and the stocking of streams. In other words, inland fisheries were increasingly managed. As early as 1872 the federal government created the first federal fish hatchery, and in 1903 it established the Bureau of Fisheries, in the Department of Commerce, since it would be primarily concerned with commercial fishing. The early concerns were almost entirely limited to game fish valued by anglers, or birds and animals valued by hunters. Scarcity of game, not threatened extinction or ecological balance, was the primary issue, or a parallel to the sustained yield idea that guided forest management. But, obviously, some fish and most waterfowl involved more than one state or even one nation, and thus required federal controls or international agreements.

Theodore Roosevelt, and subsequent presidents, continued to set aside small areas to protect vulnerable wildlife, but only by executive orders and with almost no funds for management. In 1913 the federal government federalized control over all migratory and insect-eating birds, and in 1916 it signed a treaty with Canada (technically with Britain) for their protection (the Convention for the Protection of Migratory Birds). In 1918, Congress enacted the Migratory Bird Treaty Act to make domestic policies conform to this new treaty. In 1924 Congress passed the Upper Mississippi River Wildlife and Fish Refuge Act. It enacted the Migratory Bird Conservation Act in 1929. This act authorized but did not directly fund a system of refuges, most intended to protect migrating waterfowl (geese and ducks) in the upper Midwest. (The funding would have to come from individual acts by Congress.) In 1934, under another conservation president, Franklin D. Roosevelt, Congress approved a permanent funding provision involving stamps charged for hunting privileges, or what were soon referred to as duck stamps. This allowed the Department of the Interior to buy needed habitat to protect waterfowl (small lakes and wetlands), or soon a mosaic of small refuges, many with regulated hunting. In 1934, Aldo Leopold, already an expert in wildlife management, and soon to be famous as an early and sensitive ecologist, served on a three-member committee to study the plight of water birds during the dust bowl years. In 1935 Congress made the Bureau of Biological Survey in the Department of Agriculture responsible for the growing refuge system, even as it continued to lead the war against unwanted varmints. In a major governmental reorganization in 1939, Roosevelt placed both the bureau and the Commerce Department's Bureau of Fisheries in the Department of the Interior, and the next year merged the two into the present FWS. This still left conservation agencies in different departments—national forests in Agriculture, commercial fisheries in Commerce, and national parks and the FWS in Interior.

After World War II, the FWS expanded rapidly, and with shifting priorities. Although most refuges still involved migratory ducks and geese, the concern soon embraced threatened species of all types. In 1966, a National Wildlife Refuge Administration Act expanded acquisitions and mandated refuges for threatened species. In 1965 Congress enacted the first, limited Endangered Species Act. Its much more sweeping successor, the ESA of 1973, specifically authorized purchases for the sole protection of endangered species, and over twenty-five new refuges have fulfilled this commitment. By 1997 a new act also mandated efforts to maintain the integrity of whole ecosystems that were necessary to protect one or more threatened species. The mandate of the FWS has thus expanded about as far as one can imagine, but the funds to support such a mandate have usually been all too scarce. In 2004, wildlife refuges contained over 93 million acres, but with over half of this in Alaska.[10]

THE ENDANGERED SPECIES ACT OF 1973

The United States was very active in gaining approval for CITES, and with its signing had to develop a management agency to fulfill its enforcement obligations. This alone mandated legislation involving endangered species that entered international trade. At the same time, in the heyday of environmental concern, and because of fears first stimulated by Rachael Carson's famous 1962 book, *Silent Spring*, strong support existed for better protection of endangered domestic species. Already, the FWS had this as one of its mandates under the 1965 act, and had developed a list of over a hundred endangered species, but it had limited statutory authority to protect such species. These concerns led to the enactment of the Endangered Species Act of 1973. The act recognized a series of international agreements, including migratory bird treaties with Canada, Mexico, and Japan, and several fishing and whaling agreements. It set up procedures for enforcing Appendices I and II under CITES and includes all species in those appendices as extensions of its own list of endangered and threatened species. It also mandates very large fines for any violation of CITES, with some fines for trade in endangered species as high as $50,000.

The ESA was one of the most ambitious environmental acts ever enacted in the United States or anywhere else in the world. In fact, had Congress fully realized what it was doing, the bill might not have passed (the vote for it was almost unanimous). The act provided for the protection of endangered and threatened species of fish, wildlife, and plants, because of their esthetic, ecological, educational, historical, recreational, or scientific value. Note that it does not mention economic values (it exempted insect pests). The act, following the language of CITES, defined species broadly, to encompass subspecies (such as the Florida panther), and critical populations (the bald eagle, for example, was not endangered in Alaska and parts of Canada, but was in the lower forty-eight). The FWS is primarily responsible for the development of lists and enforcement, but for coastal species the National Marine Fisheries Service, a branch of the National Oceanic and Atmospheric Administration in the Commerce

Department, has enforcement responsibility (sixty-four species were on its list in 2006). The act mandated that all federal agencies had to seek to preserve endangered and threatened species. In order to conserve the ecosystems that supported endangered species, the FWS could acquire new refuges. In behalf of the FWS, the secretary of the Interior could issue regulations needed to protect endangered species or, in cooperation with the states, implement recovery plans for such species. The act extended to all territories of the United States.[11]

When most Americans thought of endangered species, they probably thought of mammals and birds. And, indeed, in its first years of implementing the EDA, the FWS did concentrate on these most visible species. But gradually it expanded to the full scope of its authority, with plants today most numerous on its primary list of endangered species, and on its somewhat shorter list of threatened species (those that might soon become endangered). Except for microscopic life, and life-forms at the level of roundworms or nematodes, the act is inclusive. It applied to all vertebrates (mammals, birds, reptiles, amphibians, and fish), to all invertebrates (clams, snails, insects, arachnids, and crustaceans), and to all flowering plants, including flowering trees, plus conifers, cycads, ferns, and lichens. Its regulations protect listed species from any human predation, but can only fully protect the habitat of such species on public lands or on private lands that have accepted some form of conservation status within individual states. This is why, at times, the FWS has to purchase refuges to save endangered species. Note that, by federal law, all navigable streams are public property, and the courts have so interpreted the word navigable as to include even small creeks. Wild animals are also considered public property, but not plants. Any individual can nominate a species for protection under this act, and support the nomination with credible scientific data. But the final decision on acceptance, or removal, is up to the FWS, or officially the secretary of the Interior. Any exemptions to the act require the approval of a special committee made up of federal agency and department heads. The full lists have to be reviewed every five years. On June 7, 2006, the lists included 411 endangered animals and 155 threatened ones. Of the plants on the lists, 599 were endangered, and 146 threatened.[12] The list is updated daily and published on the Internet.

Note that the ESA offers protection only for animals and plants on its lists. This means that it does not protect all endangered species, however one defines this status. Some that seem to be endangered may not have been nominated for such status, or have not yet been accepted by the screening committee. The ESA keeps a list of species that are candidates for protection but which have not yet been voted onto either of its lists. Beyond these candidate species, it also has a list of nominated species, or what some refer to as species of concern. Within its area of jurisdiction, and for its lists, the ESA has proved a very tough law, and under it the FWS has promulgated and enforced some of the most far-reaching administrative law in American history. No country has been willing to commit more resources to save endangered species than the United States, and so far the effort has been very successful. Despite any action by any government, a few listed species have such a fragile or restricted habitat that some natural catastrophe or climate change may lead to extinction. This primarily involves small freshwater fish and mussels, or some Hawaiian birds and plants. For migratory birds, action within the United States may be inadequate. But consistent with what is possible, and at times at great expense, the United States has committed itself to preserve most of its officially recognized endangered domestic species. Or so it has seemed so far. But note that the George W. Bush Administration, consistent with its overall effort to lessen the burden of environmental regulation for private interests, proposed in 2005 amendments to the ESA that would relax the level of enforcement and reward private owners for any loss of property values because of the requirements of the act.

PROSPECTS FOR THE FUTURE

Species are most threatened in tropical, and largely poor, countries. Here population pressure, destroyed habitat, lax enforcement of environmental laws, and shifts in climate are taking a huge toll already. In almost all major biological groups, or biota, except freshwater fish and crustaceans, the greatest diversity of animals and plants are in the tropics, and particularly in tropical rain forests. Unfortunately, the rapid cutting of such forests, for timber or to gain new agricultural land, is probably leading to the extinction of many insects and plants not even yet identified in scientific circles. Here, on rare occasions, scientists find an as yet unidentified mammal or bird. It is for these reasons that the great challenge, in the next half century, will be identifying and saving threatened species in countries ill equipped to carry out the rescue effort for themselves.

Even in the wealthy United States, preserving the present extent of
biodiversity will be a major challenge, particularly if climate change becomes an ever more significant threat and our population continues to
expand. The present status of threatened species is reasonably clear for
the United States. The leading nongovernmental organization involved
with biodiversity, the Nature Conservancy, has published a major book
on the subject, *Precious Heritage: The Status of Biodiversity in the United States*.[13]
Because of a national data collecting effort, mostly carried out by volunteers, this book includes the most recent evaluation, and by far the most
complete synthesis, on American biodiversity, drawing from hundreds
of more specialized studies as well as from government records and field
research. I am largely indebted to this book for the following all too brief
assessment.

As for so many contemporary environmental issues, the glass is either
half full or half empty on the issue of biodiversity. Environmentalists
usually view it as half empty, because they are so aware of present and
future threats, and so committed to arousing public support for conservation measures. They do not spend much time rejoicing in recent
achievements, which are considerable. For the United States, the greatest
of these is the ESA itself, and so far the willingness of the FWS to enforce
it. Almost all polls show a strong public awareness and concern about endangered species, or exactly the opposite of even fifty years ago. Despite
threats to animals and plants, the United States is still a very large country, with up to two-thirds of its land in forests or relatively undisturbed
grasslands. Private forest acreage is expanding annually, and areas under
reasonably secure conservation controls are growing each year. With two
possible exceptions—endemic Hawaiian birds and plants, and aquatic
life in the freshwater streams of southern Appalachia—the pace of extinction has slowed in recent years, in large part because of public and
private concern and action. Compared to most of the world, the United
States is in an enviable position on the issue of species preservation.

But the preservation of endangered species has costs, and some have
had to bear more of these than others. In its first highly publicized case,
the FWS almost blocked a TVA dam to protect a small fish, the snail darter.
Congress intervened to exempt this fish, and fortunately other populations were soon discovered. In the Northwest, the efforts to protect the
habitat of the northern spotted owl led to years of controversy and a tense
compromise between environmentalists and timber interests brokered by

President Bill Clinton. Less controversial have been other, sometimes very expensive efforts to save species on the brink of extinction, most notably the whooping crane, the California condor, and the red-cockaded wood-pecker, whose fate is tied to the survival of the majestic southern longleaf pine. This tree reproduces only after fires, and thus has virtually disap-peared except in a few protected areas, some on military bases.

The United States, because of size and diversity of geography and climate, has the most diverse flora and fauna of any largely temperate zone nation. It contains around 250,000 identified species (out of about 1.75 million worldwide), though its share pales in comparison to the plentitude of life in tropical climates. Because of Hawaii and Alaska, the United States has species representing twelve of the generally recognized fourteen biomes, or more than any other country. Two of these reflect the large area of tundra in Alaska and a small area of tropical rain forest in Hawaii (because of its recent origin and isolation, this forest has a wealth of endemic species but not nearly the diversity of life present in continental rain forests). The U.S. diversity is measured by its proportion of world species: 9 percent of mammals (416), 10 percent of freshwater fish (799), 29 percent of freshwater mussels (292), 61 percent of cray-fish (322), and 17 percent of freshwater snails (661). It leads the world in the last three. It is not as rich in birds (8 percent) and amphibians (5 percent), except for salamanders, in which it leads the world with 40 percent (140). It has only 7 percent of flowering plants, but next to China the most conifers, and among them the tallest (Redwood), largest (Sequoia), and oldest (Bristlecone Pine). Hawaii is a unique ecoregion. Most of its plants and insects are endemic (it has over 1,000 species of fruit fly), and it once had over 8,800 endemics in all (more than the rest of the states combined, but many are now extinct). The United States has about 100 endemic mammals, largely rodents, and 65 of its roughly 768 birds are also endemic. (These numbers would be higher if it were not for the large overlap with Canada or Mexico.) The United States has over 4,000 endemic plants. It leads the world in endemic crayfish, snails, mus-sels, salamanders, and many species in different families that live in our large number of caves.[14]

How many species, at least those above microorganisms and round-worms, have become extinct in the United States since European settle-ment? No one can know for sure, particularly at the level of plants and insects. Only one mammal seems to have vanished, the monk seal. At least twenty-five birds are extinct or probably extinct, but nineteen of those lived in Hawaii. Four in the rest of the United States are clearly extinct (Carolina parakeet, passenger pigeon, great auk, and Labrador duck). Only two amphibians and seventeen freshwater fish are extinct or probably extinct. Thus, the loss at the most visible level, and at the level of the most popular awareness and concern, is surprisingly low. The estimates for other species are less firm, particularly for insects (around 166) and flowering plants (137). Some of these species, many long considered lost, turn up almost every year, and undoubtedly plenty of unknown extinctions are not listed. More certain are the critical losses in the one area of American exceptionalism—132 snails and 37 mussels. In all, 249 of an estimated 978 extinct species are from Hawaii. For some insects that pose threats to health, humans have tried for decades to gain extinctions (ticks, cockroaches, mosquitos), and likewise for those that threaten crops or trees. Note that these listed extinctions involve native species, not invasive species, few of which have become extinct in America despite often costly efforts to destroy them.

How many species in America are threatened with extinction? This question begs a complex answer. For mammals, birds, and possibly reptiles and amphibians, one can give a reasonably informed answer. Not so for insects and some plants. Beyond the FWS lists of endangered and threatened species are its candidate species, many of which it will eventually add to the endangered and threatened lists. Note that these lists derive not from any broad survey of species, but by nomination of concerned people. It is not fully inclusive, particularly below mammals and birds, and probably is not at all comprehensive for insects, ferns, and lichens. No full inventory of species exists for the United States, and only the first effort at intensive local surveys are under way, the most ambitious being in the Great Smoky Mountains National Park.

The only comprehensive effort to list all imperiled species was the one conducted by the Nature Conservancy and published in *Precious Heritage* in 2000. But its categories do not match those of the FWS. Its first two categories, critically imperiled and imperiled, come close to the FWS's endangered and threatened, but are not exact fits. The Nature Conservancy defines critically imperiled as species with a population of under 1,000 and those clearly threatened in the present. Imperiled includes those with a population of from 1,000 to 3,000, plus other criteria. These two categories include 2,758 species (917 animals and 1,841 plants), or more than double the 1,311 on the combined FWS list. If one included candidate and nominated species for the FWS, then the lists would be closer in size, but far from identical in content. In some cases, the Nature Conservancy gives a less critical status to species than does FWS. Beyond imperiled species, the Nature Conservancy lists a third category, which it calls vulnerable, and here lists species that generally have a population from 3,000 to 10,000. It uses the term "at risk" for all three categories. Also, unlike the FWS, it tries to determine how many ecocommunities or associations are at risk. Its survey is more inclusive, its categories at least as well-justified as the federal ones, and the final result possibly more useful, but the amount of scientific documentation is considerably less. Like the FWS, it breaks down its lists to the state level.[15]

Biodiversity, as a goal, is broader than simply preventing extinction. Effective biodiversity means not just the isolated presence, somewhere, of any single species, but a complex mix and balance among species in any one environment. If in the past the number of mammals in a given ecosystem had been thirty, and it is now only fifteen, then one has a measure of what has been lost, even if none of the now absent mammals are endangered. One cause of such a loss could be the shift from mixed woodlands to the monoculture of tree plantations. And note that such a shift, which might displace half the mammals, has effectively displaced almost all species of trees. Imbalances are also created by displacements caused by the exploding population of one species, possibly from the destruction of key predators or human-induced shifts in food supplies. One thinks of the explosion of raccoon and opossum numbers in suburban neighborhoods, based on plentiful garbage and an absence of predators, including any hunting by humans. Or the surge of bison in Yellowstone Park, only now being challenged by a new gray wolf population. Or the often dangerous explosion of alligators in the Gulf states because of the cessation of human predation based on an endangered status. But, by far, the most critical ecological threat posed by a radical imbalance in the United States is the artificially large population of white-tailed deer. In some areas, their winter browsing prevents the reproduction of any trees, thus endangering future forests. Ironically, the past danger of overhunting has been replaced by effective lobbying by hunters to so limit the annual kills as to maintain a large population of deer, since humans now are the only effective predators of deer.

Today, unlike a hundred years ago, hunting, fishing, and trapping in the United States are not major contributors to extinction, but, as suggested above, the interests of hunters and anglers may have a lot to do with imbalances in an ecosystem. The greatest threat to biodiversity is habitat loss, mostly caused by human action. As it has always been, the one largest cause of such loss is agriculture, both farming and grazing. Just below this is human development projects, such as new housing developments, military bases, major water projects, beginning with dams, and road construction. Water pollution and siltation are major causes of lost habitats for aquatic species. Outdoor recreation, logging, mining, oil exploration and drilling, and bad fire management in forests are other causes.

Displacement by imported alien species is second only to habitat loss, and a rapidly growing threat to biodiversity. In the future it may be the largest problem. Such a recent invader as the Asian longhorned beetle makes this clear, for if not checked it may threaten all our forests. The Great Lakes have been doubly endangered, first by the alewife, and now by the prolific zebra mussel. Florida lakes and streams have suffered terribly from the imported water hyacinth, Texas waters from hydrilla, while the South American nutria, larger and more prolific than the native muskrat, is playing havoc with the bayous of Louisiana. America has already all but lost two of its most important trees to aliens, the chestnut and the American elm, and several other species are now at risk. In the eastern United States, everyone is familiar with the ravages of the Japanese beetle and the gypsy moth. The list could go on, for the United States already suffers from over five thousand aliens, including many of our most imperialistic weeds and vines, with kudzu leading the list.

The geography of American biodiversity is, in most respects, favorable to efforts to mitigate extinction. Alaska and formerly glaciated northern states have few endangered species. In fact, in much of the upper Midwest, the only endangered species in many counties has been the bald eagle, and it is now recovering almost everywhere. The reason so few endangered species are there is that the diversity of species is much lower, in part because in glaciated areas not so many species have reoccupied the area in only ten thousand years. The areas of greatest species diversity, and the most endangered species, are regionally concentrated, which can help focus conservation efforts. The Nature Conservancy estimates that only 6 percent of the land area of the country includes all imperiled species, and that effective conservation efforts in only 10 percent of the land area could prevent most likely extinctions. The United States, as made clear by a flyover, still has a large share of forests (on almost 40 percent of the land) and of open countryside. It has lost up to half of its wetlands, but present regulations should prevent much further loss. The land devoted to agriculture is steadily declining, while urban-type development still involves no more than 1 percent of land. Suburban development can endanger species, but if well-planned it can often shelter more species than open farmland. In fact, some suburban areas, after a few years, are mostly forested.

The Nature Conservancy has used its surveys to identify what it calls hot spots, or six areas with the greatest diversity of species and those in greatest danger. One hot spot is the southern Appalachians, particularly a region in Southwest Virginia and Northeast Tennessee that is home to so many threatened freshwater snails, fish, and mussels. A second is the Florida panhandle and parts of southern Alabama, again an area rich in aquatic species. A third is the Death Valley area, and much of the Great Basin around it. A fourth is the coastal area of southern California. A fifth is the San Francisco Bay area. The last is Hawaii, a unique challenge in itself.

What are the tools for protecting endangered species and for supporting biodiversity more generally? Once again, the United States is fortunate. The most powerful tool for controlling land use is ownership. The federal government owns over 25 percent of all land, and state and local governments at least 5 percent more. The federal land is heavily concentrated in the West, with 80 percent federal ownership in Nevada. Almost one-fourth of endangered or imperiled species are exclusively, or largely, on federal lands. Three-fifths are present on federal lands. The largest number are on military reservations (widely distributed) and in national forests, not in wildlife refuges (most of these predated the ESA, and protected only select species, including a large number of ducks and geese). Except for the FWS, few federal agencies acquired land in order to protect biodiversity, not even the national parks. Such protection was incidental in many cases, but under the ESA all federal agencies, with certain exemptions involving treaties or national security, have to give protection to endangered and threatened species. By this backdoor route, biodiversity is now a mandated goal for the management of all public lands, including state parks and forests.

Such governmental ownership will not be enough to protect some species, and above all will not insure that ecoregions or hot spots receive protection for a range of mutually related species. This will have to involve privately owned lands. Over half of all endangered species live on private lands, and about 10 percent are exclusively or largely on private lands. But private lands are not exempt from governmental regulation tied to biodiversity goals. Ultimately, land is owned by the sovereign entity, which in America means the federal government as a representative of a sovereign people. What private citizens own, legally, is a title to land granted by a government, but such never gives any absolute control over land. In fact, when needed, governments can take private land for public uses (eminent domain), but in this country the constitution requires compensation for private owners. But short of reclaiming land, governments can place limits on what owners can do with their land, and governments have always done so. For over a hundred years, states have controlled hunting and fishing on private lands. For an even longer period, cities have used zoning laws to control use. Today, the constraints on private use number in the dozens. Many of these involve the Clean Air and Clean Water Acts or the National Wetlands Conservation Act of 1989. The ESA is simply one of the most stringent. Landowners have to protect endangered species on their land and desist from new development or uses that threaten such species, and in some cases the FWS can even require owners to make habitat changes to protect a species. But all such controls have involved extensive litigation and claims for loss of land values occasioned by such laws.

Other means of protecting endangered species involve private conservation organizations, such as the Nature Conservancy, which has bought or received by gift over 10 million acres with the primary goal of saving species. Smaller private conservation agencies have bought smaller parcels of land. The Nature Conservancy has also solicited, or bought, conservation easements from private owners, easements that prevent development and certain uses. This is among the least expensive of ways to gain protection for species at risk. Some land developers have adopted habitat conservation plans for subdivisions, and often used this to appeal to environmentally concerned buyers. Most states offer tax incentives, particularly to farmers and forest owners, to sign a covenant that precludes any development of the land, thus keeping it rural and more open to wildlife. For almost a century, the Department of Agriculture has offered subsidies for conservation practices (terraces, ponds), and since 1985 it has paid farmers to place land in a Conservation Reserve, a contractual agreement that today keeps over 40 million acres of farmland idle and more hospitable to wildlife (the primary purpose is to reduce agricultural surpluses). Beyond all this, private owners often, out of conviction, take action to protect species without any financial incentives.

Legislation and public concern have helped slow extinctions, particularly in developed countries, and will minimize them in the near future. But success in preserving small, sometimes marginal populations of threatened species may be misleading. The next step, already followed for some exotic mammals, is to preserve threatened species in zoos. The most popular of all mammals, the panda, is close to that status already. Reintroduction of captive populations into the wild has proved difficult and very expensive. All such efforts only document the fact that growing human populations, and types of consumption, are often not consistent with the unaided survival of many species. They have no place, no role to play. Humans can, if they want, save many of these species from final extinction. But they cannot easily restore the habitats that enable them to survive without aid and protection. Functionally, a growing number of species are extinct, even though individuals survive. Note that the phrase "wildlife management" is, from a certain perspective, an example of human dominance and even arrogance.

Where humans have massively changed an environment, as in the introduction of intensive agriculture, or even more the building of cities, they have created new ecosystems. The new mix of species that resulted is not unnatural, just different. It makes little sense to try to reconstruct ecosystems that existed before human settlement, unless one wants to move humans out and somehow regain the old mix, which in most cases would be impossible. The nearest approximation of older biocommunities would be large, set aside wilderness areas, but even here the human impact would be inescapable, since air pollutants and acid rain could blow in from the outside. To that extent, humans are implicated in all present ecological communities. One could add, for better or for worse. But this evaluative language begs criteria. Better for whom? For humans or for species either threatened or displaced? Most human rearrangements of an environment favor humans, at least in most respects, or in the short run. Yet, in some cases, such rearrangements may pose dire threats to humans in the future. Maybe some of the extinctions now under way around the world will eventually even threaten human survival. If we knew which ones could have such impact, humans would be hard at work trying to save those species. We do not know, and caution may indeed mandate that we try to keep as much bio-diversity as possible. For humane and esthetic reasons, this is imperative, but it is not now clear that human survival is at stake in the case of most threatened species.

PART FOUR

Climate Change

Today the most complex environmental issue facing humans is the threat of rapid climate change. Warming has clearly occurred over much of the earth during the last three decades. Will it continue? What are its causes? How much has human action been a vital, necessary condition for such warming? And what can humans do to slow the warming, or to deal effectively with its consequences? It is not easy to clarify these issues, but I will try to do as much as possible in two chapters. In chapter 7, I will look at the dynamics of climate and survey long-term trends. In particular, I will consider the implications of our present glacial cycles, and the possibilities of very rapid climate change in the near future. In chapter 8, I will try to clarify the range of complex issues that are involved in the present warming of our climate, and the degree to which human emissions of greenhouse gases are necessary conditions of such warming.

Climate Change in a Glacial Epoch

The earth is now subject to cyclical periods of extensive glaciation. We are approaching what, if past patterns prevail, will be the end of a very stable and warm interglacial period. These have rarely lasted over eleven thousand years, and make up only 10 to 15 percent of the time in the last million years that the earth has enjoyed a very warm climate. In fact, based on historical patterns, we should already be in the first stages of a new age of rapid cooling. It is possible that we will in this century see evidence of what could be a rapid change in climate, probably one based on major shifts in ocean currents. It is also possible that the human impact on climate, based largely on the burning of fossil fuels, will delay or prevent any early shift to cooling, but it is equally conceivable that it will hasten that onset. These are among the most fascinating and significant issues affecting our present earth and its prospects for the future.

THE BASICS OF CLIMATE

Essentially, climate involves temperature and precipitation, the average annual distribution pattern of each, and the many conditions (air pressure differences, wind, and ocean currents) that shape and control both. Meteorologists have developed various ways of classifying climates. For precipitation (rain, snow, sleet, hail), the variables range from humid to semiarid to arid, with qualifications for annual distribution (wet and dry seasons rather than a uniform or near uniform annual distribution).

Setting quantities for each of these variables is to some extent arbitrary. Temperature categories range from tropical (or hot), to subtropical, to temperate (or mid-latitude), to cold or polar. One special climate, often called marine west coast, features cool summers and mild winters, as in Britain or the northwestern coast of the United States. When the temperature and precipitation are combined (such as humid tropical), one can plot the major climate zones, or in most classifications from about sixteen to twenty-four zones. Because of Alaska and Hawaii, the United States has representations of most climate zones however they are classified.

The determinants of any local climate are many. First, of course, is the energy reaching the earth from the sun. Uneven heating leads to wind and to varying levels of air pressure. The pressure of air is its weight, or how much gravity leads it to press down on the earth's surface. For every square inch, this is about fifteen pounds at sea level. Its weight is progressively less as one moves above sea level. Barometers measure the weight of the air, usually with adjustments to reflect what the pressure would be at sea level. By convention, based on the earliest and still easiest mode of measuring pressure, levels of pressure are calibrated according to how much the air will raise a column of mercury in a vacuum tube. At sea level, this is just under 30 inches (or 1013 millibars).

It is rare that air pressure, at any one point, exactly matches the sea level average. Heated surfaces warm the nearby air either by conduction or by longwave radiation. This heated air is lighter, rises, expands, and cools, both as a physical effect of the expansion and because of the lower pressure that exists at higher altitudes. In areas of warmer and rising air, the pressure is lowest. The air around such low pressure moves in toward the low, creating wind. The sharper the pressure difference or gradients, the faster the wind. Because of the effect of the earth's speed of rotation (fastest at the equator, diminishing toward the poles) on observations of relative motion (the so called Coriolis force), in the Northern Hemisphere the winds moving into and upward in a low, from the perspective of the earth's surface, deflect to the right, and thus create the counter clockwise winds of a cyclone (one moving with the wind would be following a natural geodesic, would feel no centrifugal effects, but would see the earth swirling below her). Areas of cooler and heavier air make up a high-pressure system. This cooler air moves downward from a high and, again deflecting to the right in the Northern Hemisphere, moves clockwise. These wind directions reverse in the Southern Hemisphere.

One could predict that temperatures would cool as one moves from the equator to the poles. But so many other factors intervene that no generalized temperature gradient ever fits any part of the earth, not even over the oceans. As a general rule, land temperatures vary less during the year near oceans than farther inland, with the greatest variance in the center of large landmasses (such as Siberia or central Canada). This is simply because land heats and cools much faster than water. But because of the effect of ocean currents, ocean temperatures do not always reflect latitude, and thus can warm coastal areas (as in western Europe because of the Gulf Stream) or cool them (as in the case of the Labrador current that flows down the eastern coast of Canada or the Humboldt that flows up the western coast of South America). In stable air, altitude has a direct effect on temperature. With each thousand feet up, the temperature drops $2\,°C$ ($3.6\,°F$). But even this rule allows exceptions, such as air inversions (a layer of warm air above cooler surface air) in valleys or basins or under stagnant high-pressure systems.

Dry air, as it rises in the atmosphere, cools most rapidly ($3\,°C$ or $5.5\,°F$) for each thousand feet. This is known as the adiabatic lapse rate. What heats air is molecular activity. The more pressure, the greater this activity, and thus the hotter the air. As air becomes lighter, it expands, with a loss of heat. Thus, an upward-moving column of air, unlike the stable air already in place, undergoes expansion, and thereby cools faster. But if the rising air is humid, with altitude the temperature will soon reach the dew point (the point at which the humidity reaches 100 percent). At this point condensation begins, with water vapor turning into water droplets, in fog or clouds (they may or may not reach the ground as precipitation). Condensation warms the air (evaporation cools it), in the same sense as the formation of ice warms the surrounding water. This means that the loss of heat in rising, humid air may be as low as $1.2\,°C$ for each thousand feet. Warm, humid air that moves up and over mountain ranges loses most of its moisture in condensation and precipitation, even as it cools slowly, but on the way down the other side of the mountain it warms at the full adiabatic rate. Thus, after crossing the Sierra Nevada, air from over the Pacific can be as much $16\,°C$ warmer than when it moved in from the Pacific (this dry hot transmontane air is called a Chinook in the United States).

Water vapor mainly results from the cooling evaporation of water, mostly over the oceans (presently 97 percent of all the earth's water). Other sources of water vapor, such as the transpiration of trees, have a limited impact on humidity levels. The movement of humid air from the oceans over land accounts for most terrestrial precipitation. If the terrain is level or near level, like the Mississippi valley in the United States, warm, moist air is free to move far inland, if winds are available to so move it. This means a large area with a wet climate, if prevailing winds carry the moisture inland all during the year and enough cyclonic activity (low pressure with rising air) is present to insure precipitation. It means a wet and dry climate if the incoming winds are seasonal. If mountain ranges impede the movement of warm, moist air, the rising air mass loses most of its moisture on the way up, creating lush growth on the windward side but a rain shadow on the other side. This is true for the arid great basin in the western United States and for areas of central Asia beyond the Himalayas. However, most deserts result not from the rain shadow, but from a lack of moisture-ladened air. In areas with a seasonal monsoon, the presence of a large continental high during the winter pushes dry and cold winds seaward, with no moisture to support precipitation. This winter high gives way to low-pressure zones during the intense summer heating in continental areas, allowing warm, moist air to flow on land from nearby oceans, creating a monsoon, as in India (many other factors are present in this and most other famous monsoons).

Winds correlate with air pressure gradients, and these in turn reflect variations in temperatures. If the world were only oceans, one could create a very useful model reflecting normal prevailing wind patterns. The land areas mess up such a model, most of all the very turbulent weather patterns of North America. Only two climates are highly predictable—along the equator and over the poles. The heat at the equator, over both land and oceans, creates a permanent area of low pressure. Here the warm air rises and moves out from what amounts to a world-circling low trough. Although the pressure is low, it is usually uniformly so. Thus the center tropics is not an area of violent storms. The cold, ice-covered polar regions each create a near permanent high-pressure area, with air moving down and out from the high. Nowhere else on earth is the air pressure as constant, and the weather as predictable, as in these two zones. But at least over the oceans one can chart other rather stable patterns. The high-level warm air that moves out from the equator reaches a limit at about 30° north and south. Here are likely areas for large high-pressure zones, such as the Bermuda high that so affects summer weather in the United States. These rather narrow bands of high pressure are not as stable as the equatorial lows, nor as uniform. Called the horse latitudes, they are areas of relative calm over the oceans.

Both the equatorial lows and the horse latitudes shift with the seasons, moving north in the Northern Hemisphere's summer, but the shift is never as much as the present 23.5 degrees of inclination. From the horse latitude highs, air moves down and out, some toward the equator. In the Northern Hemisphere, the Coriolis effect diverts this air to the right, creating prevailing winds from the northeast or east. These winds, called trades, had a vital role in the age of sailing ships. European ships, headed for the Americas, could move down to the Canaries, pick up the trades, and sail at good speed to America. The Atlantic trade winds are very reliable, but if sailing ships moved too far north in the Atlantic, under the horse latitude highs, they could be becalmed for weeks and the occupants could die of starvation. One almost continuously calm area is the Sargasso Sea. The trades are also present in the Pacific, but not as reliable as in the Atlantic Ocean.

From the horse latitude highs, other downward-moving air moves north in the Northern Hemisphere, or into the North Atlantic and Pacific and onto the great North American and Eurasian landmasses. The Coriolis shift means that these winds move from the southwest and west, creating the prevailing westerlies of the United States. These westerlies led sailing ships, returning to Europe, to sail north and then east across the North Atlantic. But over land these Northern Hemisphere westerlies are very turbulent and erratic. They are often moved out of their westerly path by moving air masses, cyclones, or major high-pressure areas, plus at times wild aberrations in the jet stream.

In a sense, the mid-latitude or polar front jet, the most powerful of all known upper air winds, is simply a concentrated part of the prevailing westerlies. Surprised pilots of high-altitude propellor-driven airplanes in World War II first noted a jet stream; they sometimes made no progress as they tried to move west, or attained up to 150 miles of extra speed (in relation to the ground) as they flew east. This mid-latitude jet can reach speeds of over 300 mph in winter, when it moves down to around 27,000 feet. In the summer it is higher (36,000 to 40,000 feet) and rarely reaches even 100 mph. This stream of fast-moving air has a powerful impact on the movement of surface low-pressure systems, and thus on the placement and intensity of storms. The charting of the jet stream has become indispensable to weather forecasting. The jet stream can move surface lows across the United States at great speeds. But these upper level winds have an interactive relationship to upper air highs and lows. In a sense, the jet stream wends its way around both powerful high-pressure and low-pressure upper air masses, helping nudge them along even as its own direction is shaped by them.

This generalized model of prevailing winds ignores often quite different upper air wind patterns that complement the surface movements, and it also ignores some smaller wind zones around Arctic areas. Yet, even such a simplified model identifies not only some determinants of climate, but also the sources of major weather systems. Over water, where cooler trade winds meet warm equatorial air, in what is called the intertropical convergence zone, most of the world's hurricanes (called typhoons in East Asia and cyclones in the Indian Ocean) originate. One spawning ground is just off the west coast of Africa, another is off Guatemala and southern Mexico, and a third is in the area east of the Philippines. The United States east of the Rockies, which suffers some of the most turbulent weather in the world, including the largest number of tornados, is a battleground for warm and often moist air from the Gulf or southern Atlantic that collides with cold and dry air moving down from Canada. In the winter, polar air moves south from its cold, continental high in both northern North America and in Siberia. Periodically, this air mass shifts far to the south, creating the northers that cause frigid temperatures in the Midwest and even into the American South.

During the winter months the humid air over the Aleutians spawns an almost continuous series of storms (centers of low pressure) that move in from the Pacific over the west coast of Canada and the United States, bringing snow to the Northwest and the mountains and winter rain into California costal areas. In the spring and summer, as jet stream winds move north but with frequent dips (troughs) and humps (ridges), cold and warm air masses constantly battle in the middle states, leading to intense lows, cold fronts, squall lines, violent thunderstorms, and, when conditions are right, major outbreaks of tornados. An upper air, often stagnant Atlantic high off the East Coast helps pump warm, moist air into the central United States, where it meets cool, dry air, fueling intense storms. In some summers, stagnant upper air high-pressure systems over the south central United States lead to major heat waves, storms around the edges of the high, considerable air inversion, unhealthy haze and smog, and extended droughts beneath them.

The oceans variously affect climate. Circulation patterns in the oceans are almost as important as prevailing winds. Here much is still unknown, particularly about deep ocean currents. But in the Atlantic and Pacific, there are patterns. In both hemispheres, because of wind patterns and topography, a large circular movement of surface water prevails. In the Northern Hemisphere this means a clockwise direction of flow caused by the Coriolis effect. It is most pronounced in the North Atlantic, where the Gulf Stream (the world's most powerful current) flows north along the Florida coast and as far as the waters off Cape Cod, then across the North Atlantic to the British Isles and Scandinavia. In geological terms, the rather recent closing of the Panama isthmus (about 3.5 million years ago) because of plate movements was probably responsible for major climate changes in Europe, as this made possible the Gulf Stream. To complete the North Atlantic circulation, cooler surface water flows down the west coast of Europe and then back across the Atlantic, but not in as focused or as fast a current. Supporting the present path of the Gulf Stream is an earth-spanning, millennium-long exchange of surface water and deep cold water, or what is called the thermohaline circulation, which I will explain below. A similar circulation pattern, but without the same degree of deep water involvement, and with the opposite direction, prevails in the South Atlantic. In the Pacific, two even larger but in most cases less coherent circular patterns prevail, with the most focused and significant flow up the west coast of South America (the cold Humboldt current). No such clear pattern exists in the Indian Ocean.

More localized currents variously feed into these major circulations (the Labrador current that cools eastern Canada, and whose nutrient rich waters help create one of the greatest fishing banks in the world), or spin off from them (the part of the Gulf Stream that moves above Scandinavia and into the Arctic). Such currents mean that, at places, high-latitude regions are warmed and ports are ice free (Norway), while areas at similar or even lower latitudes (Labrador) are very cold. Except in El Niño years, when the Humboldt current moves away from the coast, waters in the eastern mid-Pacific are quite cold, even allowing penguins to survive in the equatorial Galapagos Islands. Because of the Gulf Stream, people flock to the East Coast's 75° water as far north as Massachusetts, while as far south as Santa Barbara the Pacific is too chilly for comfortable bathing because of the cold Alaskan (or Californian) current.[1]

GLACIAL CYCLES

We would be better able to understand our present climate if we knew more about the long-term dynamics of climate change. We now live in the warm or interglacial phase of a major cycle in world climate, a cycle that completes itself approximately every hundred thousand years. During this cycle, the warm interglacial period can be up to 10° to 12°C warmer in the higher northern latitudes and up to 4° to 6°C warmer in the tropics than during the ice age that precedes it. In the past, geologists adopted the label Pleistocene to designate what they believed to be the epoch of glaciers, or a period stretching from about 2 million years to the end of the last glacial period, the Wisconsin, which by convention they dated at ten thousand years ago. The label is doubly misleading—glacial cycles clearly predated the beginning date, while nothing suggests that the "ice ages" ended ten thousand years ago. It is now reasonably clear that the earliest major glacial cycles go back to nearly 2.5 million years ago (still recent in geological time), and that less frequent and milder cycles may go even farther back.

It seems that the glacial cycles have been colder, with deeper but not more extensive ice, since about 730,000 years ago (eight in all). In the United States we now identify the most recent near-similar cycles by state names—Nebraska, Kansas, Illinois, and Wisconsin. For the United States and Canada, the very recent Wisconsin glacier is all important, for it shaped so much of the present physical map of the continent (the great lakes, the fertile prairies of the central and upper great plains, the exposed rock and thin soils of the gouged out Laurentian plateau, most of the thousands of lakes in the northern United States and Canada). It was a humdinger of a glacier, with ice covering 30 percent of the land surface of the earth at its climax. It was also the only glacier to last until the arrival of Homo sapiens in the high-latitude areas of the Northern Hemisphere, and thus the first to be directly experienced by humans.

What no one knows is why the glacial cycles began, or before them a gradual cooling of the earth that goes back about 40 million years. We have several theories, but nothing close to certain knowledge about what triggers each new shift back into an ice age. Since these glacier cycles are so recent, one cannot explain their origin by any major movements of surface plates. The continents were in roughly the present configuration long before 2.5 million years ago. The plates still move (the North American plate moves westward each year, even as the Atlantic grows wider), but the time frame is so much larger than glacial cycles as to preclude direct correlations. It is possible that some relatively recent plate effects (the opening of a wider stretch of ocean between Antarctica and South America, the closing of the Panama isthmus, and the continued upthrust of the Himalayan chain) had enough impact on ocean and wind currents to inaugurate a new climate regime, but the full evidence is lacking.

The isolation of Antarctica, because of plate movements, created ocean currents and wind patterns that ended most mixing of water and air with the warmer areas to the north. This led, about 25 million years ago, to its enduring ice cover. The closure of the Panama isthmus about 3.5 million years ago made possible not only the Gulf Stream and the cyclical currents around the North Atlantic, but also what may be a major determinant of climate worldwide, the location of deep ocean mixing, the thermohaline circulation. The uplift caused by the collision of the Indian subcontinent with Asia created the large Tibetan plateau, exposing huge amounts of igneous and sedimentary rock. This helped create the icebox of northern Asia, and exposed so much silicate rock to chemical weathering as to help reduce atmospheric CO_2, which meant fewer greenhouse gases and cooler temperatures. A vastly increased volcanic activity could also explain the cooling (the aerosols thrown into the stratosphere could so screen the sun as to cool temperatures by several degrees), but we have no evidence of such cyclical volcanic action.

In any case, by about 2.5 million years ago, Northern Hemisphere ice began to accumulate, year after year, and migrate southward. For the next 1.5 million years, it moved and then receded in what seems to have been a symmetrical cycle, over about 41,000 years. Beginning about 1 million years ago, this pattern shifted to very asymmetrical cycles that average about 100,000 years, with most but not all interglacial periods lasting only about 10,000 years. Recent ice cores from Antarctica reveal an interglacial warm period of about 28,000 years just four glacial ages back in time, or around 430,000 years ago. Since the conditions that influenced climate then were very close to those today, one might hope that we are now in only the middle of an untypically long and stable warm period.

During the glacial cycles that the earth is now in, the cooling seems to begin slowly, with somewhat erratic periods of warming and cooling. The climate then moves to a sustained cold period, but not a stable one, for during the last glacier there were twenty-three periods (called interstadials) of abrupt warming, some sufficient to stop or even temporarily reverse the advance of glaciers. This long but undulating glacial period then gives way quite rapidly to a period of dramatic warming, with much of the global warming taking place abruptly, perhaps in one decade. This burst of warming seems to be the most sudden and dramatic episode in the glacial cycle, one that can lead to major extinctions of both plants and animals (the more gradual cooling allows an easier migration of species over many millennia). The Wisconsin glacier climaxed as recently as eighteen thousand years ago, in what may have been the coldest period in the recent history of the earth, when glacial ice moved farther south than in most recent ice ages.

We now know a great deal about the climate during the Wisconsin glacier. This knowledge has required a complete reassessment of older theories about glaciers, and even in a sense loosened the very meaning of a glacial age. Ice cores from Greenland that reach back 110,000 years allow the first rather detailed climate history of the Wisconsin. An isotope of oxygen (^{18}O) has provided a good proxy for the amount of glacial ice at any one time, and also for sea levels. These have allowed a reconstruction of the climate, at least on Greenland and in the Northern Hemisphere, stretching back over a hundred thousand years. What it reveals is a climate pattern that is completely the opposite of the stable climate of the last ten thousand years. It was a climate marked by continual turbulence, with periods of very rapid warming (such as $10°C$ in a decade or two), with some periods of almost equally rapid cooling, but more often extended periods of gradual cooling. It is hard to identify any period of even one millennium with a stable climate (with shifts of no more than $2°C$). This meant a difficult time for both plants and animals, with a continuous migration of each to remain in a habitable climate zone.

Fully reliable climate data, unfortunately, is almost impossible to find for most of earth's history. Theories abound, but most are contested. One very broad generalization survives: the earth, despite warm and cold intervals, has gradually cooled from the beginning of life (or around 3.8 billion years ago), even as the energy from the sun has risen by at least 25 percent. Changes in the atmosphere, most due to the effects of living organisms, have supported the cooling. Beyond this, it is still impossible to determine the shifts in temperature over long periods of time, or to discern any clear dynamic that accounts for major shifts in climate. Some correlations are suggestive, including those involving shifts in the orbit of the earth around the sun and greenhouse gas concentrations, but none fit all cases. Unfortunately, the Greenland ice cores do not provide reliable data on the warm interglacial period that preceded this glacier. Air bubbles in the ice allow rather exact calculations of levels of methane and carbon dioxide and of various aerosols. One problem with what would seem to be causal mechanisms is that they often correlate with warmer or colder periods, but do not clearly precede such. This is most true of carbon dioxide, which was at its lowest ebb at the end of the Wisconsin glacier, but then began to rise with the warmer temperatures, reinforcing the warming but not triggering it.

Some plausible theories about the waning of the Wisconsin glacier may help clarify our present climate. Around 20,000 years ago, the Wisconsin glacier reached its final climax in temperature. A slow, irregular warming began and, despite interludes of cold and warm, never really reversed for the next seven thousand years. By 18,000 before the present (B.P.), the great glacier began a retreat from its last maximum. Gradually, and sporadically, the earth's climate so warmed that glaciers continued a gradual retreat. By 13,000, large interior lakes had formed, blocked on the way to oceans by huge ice dams (one was in the Rocky Mountains, another in the great lakes area), and by then the pace of warming had quickened.

By 12,800 B.P., temperatures were close to present levels. The last half of the glacial cold had vanished quickly. Climatologists often list this as the last of the Wisconsin interstadials, but it was warmer than any before. Then, as with earlier interstadials, cooling resumed, soon with a vengeance—perhaps because of shifts in deep water overturning in the North Atlantic. This Younger Dryas (Dryas is the name of a flower in polar areas of Scandinavia, and it has been adopted as a name for glacial periods) meant temperatures near the glacial low of 18,000 years ago. This lasted for about 1,200 years. In about 11,600 B.P. a sudden warming occurred, with temperatures reaching near modern levels in as little as a decade. Our present interglacial interlude had begun. Whether the Younger Dryas led to similar cooling in the Southern Hemisphere is not as clear, with evidence on both sides, but at present the evidence suggests a warming in the southern oceans during this last dying gasp of the Wisconsin glacier. The problem is explaining such radical temperature shifts in a short period. Could we do so, we might be able to offer plausible hypotheses about what initiates a glacial period, and what ends it so suddenly.

We do have some plausible theories about the reversal of warming around 12,800 B.P. The rapid warming before this, although still unexplained, led to a rapid melting of continental ice, including some from the glaciers on Greenland. One likely explanation of this first warming was a resumption of what is now present, but not so during the coldest interludes of the Wisconsin glacier, a massive turnover of surface and deep waters in the North Atlantic. The surge of melt water, possibly combined with increased rainfall, would have dramatically reduced the salinity of the North Atlantic. Tropical waters are more salty because of higher rates of evaporation, and all ocean waters were more salty than today during the periods of maximum glaciation (the salt does not enter the precipitation that creates glaciers, but remains in the oceans at higher concentrations). In the Atlantic, today's circulation pattern carries this more salty water northward to the areas south of Greenland. There, because the salt makes the water more heavy, it sinks, and in so doing draws north a continuing supply of warmer and more salty surface water, and also propels southward ice-cold Arctic deep ocean water that flows over the sill that separates Greenland from Iceland. This begins a thousand-year circulation pattern that carries the deep cold water to the southern Atlantic, across the Indian Ocean, and into the northern Pacific. Without any one local point of turnover, this deep water in the Pacific slowly warms and rises, creating a warm current that eventually flows back to the North Atlantic. We call this the thermohaline circulation, or the global conveyor belt (see figure 10). This overturning of surface water and mixing with deep cold water occur at only a few places, with the only other extensive mixing around Antarctica. Any major reduction or southward relocation of this North Atlantic mixing has major effects on climate worldwide.

If the increased fresh water in about 12,800 B.P. so lowered the salinity of the North Atlantic as to drastically reduce or even end the thermohaline mixing, this would have meant much colder weather in areas formerly warmed by air that passed over the relatively warm North Atlantic. Note that such a shift in ocean circulation, tied to a critical threshold, could be sudden, even occurring in one year. Such a rapid cooling would, at least so long as it lasted, stop glacial melt in the Northern Hemisphere. It would also plunge temperatures in western Europe back toward glacial averages. But this effect is eventually self-correcting, for with the slowing or reversing of glacial retreat the supply of fresh water is cut off, and in time the normal flow and thermohaline mixing would resume, as it

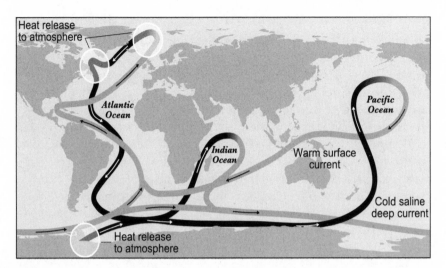

Fig. 10. Great ocean conveyor belt. (IPCC, *Climate Change 2001, Synthesis Report*, 83.)

apparently did in about 11,550. During the Younger Dryas the glaciers stopped retreating, but without the required precipitation they did not advance (the ice cores reveal a very dry period). However, plenty of glacial ice remained, and would continue to flood the oceans for the next three thousand years, though apparently not enough to stop the deep water mixing. Around 8200 B.P., a likely period of very cool weather may have resulted from a slowed, but not halted, thermohaline circulation. After that the melt water decreased. Without a major supply of new glacial melt, the cyclical cooling did not recur. Thus, for the last ten thousand years, and particularly the last eight thousand, the earth has enjoyed an unusual period of climate stability. Yet, even during our relatively stable interglacial period there have been smaller cycles, including a so-called little ice age in western Europe and North America that lasted from the fourteenth to the nineteenth century. These cycles, which have usually reflected a temperature shift of only 1 °C above or below the mean, have had major impacts on rainfall patterns, with prolonged droughts at least contributing to the decline of several past civilizations.[2]

This relative stability may be about over. The warming of the last century, however caused, has contributed to a rapid reduction of Arctic ice. Recent measurements by submarines indicate that over the last thirty years the perennial ice sheet in the Arctic has thinned by about 40 percent. At the same time, recent satellite surveys indicate that the geographical extent of Arctic ice in the summer has shrunk by about 30 percent. If present rates of thinning should continue, the Arctic will be open during summer months in about thirty years. The rapid melting may not continue, for the recent thinning has been affected by a cyclical shift of wind patterns to a warm phase (these relate to major northern Pacific and Atlantic oscillations). But in 2006 all the evidence points to an increased rate of melt with each passing year.

If this present thaw continues, and the Greenland ice cap continues its recently double rate of melting, then the North Atlantic will continue to be flooded with fresh waters, which will contribute to what is already apparent in a small way—lower salinity. As in so many areas of climate, this involves a buildup of factors that can suddenly lead to major climate shifts—in this case a disruption of the warm water flow into the North Atlantic and the worldwide circulation of deep cold water. In other words, the warming and the melting could initiate a period of rapid cooling in the Northern Hemisphere. An open Arctic would, given certain wind patterns, dramatically increase precipitation around much of the Arctic Ocean (the so-called lake effect). And one necessary condition of new glacial development in that area is more snowfall. In the most extreme scenario (unlikely but theoretically possible), the present warming could trigger a new, self-reinforcing era of glaciation. But note that a closing down of the thermohaline circulation today would in all likelihood not soon lead to increased glaciation. The present pattern of warming, the inertia of the now warming ocean waters, and the high level of greenhouse gases would at least postpone, possibly for centuries, the beginning of a new glacial cycle despite a switch to a much colder weather pattern in western Europe.

Why the glacial cycles? It is easy to assume that the aberration needing explanation is the onset of glacial ice. This could be wrong, since the cooler periods are longer than the warm ones. But, in any case, certain conditions must trigger the cooling, or what we date as the beginning of a new cycle. A cessation of the thermohaline circulation in the North Atlantic is now the most persuasive among possible necessary conditions. Others are cyclical changes in the earth's orbit and inclination. Among climatologists, these shifts in orbital patterns had long remained about the only widely accepted theory, to the extent that indirect data series on past climate were often modified to bring them in line with what is called the Milankovich pacemaker.

The name derives from a Yugoslav astronomer, Milutin Milankovich, who developed the theory, and the mathematical calculations to exemplify it, before World War II. He believed that the problem to be explained was glaciation in the Northern Hemisphere. For glaciers to grow and advance, all the annual snowfall could not melt during the short Arctic summer. The possibility of such carryover meant one of two scenarios, or both—more winter precipitation and cooler summers. He believed the main cause was cooler summers caused by orbital shifts, or in brief much less summer cooling and thus melting when certain cycles so meshed as to lower Northern Hemisphere summer temperatures.

Over a period of roughly 95,000 years, the orbit of the earth around the sun shifts from near circular to up to 6 percent away from circular, with a slightly greater eccentricity in every fourth cycle (every 400,000 years). This is not a great amount, and even at its greatest eccentricity the amount of annual solar insolation (or radiated energy) is only slightly decreased, or not enough in itself to have much impact on annual temperatures. The loss of energy when the earth is farthest from the sun (aphelion) is compensated for by the extra energy absorbed by the earth when it is closest to the sun (perihelion). But what Milankovich was interested in was not the annual insolation, but that of the Arctic summer, which was lowest when summer coincided with the aphelion (far away from the sun). The seasons precess (move) about the orbit in a cycle of 105,000 years, meaning that the mid-summer is at its lowest energy level only for a few thousand years in every 105,000-year cycle. It is lowest whenever it is at the aphelion, however eccentric the orbit, but lowest of all when the eccentricity is at its maximum. But even this loss of summer energy can account for a cooling of only a degree or two. Other factors must reinforce this small cooling for a glacial age to begin.

The inclination of the earth (the tilt away from the plane of its orbit) varies through time, from 21.8° to 24.4°. The earth cycles from one extreme to the other every forty-one thousand years. At present the inclination is approximately 23.5°, or closer to the maximum. But the present trend is toward a lower inclination, with the Tropic of Cancer moving south by about twenty-three feet each year. When the inclination is greatest, the sun moves higher in each hemisphere at the summer solstice, meaning that the seasonal differences in temperature are then the greatest. When the inclination is at 21.8°, or the lowest, seasonal differences are less. For the northern summer, the low inclination leads to less warmth, and thus cooler temperatures, and this effect (or obliquity) has a more powerful impact on temperatures than changes in eccentricity. Milankovich combined these two cycles with precession (the axis of the earth wobbles, slowly shifting the location of the seasons) to locate periods when summer insolation was lowest in the Northern Hemisphere, and argued that this low temperature should correlate with the beginning of a new ice age, possibly after a lag of a few years. Note that the Arctic would be coldest when the eccentricity was greatest and summer coincided with the aphelion, and at the same time the obliquity was lowest, a rare event almost duplicated about two hundred thousand years ago.

Most scientists did not take Milankovich seriously until later inquiries revealed a much longer history of glaciation than previously thought, and until it was possible to measure, with a rather high accuracy, the patterns of sea ice during the whole age of glaciers. These measurements are based on an isotope of oxygen (^{18}O), which is a molecule (two atoms) of oxygen with two more neutrons than the sixteen in most oxygen, and which proved to be a marker for past levels of sea ice (^{18}O does not evaporate as rapidly as normal oxygen, and thus in times of glacial advance becomes more concentrated in the now lowered level of ocean water). To a large extent, Milankovich's calculations seemed to correlate better than any other data with glacial cycles, at least until 1 million years ago.

But, tantalizingly, the correlation was rarely exact, at least in some cycles. The best fit was between obliquity cycles up until about a million years ago, with some smaller cycles correlating with precession. These were large enough in their impact on temperatures to suppress most effects from eccentricity. But in the present glacial cycles, or since 1 million years ago, the only close correlation is with the roughly one-hundred-thousand-year eccentricity cycle. It is now too weak in its impact on even summer temperatures in the north (not even 1°C) to account for a temperature drop of up to 10°C in the Arctic during early stages of a new glacier. Even less can eccentricity account for the sudden surge of higher temperatures that mark the termination of a glacier. Thus, at best, the Milankovich pacemaker is a rather weak trigger for a glacial cycle. It has to have several feedbacks or reinforcing conditions to do its heavy work. The best candidate is a cessation of the North Atlantic thermohaline circulation. Another change that could reinforce cooling is a much higher precipitation in the Arctic, which begs another difficult problem of causation. One reinforcing mechanism would be a very rapid drop in greenhouse gases; however, it seems that this does not precede but accompanies glaciation. Another would be a series of super volcanoes, but it is impossible historically to correlate such with eccentricity. Ironically, if global warming has the effect of indefinitely delaying the onset of a new ice age, it could be a blessing to humans in the temperate zones of the Northern Hemisphere. If instead it so changes the thermohaline circulation as to trigger a new period of rapid cooling, it could be a double curse, particularly in the Northern Hemisphere (life would have to adjust to rapid warming and then, in time, to a new glacial age). In past periods of climate instability it has been rapid shifts in climate regimes that have caused the most extinctions. Such a flickering climate could pose the greatest danger to humans in the future.

Once the cooling begins, or the snowfall starts accumulating, it is not hard to find reinforcements. As glaciers grow, their white surfaces reflect more and more of the sun's energy, with little surface warming and little longwave radiation. The process feeds upon itself, and it seems it might continue indefinitely. Thus, the major question is what so quickly halts the glaciers? The best guess, and about the only credible one, is a sudden resumption of the thermohaline mixing in the North Atlantic, possibly linked to a period of increased solar flares (a hotter sun).

The concern today is the effect of human activity on a recent increase in the mean earth temperature. We have not reached the likely climax of such warming. The Wisconsin glacier lowered mean temperatures, worldwide, by about 6 °C, compared to the present (to a mean of 8 °C instead of 14 °C), and lowered the sea level by an astounding 350 feet. The continental shelves were mostly exposed. But in the interglacial period that preceded it, ocean levels rose over seven feet above present levels, and average temperatures were probably as much as 2 °C above present levels, meaning major shrinkage in Greenland ice sheets.

Present maps of the earth reflect, from the perspective of the last million years, an untypical view of oceans and land. For all but the early phases of the Wisconsin glacier (before seventy-five thousand years ago), and for two long interstadials before thirty-five thousand years ago, the land area of the earth was so much larger than at present as to amount to an additional, very large, and almost level continent, or land that, in tropical areas, sustained an enormous amount of plant growth. One can view the extent of such an earth in the attached map (figure 11), or by tracing the 120-meter contours of present ocean depths, which enclose areas then above sea level. The Gulf of Mexico and the Mediterranean were less than half their present size, the Adriatic and Black Sea were missing, and most of the islands of Southeast Asia were conjoined in a large subcontinent. Many today refer to a former land bridge connecting Asia and North America. The image is very misleading, for almost all the present Bering Sea and much of the Arctic Ocean north of the present Bering Strait were above sea level. The so-called bridge was as wide as western Alaska (one thousand miles), and Eurasia and North America one giant land area. Humans and large mammals freely moved through this continental landmass; humans were likely unaware of an ocean that could have been over five hundred miles away in either direction.

A key term in most present discussions of climate is "natural variability." The phrase is a bit loaded. It usually designates changes in climate that reflect no well-understood physical causes, or those that reflect reasonably stable oscillations. This would seem to make human influences on climate unnatural, which is absurd. Actually, almost all living beings have some impact on climate. Our present atmosphere is, to a large extent, the product of living organisms, including almost all of its oxygen content. The human impact is now much larger than that of any other species, but hardly unnatural. The problem, one that can never be definitively resolved, is exactly how much does human activity contribute to changes in the climate. Any approach to answering this question begs information we do not have at present, and may never have. Often, all we can do is record what seem to be significant patterns and correlations. In a sense, the most important pattern in climate now is the glacial cycles, which we can document but not fully explain. It is not likely that human action has, in the past, helped shape glacial patterns, but human action might do so in the future. To specify how simply demands much more understanding of the dynamics of climate change. The second most critical pattern, and one that may relate to glaciation, is the roughly eleven-year cycle of increased solar flares. A short-term oscillation, the El Niño warming of the Pacific (or formally the El Niño Southern Oscillation, or ENSO), is today the best understood of at least a dozen oscillations that climatologists have identified, including major ones in the North Pacific

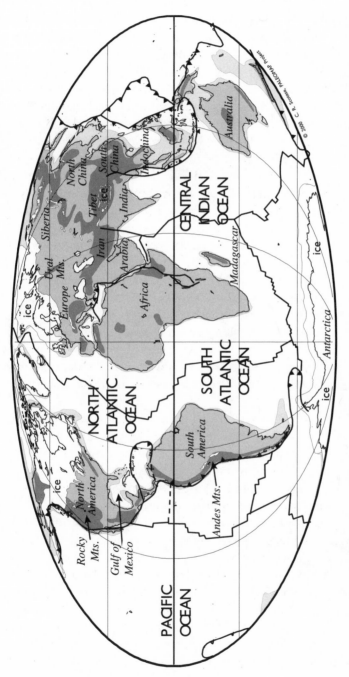

© 2000 C. R. Scotese, PALEOMAP Project

Fig. 11. Last glacial maximum, 18,000 years ago. (C. R. Scotese, © 2006, PALEOMAP Project, all rights reserved.)

and North Atlantic. Some of these patterns seem to be interrelated, but in ways that so far defy an exact explanation.

The North Atlantic Oscillation (NAO) has long been noted by climatologists, and is present in observations that go back centuries. It involves air pressure gradients in the northern Atlantic, with the greatest effects in the winter. This involves high pressure in the Atlantic off Iberia and the Azores, and low pressure off Iceland. These pressure zones are almost always present, particularly in the winter, but at times each pressure zone is weak, at other times very intense. With no exact pattern, but in rough cycles of twenty to thirty years, the northern Atlantic shifts back and forth from weak to intense lows and highs. When intense, or what is known as the positive phase, the sharp difference between the high and low pressures creates high winds and intense storms, which move across the relatively warm North Atlantic toward Britain and northern Europe, bringing mild temperatures but high precipitation. At the same time, southern Europe and the Mediterranean area have lowered rainfall, the eastern United States mild and wet weather, with Greenland and northern Canada colder and drier. In the negative phase, the lows and highs are both weak. The winter storms are then less severe in the Atlantic and oriented more toward southern Europe, meaning more rain in the Mediterranean areas, more cold and dry weather in northern Europe, warmer in Greenland and Canada, and cooler and drier in the eastern United States.

Since 1970, the NAO, with only two or three brief exceptions, has been in the positive phase. This has meant a warmer northern Europe and increased snowfall in Scandinavia, or one of the few areas of the world in which glaciers have been advancing. The winters in the eastern United States have been wet and mild, while southern Europe has been dry, with Alpine glaciers in rapid retreat. It is a testimony to the degree of recent warming in the Northern Hemisphere that the ice on Greenland has continued to decline in spite of this phase of the NAO. A shift to the negative phase is now overdue. This would cool northern Europe and the eastern United States. But the long reign of a positive phase has begged an explanation, and suggested the possibility that it is linked to global warming. The NAO may be linked to a related oscillation in the northern Pacific, but it is not clearly linked to ENSO. Those who doubt human causes for the recent global warming cite these oscillations as evidence for natural variations as the likely explanation, but the NAO is not, in itself, sufficient to explain the extent of overall warming since 1990 (the regional warming and cooling tend to balance each other). And no one can determine for sure if a positive NAO has been an effect, or a cause, of the warming.

It seems that aspects of both climate and weather are inherently random. If so, no physical mechanism may fully account for often abrupt changes. But plenty of mechanisms at least influence climate and weather, and some of these we know very well. In fact, weather forecasting is based on such knowledge. We know the role of greenhouse gases in warming the atmosphere. What is lacking, in almost every area, is sufficient data about the enormously complex subject of climate. In particular, we need much more information about ocean currents. The ideal would be a very complete model of the earth's climate (called a General Circulation Model), a model that would allow fairly exact predictions about the future, given certain inputs. We have many such models, but none are nearly complete enough to allow anything close to exact predictions. For example, we cannot yet measure all the implications of increased CO_2 in the atmosphere, simply because of so many feedback mechanisms, such as increased plant growth. But these issues are best left to the next chapter, on the role of greenhouse gases.[3]

GLOBAL WARMING

Frequent, rapid climate change has been the norm for most of the last million years. A growing awareness of this has revealed how abnormal has been the relative stability over the last eight thousand years. This stability made an important contribution to the rise of human civilizations. That the stability may be over has raised justifiable fears over the last two decades. And, unlike in the past, maybe human activities are intimately involved with the pending changes. The phrase "global warming" has come to symbolize the concern. And, no doubt, many parts of the earth, including all the higher latitudes of the Northern Hemisphere, have warmed over the past two decades at a rate that is unprecedented for the period for which we have instrumental records. It seems likely that we would have to go back to the end of the Younger Dryas to find warming of this magnitude. It seems more likely all the time, as research and model building goes on at an unprecedented pace, that one necessary condition for this recent warming has been the increasing quantity of greenhouse gases in the earth's atmosphere. The increase has been almost entirely a product of human action, most of all in the burning of fossil fuels. I will postpone, to the next chapter, the enormously complicated problem of explaining the recent warming, and of making predictions about the next century. Here I will simply note the extent of warming, and some of its early effects.

It is not easy to collect climate data for the whole earth, particularly over parts of the underdeveloped world and over the oceans. The best global climate data we now have has been collected and analyzed by the Intergovernmental Panel on Climate Change (IPCC). By its 2001 estimate, the earth's climate has warmed over the last century by 0.6°C (or 1°F), with a possible 0.2°C higher or lower than this number. Since 1990, the climate has been warming at the rate of 0.2°C per decade. This may seem small, but it is not, because the warming has varied from area to area. It has pushed the mean earth temperature close to 14.4°C. Some areas in the Southern Hemisphere even cooled during the twentieth century, while the greatest degree of warming has occurred in the higher latitudes of the Northern Hemisphere (up to 5°C in some Arctic areas). Also, the warming has not been uniform, with the first clear increase between 1910 and 1945, and by far the most rapid warming from 1976 to 2005, with 1998 and 2005 being the warmest years since we have had instrumental records (2002 was next warmest, and 2003 just below that), and probably the warmest in the last 100,000 years. The record warming in 2005 is more ominous than that of 1998, an El Niño year (see figure 12).

The recent warming has caused more rapid glacial melt on most (but not all) mountains, a gradual rise in ocean levels in most parts of the world, and an expansion of tropical and subtropical climate zones. The Arctic area has been impacted the most. The warming may have contributed to a near doubling of severe weather events over the last two decades (floods, droughts), although the evidence is not conclusive. Warmer ocean surface waters have very likely increased the intensity of hurricanes. Warming increases the frequency of infectious diseases, particularly those with a tropical source. It may lead to major shifts in ocean currents, including even changes in the thermohaline circulation. Rapid warming will dramatically increase the present high rate of species extinctions. The recent increase in the intensity of periodic mid-Pacific warming (El Niño) may be one effect of global warming, one with a major impact on climate almost worldwide, with some land areas ex-

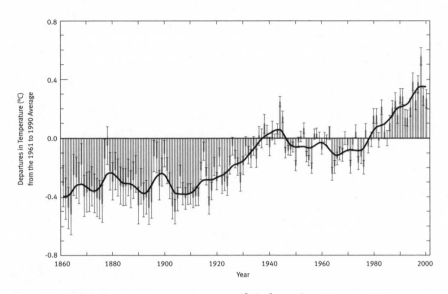

Fig. 12. Global departures in temperature (°C) from the 1961 to 1990 average. (IPCC, *Climate Change 2001, The Scientific Basis*, 26.)

periencing devastating floods, others extended droughts. One estimate of the cost of the unprecedentedly warm El Niño of 1997–1998 was $100 billion worldwide, with up to twenty-one thousand people killed by floods or drought.

The impact of warming varies widely, with the countries eventually most effected being those with extensive areas at or just above existing sea level. Even the rise of up to almost one foot in ocean levels (because of thermal expansion and glacial melt) over the last century has already worsened delta flooding in countries such as Bangladesh. Small, low island countries are most fearful of such warming. Affluent countries will be able to build dikes and levies, and install huge pumps, to protect coastal cities (a majority of the world's largest cities are at or near sea level); developing countries cannot afford such an expense.

Not all effects of warming will be harmful to humans. In part, that will depend on where one lives. In Canada and Russia, for example, agriculture may benefit, with a northward expansion of crop zones and forests. Some arid areas will enjoy increased rainfall. The buildup of CO_2 in the atmosphere, which has accompanied, and probably contributed, to the warming, will increase crop yields. In temperate climates, winter heating bills will drop, with a saving of energy that may exceed the increased costs for summer air conditioning.

In any case, global warming, because of its possible implications, is now not only the most pressing issue in climate research, but the one issue with the greatest potential implications in all areas of environmental studies. It is an issue that has incited deep political divisions and enduring controversy. The next chapter will address most of these issues.[4]

Greenhouse Gases
and Climate Change

Today, it is increasingly clear that human emissions of greenhouse gases have contributed to a recent warming in most areas of the earth. Even more rapid warming is very likely during this century. Unlike the largely successful international response to ozone layer thinning, parallel efforts to reduce emissions of greenhouse gases have largely failed. Almost every factor that has favored ozone agreements has been absent in these efforts. Although it is clear that human actions affect climate, the extent of that impact is very difficult to assess, for some human actions help cool as well as warm the climate. The effects of the present warming, which so far are most concentrated in the higher latitudes, are not fully clear. It may already be too late to arrest many of the long-term climate effects of a buildup of greenhouse gases that has already occurred, leaving only adaptive options. But above all, any effective international agreements to reduce greenhouse emissions will have quite varied impact on different countries, and a major impact on patterns of consumption and how people live in all high-income societies. The earth cannot sustain its present population without the continued use, possibly even an increased use in the near future, of fossil fuels, which will probably continue to supply up to 70 percent of all energy until at least 2025. Perhaps most important of all, the United States, which took the lead in gaining agreements on ozone-depleting gases, has come very close to sabotaging international efforts to reduce greenhouse gases.

Whatever the causes, the recent warming in most areas of the Northern Hemisphere has already led to some irreversible effects. Even if the

189

nations of the world were able to stabilize greenhouse gas emissions at 1990 levels, the amount of greenhouse gases in the atmosphere would still increase until 2100. And the warming trend would, because of the time the well-mixed greenhouse gases remain in the atmosphere and the necessarily slow warming of the oceans (thermal inertia), only gradually decline to zero over the next few centuries.

THE SCIENTIFIC BACKGROUND

Recognition of a major human contribution to warming came only recently. It was in 1896 that a Swedish chemist, Svante Arrhenius, first argued that human emissions were causing warming. By 1910 scientists were able to get some early, if inexact, measurements of atmospheric CO_2. Speculations about the effect of human-caused increases of CO_2 go back to the hot 1930s, but significant warming in the period before 1940 did not continue. A warmer than average 1930s was followed by three decades of sightly lower than average global temperatures. In fact, as late as the 1970s, many meteorologists continued to predict imminent cooling, based on such human causes as industrial pollutants, which reduce the intensity of the sunlight that reaches the earth's surface. Meteorologist Reid Bryson of the University of Wisconsin became a near celebrity for his almost apocalyptic warning about global cooling and the possible beginning of a new ice age.

Beginning in 1956, scientists on Mauna Loa in Hawaii began monitoring the exact level of carbon dioxide in the atmosphere, which demonstrated its annual increased concentration. But would this be enough to cause significant warming? No one was sure, though the concerns increased each year. In the very influential and controversial 1972 Club of Rome (and MIT) econometric study *The Limits to Growth*, the authors cited the buildup of CO_2 and noted a possible climatological effect. But the report emphasized early resource scarcity and deadly levels of pollution, not global warming. However, continuing climate studies, some based on core samples from Greenland ice, suggested a close correlation between atmospheric carbon dioxide and world temperatures.

In 1975, Wallace Broecker published a paper in *Science* that predicted imminent climate change because of greenhouse emissions. He noted the short-lived cooling caused by aerosols, but believed the more extended effect of well-mixed greenhouse gases would dominate over the long haul. In 1981, James Hansen, chief of the Goddard Institute for Space Studies, along with seven colleagues, published an article in *Science* in which they used a sophisticated model and computer simulations to predict that the growing emission of greenhouse gases would soon result in greater climate variability and cause the average global temperature to rise. By then more extensive research efforts were under way. By the late 1980s, widespread concern about ozone depletion led to renewed attention to atmospheric dangers, while a severe drought in the United States in 1988 began to sway public attitudes. Perhaps most important, the global climate began to warm at an unprecedented rate, at least in recent history. Ironically, such a rise may have largely reflected a short-term natural variation and not the effect of increased greenhouse gases, but such warming gave added prestige to early models that seemed to predict just this effect. However, it now seems very likely that the warming in the 1980s and 1990s was a rather sudden effect of the gradual buildup of long-lasting greenhouse gases, enough over time to reverse a stable or even cooling trend in global temperatures.[1]

At present there is a high level of uncertainty about, and no full consensus on, many of the scientific issues that involve our climate system. But on some issues the level of uncertainty is small. This includes the rather firm estimates of the present concentration of carbon dioxide and most other well-mixed greenhouse gases. What is not nearly as clear is the level of climate-affecting aerosols (material particles or droplets) in our atmosphere, including those of human origin; the extent of added vegetative growth caused by higher levels of carbon dioxide; and the exact amount of increased atmospheric carbon absorbed by vegetation and the oceans. That greenhouse gases help warm the atmosphere is clear, but how much is still far from certain. We cannot, at present, estimate exactly how sensitive the climate is to a given quantity of greenhouse gases. One way of estimating climate sensitivity is to try to calculate how much the climate will respond to a doubling of CO_2. Based on a wide range of climate models, the Intergovernmental Panel on Climate Change (IPCC), in its third assessment (*Climate Change* 2001) offered a range of predicted warming of 1.5° to 4.5°C, with its best estimate at 2.8°C.[2] Early indications are that the fourth assessment, due in 2007, will not reduce by much this degree of uncertainty about sensitivity.

Even the term "greenhouse gases" can be misleading. If one counts human-synthesized gases, mainly halocarbons (gases containing carbon plus chlorine, bromine, fluorine, or mixtures of more than one of these three halogens), and the large number of molecularly distinct hydrocarbon trace gases that coexist with methane in natural gas, then over a hundred gases allow the passage of most shortwave solar radiation to the earth's surface and absorb part of the longwave or infrared energy it radiates back. Warmed by this radiation, the greenhouse gases radiate a part of this heat back to the surface, helping further warm surface temperatures. Two of the major greenhouse gases (water vapor and ozone) survive only for a short while in the troposphere. Other gases survive for years and become well mixed in the atmosphere. These gases, led by the big four—carbon dioxide, methane, CFCs, and nitrous oxide—are what most people refer to by the label greenhouse gases. A few of the rare gases, including mainly halocarbons, absorb as much as fifty thousand times as much heat, per molecule, as carbon dioxide, but so far only ozone-depleting CFCs exist in large enough quantities to pose a major threat. All the well-mixed greenhouse gases absorb infrared radiation throughout the middle and upper troposphere, and to a limited extent in the stratosphere (the "glass" is many miles thick). But many particles, like soot, or droplets, such as sulphates, also absorb infrared radiation and radiate heat back to the surface, although most reflect more incoming radiation than they absorb from the surface, and cool more than they warm. But, in any case, these are "greenhouse" aerosols, and they have to be taken into account in any estimate of atmospheric warming.

   Without infrared-absorbing gases and aerosols, the earth would be a frozen planet. Thus, the so-called greenhouse phenomena is a blessing. Without it, humans would not be here (Mars is an example of a planet without such gases). But too much of a heat-absorbing blanket would mean an earth too hot to sustain life, or even to leave any liquid water at its surface (here Venus is the model). Of all the greenhouse gases, the most important by far is water vapor. It largely accounts for the earth's surface temperature, and works as the main thermostat of global temperatures. Since water vapor remains in the atmosphere for only an average of nine days, it cannot become well mixed, and thus its impact varies from region to region. In hot, humid, tropical climates, the water vapor in the air may climb as high as 4 percent, or 40,000 parts per million (in 2006 the second most concentrated greenhouse gas, CO_2, was only 380 parts per million). In humid climates, the other greenhouse gases have a proportionately smaller role in warming the atmosphere than they do in cold, very dry, Arctic-type climates, where water vapor may be less than 1,000 parts per million. This in part explains why the recent warming has been so much greater at high latitudes.

The most important necessary condition for high-latitude warming has been the enormous warming potential of major reductions in snow and ice cover. Ice and snow reflect most of the limited high-latitude so-lar radiation back into space. Melting of snow and ice also increase the water vapor, and this reinforces the warming (the increased snowfall that may result can in part negate this warming). At present, most glaciers are retreating and Arctic ice is both shrinking and thinning. Only in areas of no warming, or of increased snowfall, are glaciers stable or still growing. In the areas around the Arctic, where temperatures in the 1990s were often 5 °C above earlier averages, the permafrost line is moving north-ward, with threats to the stability of buildings and roads as soft soil or bogs replace the foundational ice. Possibly more significant, the thawed permafrost, with its organic content, could release a surge of CO_2 and frozen methane, both of which would join with water vapor to reinforce the warming.

Many people wonder why the IPCC and most other agencies that deal with global warming do not include water vapor in their list of green-house gases. They also do not include among listed aerosols what is, by many times over, the most important—the condensed droplets of water or pellets of ice that make up fog and clouds. The reason for this is simple. Water vapor and clouds are part of the earth's hydrological cycle. They are internal to, and at the core of, our climate system. In small ways, humans can directly increase humidity, but compared to the evaporation of ocean waters, or even the transpiration of plants, this is only a drop in a huge bucket. Thus, climatologists treat water, in all its forms, as a dependent variable. When the well-mixed greenhouse gases increase in the atmo-sphere, the resulting warming raises the level of water vapor and changes the amount and nature of clouds. Thus, in climate studies what one is concerned with is the effect of the other greenhouse gases or aerosols on these most powerful regulators of climate. Water vapor and clouds are thus considered as feedbacks from the warming or cooling caused by new inputs of the other greenhouse gases and aerosols, and particularly those inputs of human origin. The increased water vapor that results from warming and from higher rates of evaporation at least doubles the warming potential of other greenhouse gases. It is in this sense that water vapor is a vital aspect of all attempts to measure the impact of increases in the well-mixed gases.

The atmosphere does not warm in direct proportion to the quantity of any greenhouse gas. This is because of indirect effects and numerous feedbacks. By convention, we now refer to the effect of atmospheric gases and aerosols on climate as "radiative forcing," or just "forcing." If the effect is to raise temperatures, it is a positive forcing. If cooling, then negative. Also, the IPCC and most other agencies emphasize not the total amount of forcing by an agent, but the added annual average amount of forcing in comparison to the pre-industrial level, or 1750, and also those additions caused by human perturbations, such as extra emissions of CO_2. The unit of measurement used is one of energy, or the watts per square meter (Wm^{-2}), which allows a comparison between the effect of added greenhouse gases and changes in solar insolation. Because some of the most numerous aerosols, such as sulfates, reflect and scatter incoming solar radiation, and thus cool the climate, any increase in such aerosols has a negative effect. Thus, most of the aerosols that pollute the air, and that cause smog, have a locally cooling effect on climate. They dim the sun at the surface. According to some recent estimates, the average amount of solar insolation over land areas declined from 5 to 10 percent from 1950 to 1990, with a major cooling impact on climate. Increased greenhouse gases at least balanced this by their role in warming the atmosphere. Since 1990, the amount of air pollution has declined in many industrialized areas because of more stringent clean air regulations. This has lowered the cooling impact of air pollution. Ironically, the more effective are future controls over air pollution, the more rapidly the climate will warm.

Ozone is a unique greenhouse gas. Most heating of the atmosphere comes from infrared radiation, which is captured by greenhouse gases. But several gases in the atmosphere directly absorb, and are heated by, incoming, shortwave radiation. These include limited absorption by CO_2, NO_2, and water vapor, but much more absorption by ozone—that molecular variant of oxygen. Ozone not only screens out ultraviolet radiation harmful to life on earth, but it has a vital role in the heat balance of the atmosphere. Its absorption of a portion of the ultraviolet spectrum warms the air in what we call the stratosphere (the zone in which temperatures increase with higher altitudes) and also in the troposphere, where the quantity is much less. At the same time, ozone absorbs infrared radiation from the earth's surface in both the troposphere and stratosphere. It thus warms in two ways. Without ozone, and its role, the earth would be much cooler. But tropospheric ozone, unlike that in the stratosphere, is locally produced and very short-lived. It is thus largely a local pollution problem. And because of its danger as a pollutant, most governments are already doing what they can to reduce it.

Most ozone, to our great benefit, is in the stratosphere. Even there, it absorbs infrared radiation not already captured by greenhouse gases in the troposphere. The more the greenhouse gases catch, the less ozone can warm in the stratosphere. Thus, one effect of more tropospheric greenhouse gases is a slight cooling of the stratosphere, and particularly the lower stratosphere. Much more important is the cooling that results from any thinning of the ozone layer, for this means a significant drop in the absorption of both solar and infrared radiation. Thus, the recent human impact on ozone thinning has helped balance out the warming from increased greenhouse gases. Some estimate this negative effect as being as high as 20 percent of the otherwise expected warming. The IPCC has chosen a more modest number of around 3 percent (or about $-0.15\,\mathrm{Wm^{-2}}$, or about the same amount of cooling as the positive forcing by nitrous oxide), and much less than the warming caused by the halocarbons that have reduced the ozone layer. One of the complications in creating climate models, both to suggest explanations for measured changes up to the present, and even more often to simulate future climate change, is the uncertainties posed by ozone and aerosols. If one can now confidently predict an early restoration of the ozone layer and a decreased output of polluting aerosols, then these two major dampers on greenhouse forcing will diminish, and warming will increase. But at the same time, a restoration of stratospheric ozone will require a reduction of ozone-depleting halocarbons, particularly CFCs, and this will cool the climate, for all the halocarbons are powerful greenhouse gases. Increased ozone at all levels will increase the amount of HO (hydroxyl radical), which helps remove methane from the atmosphere, and thus helps cool the earth. How these positive and negative forcings balance out is the problem, for almost all these estimates have a high level of uncertainty. It is possible that the lack of significant warming in the period from 1950 to 1970, despite rising greenhouse gases, was a product of air pollution and ozone thinning. The resumption of warming in the 1980s, and the dramatic warming from 1995 to 2005, may have reflected a reduction in air pollution (particularly sulfates), which freed the climate to respond more fully to the buildup of CO_2.

Either a higher concentration of greenhouse gases, or the warming that ensues, leads to various feedback effects. Our climate system is intricate, with all types of interlinkages, some scarcely understood today. In fact, the tie to ozone is one such linkage. But, by far, the most important linkage of greenhouse gases and aerosols is with water vapor and clouds. Increases in temperature raise the rate of evaporation. The present warming has already increased evaporation, and thus the concentration of water vapor in the atmosphere. This is the most obvious feedback from warming, and so far as the warming is an effect of increased human emissions of greenhouse gases, then we have a major positive feedback to what we are doing to the atmosphere, or roughly a doubling of the effect of the greenhouse gases alone. As other gases help raise temperatures, we get more water vapor, or the main warming gas (up to 98 percent of the total greenhouse effect). Thus, the cycle of warming continues so long as human-caused emissions of the well-mixed gases keep rising (or for that matter, so long as they rise because of nonhuman causes).

But wait. Maybe this scenario is much too simple. More evaporation means more condensation, more clouds, and more rainfall, at least when averaged worldwide. All clouds absorb, and reflect, infrared radiation from the surface (some back to the surface, some upward into space), and in this way add to the warming. This is the only effect of clouds in the nighttime. But during the day clouds reflect solar radiation and help cool the planet. Dense, thick, low clouds reflect the most shortwave energy, and because they are low and not much cooler than surface temperatures, they absorb few long waves. Thin, high cirrus clouds transmit most short waves to the surface, and because they are so cold they absorb a high percentage of long waves. They help warm the earth even in the daytime. This may also be true of thicker high clouds, for they absorb more long waves than warmer low clouds. By almost all measurements, the net effect of clouds is to cool the earth. The problem is how global warming will affect the balance. Will it increase their reflectivity more than their infrared absorption, and thus cool? Or just the opposite? No one today can give a confident answer, despite an enormous amount of work on clouds and numerous complex feedbacks tied to them. That said, it is very likely that more clouds will have a cooling effect, but nothing close to the warming caused by increased water vapor.

The same heat that evaporates more ocean water can also increase evaporation over land, and in areas with barely enough rainfall for crops, that can lead to extended droughts, which lower the level of vegetation and thus photosynthesis. This warms. On the other hand, desertification will increase the reflectivity of land, and thus help cool. No one as yet can measure all these competing effects. To address these most obvious feedbacks is to suggest the enormous difficulty in developing predictive climate models, and the reason different models vary so much from one to another. It is presently impossible to gain all the data needed to take into account, with any degree of precision, all the climate feedbacks. And believe it or not, even today we do not have the computer capacity to deal with all the data. The models all involve simplifications and the compounding of several empirical assumptions, many with a wide margin of error.[3]

CARBON CYCLES

Most climate feedbacks involve CO_2 and the complications of the carbon cycle. Of the well-mixed greenhouse gases, carbon dioxide is by far the most important. It accounts for about 80 percent of the forcing by these gases (or 1.5 Wm^{-2}), and over half of all the forcing from well-mixed gases, ozone, and aerosols. This is not because it screens infrared radiation efficiently (it is the least efficient among major greenhouse gases), but because of its high concentration in the atmosphere. Nor is it because the human sources of atmospheric CO_2 are particularly high, for humans are responsible for only about 5 percent of the carbon dioxide that enters the atmosphere each year (they are now directly or indirectly responsible for over half of the methane), but rather because of the complicated role it plays in the biosphere and the various feedbacks tied to it.

Carbon exists in six reservoirs or bins, and moves among them at different time scales. Most of the carbon on earth is sequestered, for long periods, in sedimentary rocks. Almost all the rocks began as detritus that fell to the bottom of oceans, and gradually compacted into solids, such as limestone. Some of this carbon may remain sequestered for millions, even billions of years. Effectively, it is out of circulation. About a half billion tons of carbon joins this repository each year, or only 0.05 percent

of the carbon that is continuously cycling in and among the other repositories. But if that were the end of the story, then eventually all carbon
would end up in solid form, and life on earth would be impossible. Thus,
in one of the wonderful equilibriums that mark the earth, roughly the
same amount of carbon enters the atmosphere or ocean water each year,
through the chemical weathering of rocks or the expulsion by volcanoes
of the carbon buried in the mantle.

The only other large, long-term repository of carbon is the hydrocarbons in peat, coal, petroleum, and natural gas. This carbon reenters
the atmosphere by burning, whether ignited by fermentation, lightning,
volcanism, or human action. Today, the rapid burning of fossil fuels un-
balances the equilibrium that normally exists among the other four repositories of carbon—the atmosphere, biomass (the bodies of all living
organisms), soil, and the oceans. In complicated ways, carbon moves or
flows among all four. It is impossible to measure the exact amount of carbon in these reservoirs, but clearly the oceans contain by far the most, or
about fifty times as much as the atmosphere. Of the other two reservoirs,
the soil contains more carbon than living organisms, but note that much
of the carbon in soil comes from dead vegetation. Humans add CO_2 to the
atmosphere by burning fossil fuels. But all types of burning, in the past
largely biomass (wood, dung), add carbon dioxide to the atmosphere.
The other two main sources are plant and animal respiration and the decomposition of organic material, usually through bacterial action in soil
or water. Vulcanism is a smaller source, but a vital part of the long-term
stability of our atmosphere and thus of climate. Large amounts of carbon
dioxide leave the atmosphere through photosynthesis, but most of this
cycles back again through animal and plant respiration and the bacterial
decomposition of organic matter, which frees carbon dioxide from soil
and oceans. Humans have separated carbon dioxide from the air and used
it in many processes and purposes, down to the carbonation of bever-
ages, but it usually escapes back into the air. The chemical weathering of
silicate rocks removes small but cumulatively vitally important amounts
of CO_2 from the air. The oceans and the air exchange large quantities of
carbon dioxide at their often turbulent interface, but unless an imbalance
develops, the exchange is roughly equal in both directions (over hundreds of years, with the slow mixing of surface and deep ocean waters,
a warming ocean can increase its total concentration of CO_2). The large
influx of carbon dioxide from fossil fuels has created such an imbalance

between ocean surface waters and the atmosphere that the oceans are now absorbing more CO_2 than they give out. It is in this sense that we now emphasize the oceans as a major sink for carbon dioxide. Measuring the dimensions of that sink has proved difficult.

Since carbon dioxide cycles through these four repositories in complicated paths, it makes no sense to talk about how long our carbon dioxide emissions will remain in the atmosphere. Unlike methane and nitrous oxide, where it is simply a matter of how much in and how much out, our emissions of CO_2 simply add to the total cycle, with perturbations all along the cycle. On average, a molecule of CO_2 will leave the atmosphere, either by absorption at the ocean surface, or by photosynthesis, in a decade. But almost all of this will cycle back again to the atmosphere. Only a small percentage will fall to the mixing level in the ocean, where it may remain on average for a century before most returns to surface waters. Even less sinks to the ocean bottom, where some will remain as sedimentary deposits. What is true is that, in about one hundred years, if the annual emissions of CO_2 from all sources remain at the present level, a new equilibrium will develop, which will mean stable but higher levels of carbon in the atmosphere (and also in biomass, soil, and oceans) and, all else being equal, warmer temperatures. But the impact on warming will continue for centuries.

Probably the most important feedback effect of increased levels of CO_2 is a speedup in photosynthesis, which will absorb at least part of the added emissions. This means a growth in total biomass, and thus in the amount of carbon in this repository. Evidence indicates that this is happening now. Almost one-half of the human-caused carbon dioxide emissions each year do not show up in the concentration of carbon dioxide in the atmosphere. Some have referred to this as the missing carbon. What it suggests is that sinks—oceans and more rapid vegetation growth—have increased enough to account for the difference. That more vegetation is a major added sink is evidenced by the recent 15 percent increase in the seasonal variation in CO_2 concentrations in the Northern Hemisphere (lower after a summer of growth, higher by the end of winter). The problem is one of locating the largest sinks, and measuring their increased absorption rate. One likely candidate is northern mid-latitude forests, which have been expanding.

Much research on the influence of extra carbon dioxide on vegetative growth has clarified a few issues, but left many puzzles. In a controlled greenhouse environment, growth rates have risen by 30 to 40 percent in the presence of a doubled concentration of carbon dioxide. In a natural environment, the effect varies according to circumstances—nutrient supply, water availability, temperature, light intensity—and also for different plants. Stressed plants—nutrient and water deficiencies—proportionally improve more than normal plants, but still accrue less mass. The effect of a large surge of carbon dioxide in a vegetative environment reveals an initial surge of extra growth, but this diminishes over a five-year period, and beyond that limited if any extra growth. The effects of increased growth rates soon cycle through the carbon cycle—not only more biomass, but more organic deposits in soil and water, more microbial activity, and a larger return of carbon dioxide to the atmosphere, which slowly reduces the negative forcing of exploding plant growth. Nitrogen supplies enters into the equation at several points, for nitrates, when available, fertilize the added growth. Chains of feedbacks make any final estimate of the long-term impact of enhanced vegetative growth on atmospheric CO_2 difficult. Once again, it seems that the increased plant growth will lead over time to a new equilibrium among the carbon repositories, but in this case a somewhat lower level of carbon in the atmosphere than would have occurred without the vegetation surge. If carbon dioxide emissions continue to rise by more than 2 percent each year, then the effect will be a continuous upward adjustment of the pace of photosynthesis, and thus a negative forcing on the climate. No one can estimate how much. This has become a politically sensitive issue, for the United States wants to claim a large negative forcing due to its land use changes (more new forests or shifts in farming methods). If anything, recent research indicates that earlier estimates of the increased vegetative sink, based largely on controlled experiments, were too high.

In the mid-oceans, increased levels of CO_2 in the water do not seem to have the growth-enhancing effects on vegetative growth observed with land plants. The limit for growth here seems to be iron, not carbon. But ocean vegetation may, nonetheless, have a critical role in warming. In the mid-oceans, far from land, the only likely source of condensation nuclei for clouds is sulfates derived from the dimethyl sulfide emitted by the limited amount of plankton that grows in these nutrient-starved waters. If warmer waters decrease the growth of plankton, then the loss of cloud cover will help warm the atmosphere. If ocean pollution should drastically reduce mid-ocean vegetation, and the dimethyl sulfide emitted by it, then clouds would diminish and world temperatures would rise to what could be a disastrous level. This is one of the extreme climate scenarios that produce bad dreams among oceanographers.

Next to vegetative growth, the other great carbon sink would seem to be the oceans. But, as suggested above, this is an equilibrating response over the short run. We have rather firm evidence of a presently increased ocean sink, simply because of the imbalance created by the infusion of extra carbon dioxide into the atmosphere. So long as atmospheric carbon dioxide increases each year, the imbalance will continue, and thus a considerable amount of the added carbon dioxide will be absorbed by the oceans, with this absorption in turn influenced by the amount of photosynthesis that takes place in ocean vegetation. If fossil fuel consumption continues to rise year by year, the same annual increase in ocean absorption should continue, since a stable new equilibrium is impossible. In any case, the "missing" carbon seems to indicate that the increase in vegetative and ocean sinks has, so far, balanced off almost half of the increased carbon dioxide added by human-induced emissions.[4]

NON-CARBON GREENHOUSE GASES AND AEROSOLS

The other well-mixed greenhouse gases are important, although not at the level of carbon dioxide. By most predictions, they will increase less rapidly than CO_2 in the future. While the level of carbon dioxide was around 380 parts per million in 2006, methane was only 1.8 parts. But such is its greater absorptive capacity (twenty-one times that of CO_2 per molecule) that its total impact is 12 percent that of carbon dioxide, or just over 10 percent of the total forcings of all the well-mixed greenhouse gases. Thus, methane is important in global warming, and becoming more so all the time. While carbon dioxide has risen by just over 35 percent since 1800, methane has more than doubled. And a much greater proportion of methane derives from human activity (in nature most comes from organic decay, leading to the old name of swamp gas). At present, over a third (37 percent) of human-caused methane emissions, by most estimates, comes from landfills. Recently, some municipalities have been able to capture this methane and use it as a fuel, but most simply leaks into the atmosphere. The next two major sources are farm animals and natural gas leakage (some from oil wells). Ruminants, with cows by far the most significant, create methane in their unique digestive processes (19 percent of the U.S. total), and contribute a large share of the manure that creates even more of this gas (9 percent in managed manure disposal). In New Zealand, with its huge population of sheep and cows, methane exceeds CO_2 in its greenhouse effect. Other sources of methane include emissions from coal mines and from rice paddies (a major source in Southeast Asia). It may be possible to reduce these human-induced sources, but not easily. For example, we as of yet have no way of reducing, or capturing, the methane from belching cows (some scientists are actually experimenting with food additives that may lower the methane output of cattle), and in most cases no good substitute for landfills. One desirable quality of methane is its short life in the atmosphere (only nine to fifteen years). Thus, the most rapid means of reducing the present level of greenhouse gases is to curtail methane. For example, in the United States the most potent present reduction effort involves a 1996 law that requires the collecting and using of the methane given off by our largest urban landfills.

The third largest of the greenhouse gases that have been targeted by international agreements (the Kyoto Protocol) is nitrous oxide. It is comparatively rare (only 0.312 parts per million), but because of its screening effectiveness (310 times that of carbon dioxide), it accounts for nearly 3 percent of the impact of all the well-mixed greenhouse gases. The increase of nitrous oxide, unlike methane, has been very gradual (15 percent in the last two centuries), and the human impact slight. Over two-thirds of nitrous oxide derives from the breaking down of nitrates in the soil. This activity is increased by the use of nitrogen fertilizers or the application of manure. Thus, it is largely an agricultural problem, and one not easily remedied (the world needs more fertilizer to feed a growing population). Lesser amounts come from automobile exhausts, ironically produced by the very catalytic converters that reduce other pollutants, and from stationary motors and the production of nylon. Indirectly, more nitrous oxide leads to more tropospheric ozone, and in this way further increases warming.

The Kyoto Protocol involves measurements and targeted reductions of three more sparse but very powerful classes of greenhouse gases, hydrofluorocarbons (HFCs), perfluorocarbons, and sulfur hexafluoride. The first two involve many closely related gases with slight molecular differences. Collectively, these halocarbons do not have the concentration level of even nitrous oxide. However, these gases are distinctive, and in time could be very dangerous, because of their absorptive capacity. Many of the HFC gases capture up to 11,700 times the heat of CO_2, and hexafluoride captures up to 24,000 times. It is only the scarcity of such largely human-synthesized gases (often only one or two parts per trillion) that accounts for their minute greenhouse effect (less than 2 percent). It could be different in the future, since certain forms of HFC have become a major replacement, in refrigeration, of CFCs (true for almost all refrigerants for automobiles). These HFC gases do not deplete the ozone layer, but substantial quantities could contribute significantly to global warming. Their percentage increase, beginning with a very small base, has led all others since 1990 (over 60 percent). The tradeoff, at present, seems to favor their use, but the same precautions used to keep CFCs out of the atmosphere should apply to these gases. The European Union is already trying to reduce these emissions by half by 2020. CFCs are also greenhouse gases, and by far the most important of the halocarbons (they warm more than nitrous oxide). In fact, the only reason that international conventions have not included CFCs as targeted greenhouse gases, despite United States objections, is because of the Montreal and London Protocols that will, in theory, lead to their suppression.

Aerosols add uncertainties to all calculations of warming. Apart from water droplets, sulfates seem to be the most numerous and powerful among the particles and droplets in the atmosphere. Note that many aerosols, including sulfates and nitrates, originate in emitted gases, mostly sulfur dioxide and two oxides of nitrogen, and estimates of each are closely intertwined with efforts to control air pollution. All aerosols absorb some infrared radiation, but most scatter and reflect even more shortwave radiation, thus helping cool the earth. But black particles, such as black carbon, absorb more heat than they reflect. Clearly, the total effect of all aerosols is to lower temperatures, but how much they lower them is not certain. The IPCC estimates that the net cooling effect equals the positive annual forcing for methane (0.48 Wm^{-2}), but other estimates are much lower or higher. Part of the sulfate effect is indirect, or a matter of other feedbacks. These primarily involve the role of sulfates in providing nuclei for condensation and cloud formation. These variously modify the number, density, and size of droplets, and by most estimates increase the negative forcing, but here again estimates vary widely, and only much new and difficult research can reduce the uncertainties. A few scientists have estimated that the indirect effects of the present levels of sulfate aerosols could completely balance off all the warming caused by increased levels of greenhouse gases. But note that, if this is true, then successful efforts to control SO_2 pollution (the major progenitor of sulfates) could dramatically contribute to future warming.[5]

Where does this leave us? No one is quite sure, as reflected in several simulated models of climate changes projected for this century. The best summation of recent research, as analyzed by the IPCC, is reflected in Figure 13. This complicated graph offers the best estimates of how much the added annual quantity of certain gases, aerosols, and solar insolation, above pre-industrial levels, adds to either warming or cooling (radiative forcing). Except for solar insolation, most of the added amounts, as stated in watts per square meter, reflect human activities. The only confident estimates involve the well-mixed greenhouse gases, with reasonably exact

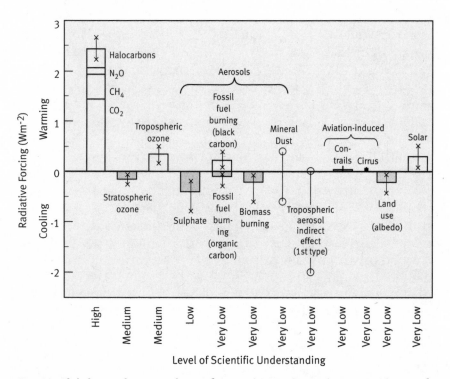

Fig. 13. Global annual mean radiative forcing. (IPCC, *Climate Change 2001, The Scientific Basis*, 8.)

measurements of tropospheric and stratospheric ozone. The estimates for the various aerosols are not at all certain, and for the indirect effect of sulfates not firm enough for any quantifiable estimate. This table does not show the amount of warming due to these forcing agents.

The degree of warming over this century will depend upon patterns of growth and development, population growth or decline, levels of political stability, and mitigating policies. The IPCC, therefore, in its third assessment in 2001, ran computer simulations based on four scenarios, or what it called families. These include various estimates for these variables (see figures 14 and 15). Note that the wide range of estimates do not so much reflect differences among climate models as uncertainties about political, economic, and cultural change. The IPCC ended up with four families (called Special Report on Emission Scenarios envelops), or A1 and A2, and B1 and B2. All too briefly, A1 and B1 assume a convergence between developed and underdeveloped societies, or more globaliza-

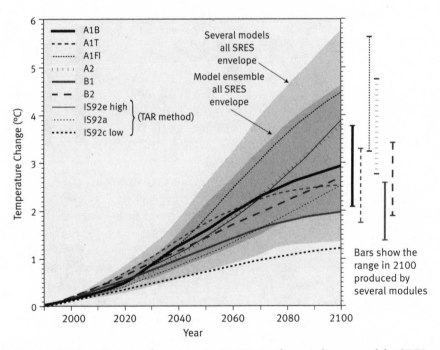

Fig. 14. IPCC predictions of warming by 2100 according to climate models. (IPCC, *Climate Change 2001, The Scientific Basis*, 70.)

tion, but in A1 much less concern for clean and resource-efficient technologies than in B1 (the sustainable scenario). A2 and B2 assume a very heterogeneous world, without political or cultural convergence, but more sustainable economic growth and less population growth in B2 than in B1. Figure 14 includes projections tied to these four models, but with the further complication that SRES A1 is divided into three parts, one to reflect a continued high use of fossil fuels (FI), a low use based on more alternative fuels (T), and a balance between the two (B). Further complicating this projection profile are three estimates from 1992. It is no wonder that such projections have confused as much as informed most lay readers.

All these simulations involve relatively small uncertainties on the forcing contributed by the major well-mixed gases, but high levels of uncertainty in measuring vegetative and ocean sinks, on the effects of warming on clouds, and in estimating shifts in the amount and effect of ozone and aerosols. They also involve different estimates of climate sensitivity, but with most averaged results based on 2.8°C (the estimated amount of warming caused by a doubling of CO_2). Representative simulations for each of the four families lead to an estimated increase of carbon dioxide from the present 380 ppm to a range from 490 to 1,260 ppm. Methane will vary from levels lower than today to around double the present amount. Nitrous oxide may rise as much as 50 percent. Given the sizeable increase of carbon dioxide in all trajectories, the climate will continue to warm even in the most favorable circumstances. How much depends on the mix of variables, while predictive success depends on how well these climate models fit reality. The same SRES series underlie the IPCC predictions of ocean rise between now and 2100, as shown in figure 15.

One of the problems with almost all earlier climate models is that they do not account for what has long seemed an anomaly. Since the beginning collection of satellite observations in the 1970s, the warming of surface temperatures has not seemed to accompany a comparable warming throughout the troposphere. This does not make sense, for tropospheric temperatures should have risen at roughly the same pace as surface temperatures. This seeming anomaly has been exploited by a minority of scientists, and by opportunistic politicians, who continue to deny any appreciable warming of the atmosphere and continuously cite stable or even declining tropospheric temperatures to prove their point. In 2005 several scientists, working with both the data received

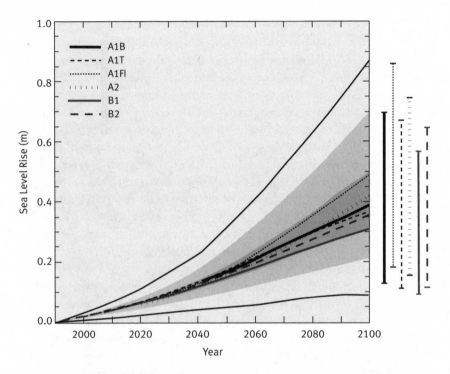

Fig. 15. IPCC predictions of ocean rise by 2100 according to climate models. (IPCC, *Climate Change* 2001, *The Scientific Basis*, 74.)

from weather balloons and from satellites, found what they believe to be errors in the formulas long used to calculate atmospheric temperatures. The data was wrong. When corrected, the troposphere is indeed warming. But given the politically charged debate about global warming, these calculations will not soon appease critics. It is worth noting that a scientific panel appointed by the Bush Administration, which is usually so suspicious of expert opinion, has endorsed these new findings.

This leads to the big questions. How much will it warm in this century, and how high will the oceans rise? The range, from thirty-five IPCC scenarios, is for a warming by 2100 of from 1.4° to 5.8°C (or 2.5° to 10.4°F). The extremes reflect variations in estimates of climate sensitivity, and are reflected only by the light shading in figure 14. Note that even the lowest estimate, which is not a likely outcome, involves more warming than occurred in the twentieth century. Even it assumes a rise in CO_2 from the present 380 to 450 ppm. The sea level is expected to rise from 0.09 to 0.94 meters (3.55 to 37 inches). The temperature rise will be greater over land than over oceans, up to 40 percent above this average in northern regions of North America and Asia, and below this average in tropical areas and in parts of the Southern Hemisphere. The warming will be greater during the night and in the winter. All scenarios include an overall increase in precipitation, but because of regional variances some areas will have less rainfall. Given present trends and the low probability of any rigorous and enforceable international agreement to limit greenhouse gases, the lower predictions are no more likely than the extremely high ones. The median predictions have received more publicity, or around a 3 °C (5.4 °F) rise in temperatures, and a sea level rise around 0.35 meters (14 inches). The greatest loss of ice and snow cover will be in the far north, with realistic prospects of an open Arctic Ocean and major glacial melt on Greenland. In Antarctica the interior ice could increase because of higher levels of snowfall, but ice shelves around the Antarctica peninsula are already declining and will continue to do so.[6] Since they float, their melting will not raise ocean levels, but their decline could allow a more rapid movement seaward of costal glaciers, more calfing along the coast, and thus more ocean rise.

What the IPCC will not predict, at present, are discontinuous, irreversible, and extreme climate events. These include such events as the melting of the West Antarctica ice sheet, a drastic reduction in coral reefs or costal mangroves, or enough ocean warming to kill off most ocean krill (basic to the food chain of almost all ocean mammals). But the one most troubling event, and one not out of the realm of possibility if our climate warms as much as 5 °C, are shifts in, or even the ending of, the thermohaline overturning of ocean water south of Greenland, which could lead to abrupt and major shifts in the earth's climate, including even the initiation of a new ice age (see chapter 7).

THE INTERNATIONAL RESPONSE

The climax of the early concern about warming came in 1988. With strong United States support, the United Nations Environment Programme and the World Meteorological Organization established the Intergovernmental Panel on Climate Change. The IPCC was, and remains, the leading international agency involved with climate change. Its impact has been immense. At least half of the information in this book derives from its reports and studies.

Since 1990, its counterpart in the United States has been the U.S. Global Change Research Program (USGCRP), an interagency panel. The USGCRP does not directly carry out research, but instead provides funds (an annual budget from $1 to 2 billion) for climate-related inquiry by several government agencies or in universities. As of 2002, the USGCRP became one of two climate-focused agencies under a new George W. Bush Administration reorganization. Under the broad rubric of a U.S. Climate Research Program, the USGCRP continues the most basic scientific inquiry, but it shares its funding with a new Climate Change Research Initiative, which fits well the Bush Administration's cautious and often hostile stance toward much of the existing climate research establishment. The Climate Change Research Initiative will carry out comparative, and policy-oriented, studies of climate change and possible strategies to deal with it. Clearly, the new agency is more oriented to business interests and to policies that offer less threats to economic growth. For several years, the USCCRP has directed much of its research to the effects of warming, and how to deal with it in various regions. This seems to reflect an implicit admission that humans may not be willing or able to do much to arrest a continued higher emission of greenhouse gases. We will have to adapt, for we will not be able to mitigate.

The IPCC helped initiate international efforts to deal with global warming. With always too limited funds (contributed by United Nations member nations), it has coordinated scientific evidence on warming, gained a high level of credibility for its cautious publications, and in a major report in 1990 offered its first but very tentative assessment of how human activities influenced or forced warming. In the first of what would, as of 2001, be three assessment reports, it offered various predictions of possible climate changes over the present century. Since the worldwide research effort has expanded in both quantity and quality, the fourth assessment (due in 2007) should decrease several of the uncertainties that still haunt future predictions of warming. The IPCC data helped create widespread concern over warming. Soon the announced goal of most industrialized nations was some international convention or treaty that would lead to a stabilization or reduction in greenhouse gas emissions. Several European countries began unilateral efforts to reduce such emissions. Among affluent nations, the United States was most cautious. Resistance to any binding treaty came from the underdeveloped countries, and at times from the former Soviet bloc. For these countries, some overwhelmed with international debts, poverty, and even hunger, the cost of reducing greenhouse emissions had to take second place to policies that promoted economic development, including an increased use of fossil fuels.

In 1991, informed by the ever cautious work of the IPCC, representatives of various nations began negotiations on a treaty to limit greenhouse emissions. At the United Nations Conference on Environment and Development (usually referred to as the Earth Summit) in Rio de Janeiro in June 1992, delegates from 179 countries completed a Framework Convention on Climate Change, but not without some diluting compromises pushed by the United States. This was only part of the ambitious agenda of this much publicized conference, but possibly the most significant. It also adopted a convention on biodiversity, considered but did not agree on a United States–backed plan to preserve rain forests, and accepted, in principle, an agreement (not a binding treaty) on a broad international agenda for dealing with not only a range of environmental issues, but also human rights and third-world economic development (the industrial countries pledged, but so far have not delivered on, an annual assistance package of $125 billion a year to aid underdeveloped countries).

At Rio, the American delegates were much constrained by the concerns of different affected groups at home. Citing the lack of conclusive scientific evidence that human-caused emissions made up the major source of warming (a standard that will not be met soon if ever), the United States supported the final, possibly almost meaningless treaty that committed nations to the reduction of greenhouse gases and set a voluntary target for industrialized countries to reduce such gases to the 1990 level by 2000. In contrast to almost all other industrialized countries, the United States would not accept any binding targets. It was soon obvious to any realist that the United States could not, or would not, be able to meet the target for 2000. In fact, despite abundant research, numerous published studies, and pious promises, the rate of U.S. greenhouse gas emissions, which had actually declined in the late 1970s as a result of new energy policies and oil scarcities, went up after 1992, at a much higher rate than in the two preceding decades (at first approximately 1.3 percent a year). At least the United States favored lower emissions in principle, and led the world in research into new techniques or strategies that might, in time, allow such a reduction. As for the developing countries, they could not in good faith even commit to the nonbinding targets. In many of these countries, and particularly in China, the subsequent rate of growth in emissions has exceeded that in the United States.

The story did not end at Rio. Those who signed the climate framework continued negotiations in follow-up conferences. Periodically, the signatories of the Rio Framework met in Conferences of the Parties, or COPS. In Berlin, in 1995, the delegates, in spite of the failure so far to meet the Rio targets, decided to up the ante. By then it was clear that a stabilization of emissions at the 1990 level would not do much to retard the rate of warming over the next century. Thus, they accepted a need to reduce emissions as much as possible below 1990 levels. To this end, they proposed binding protocols that would commit industrialized countries to specific targets and deadlines to achieve them. This set the agenda for the Kyoto Conference of 1997. Here the United States dominated the planning, and Vice President Al Gore won laurels for helping shape the final agreements. The Clinton Administration, at least in its public statements, was more environmental friendly than the two prior Republican administrations, and not quite as responsive to the various economic interests that were threatened by any mandated reductions (this included such powerful players as electrical utilities, coal and petroleum producers, and automobile firms, plus labor unions that represented workers in such industries).

Delegates of the U.S. government, after helping to craft a plan that catered to as many American concerns as possible, signed the Kyoto Protocol (a supplement to the Rio treaty, and thus, if ratified by the Senate, as binding as any other law). Not only did the Senate not ratify this treaty, but in an early advisory vote unanimously opposed its submission to the Senate until underdeveloped countries accepted quotas (greenhouse emissions are increasing more rapidly in these countries). The Clinton Administration never submitted it to the Senate, so remote were any chances of approval. In 2001 the new Bush Administration announced that the United States would no longer be a party to the Kyoto Protocol. This seemed to doom it, either to a failure to gain enough national ratifications to go into effect, or to virtual futility if it did win the needed countries (industrialized countries with a total of over 55 percent of worldwide emissions had to ratify before it went into effect). In Bonn, in

2003, Russia offered a tentative promise to ratify the accords (this would have met the 55 percent goal), and in November 2004 it finally ratified (this allowed the protocol to go into effect in February 2005). At Bonn, the member countries further diluted the goals. They dropped proposed sanctions to punish noncomplying countries and increased the amount of land use changes that could count against emission targets. By some estimates, the goals, if met, would only reduce greenhouse emissions in the ratifying countries to 1 percent below the 1990 levels. Without major reductions in emissions by the United States and China, the treaty will not stop the present annual increase in worldwide emissions, but at best will only slow or slightly retard the present rate of growth. Also, ratification did not remove the widespread international belief that the United States had, in effect, sabotaged the climate control agenda.

The Kyoto Protocol has taken on tremendous symbolic meaning. Too often, people have viewed it as the solution to the problem of greenhouse emissions and even global warming. At best, it is a small beginning. Everyone conversant with the magnitude of the problem realized that the Kyoto targets were the first, and easiest, installment on what had to be a continued, ever more expensive reduction in greenhouse emissions and in the consumption of fossil fuels. For example, Britain has projected, as a national goal, the reduction of CO_2 emissions by 60 percent by 2050. It would require at least such a reduction by all industrialized countries, and at least some reductions by China and India, to move close to what the IPCC has projected as the lowest possible levels of CO_2 (490 ppm) and of global temperature increases (1.4°C) by 2100. It is impossible to estimate the costs and the economic dislocations required to attain such goals, particularly in a high-energy, high-consumption, growth-oriented economy such as that of the United States. It is quite possible, as some hardheaded economists point out, that it would be less expensive to cope with warming as it occurs, and allow the free market to make the needed future shifts in energy use as the costs of fossil fuels mount. Such a strategy may make good sense if the lower estimates of climate sensitivity, and of projected warming, prove correct. In fact, this is the likely policy that high-income countries will follow. What it does not do is offer a solution to low-income societies, which do not have the ability to make such accommodations. It also evades the risk of extreme climate shifts if temperatures warm as much as 5°C, and thus violates what many environmentalists refer to as the precautionary principle (when so much is at stake, policies should be based on worst-case scenarios).

Until withdrawal in 2001, the United States, even without an early prospect for Senate approval, did take frustrating steps to meet the terms of the Kyoto Protocol. The early American openness to the Kyoto agreement rested on several concessions to the American delegates. The Protocol committed thirty-nine industrialized countries to specific goals, goals to be met from 2008 to 2012, or what would lead to an average annual reduction in emissions of 5 percent below 1990 levels. For the United States, the key culprit in such emissions (35 percent of the total by these countries), the goal was emissions 7 percent below the 1990 levels, based on six listed greenhouse gases or families of gases. Given the steady growth after 1990, and projected emissions levels running 25 percent higher by 2010, this goal would have required for the United States a reduction to approximately 31 percent below anticipated levels. This was an intimidating target, and little suggests anything close to compliance with such an emissions target was possible even had the Bush Administration remained on board.

The stated emissions goals were a bit deceptive. To make its goal more bearable, the United States insisted on international emission trading (the United States could buy surplus reductions attained by other countries, such as in the rapidly declining economies of the former Soviet bloc countries). The agreement also contained provisions that allowed a country to get credit for the assistance it or private firms gave to help underdeveloped countries reduce emissions (called the Clean Development Mechanism, or CDM), allowed shared reduction programs involving two or more countries (an important priority of the European Union), and provided for a balancing of land use changes, such as tree planting, against emission goals (by some interpretations in the United States, it might have been able to fulfill almost half of its targets by emission trading, foreign aid, and land use changes, thus drastically cutting the needed reductions in emissions). These various qualifying provisions alarmed many countries. Some European nations feared that the United States would largely negotiate or buy its way out of domestic reductions. Only at COPS 6, at the Hague in November 2000, did the parties finally begin to set the exact rules for trading and sharing quotas, but as of 2005 they had not set clear limits on how much of a quota a country may meet by these swapping and pooling provisions. Only at COPS 9, in Milan in

December 2003, did the delegates finally work out final plans for the Clean Development Mechanism, with the first registered aid programs going into effect in 2004.

The Bush Administration repudiated the Kyoto accords for various reasons, including the political constituencies that backed the Republican Party. At first, President Bush challenged the conclusiveness of scientific data that confirmed the human impact on warming. In 2002, after a requested and hurried evaluation by the National Research Council, the same administration conceded the high probability of human-induced warming, but still believed the Kyoto accords unrealistic and too threatening to needed economic growth in the United States. Note that the announced refusal to ratify the Kyoto accords did not cancel the U.S. commitment to the voluntary reductions required by the 1992 Convention on Climate Change. Thus, the United States has continued to submit very detailed, and honest, emission reports each year, and it usually sends more delegates to COPS than any other country (its large delegation to COPS 9 faced almost universal criticism because of Bush Administration policies). At COPS 11 in Montreal in late 2005, American delegates tried to block even any discussion of new revisions to the Convention of 1992, or of new strategies beyond Kyoto. In 2003, the Bush Administration gained promises from most corporations for a voluntary reduction of greenhouse emissions, per unit of gross domestic product, by 18 percent by 2012, but at present growth rates this will not reduce total emissions, and will mean few changes because a shift toward lower carbon fuels had already lowered greenhouse emissions per unit of GDP (1.7 percent each year after 1990).

In 2006 the United States is still committed to finding the technologies that will allow fewer emissions of greenhouse gases in the future, possibly by capturing and sequestering CO_2. The Bush Administration correctly notes that, despite all the promises, few other industrial countries have met the quotas set at Kyoto (see figure 16). At a combined meeting of COPS 11 and of the countries that have approved the Kyoto Protocol in Montreal in December 2005, the first detailed assessment of progress toward the Kyoto goals for 2012 was in most respects a confession of failure. Although total greenhouse emissions by these countries had declined by 5.9 percent below 1990 levels, almost all the reduction reflected the economic collapse in Russia and eastern Europe. In all the other member countries greenhouse emissions had risen by 9.2 percent,

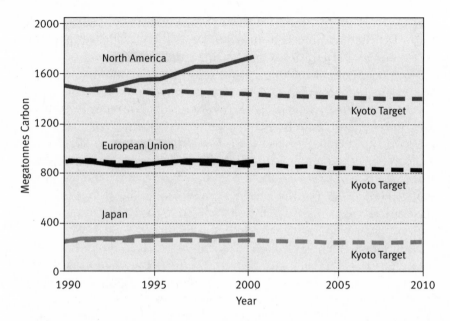

Fig. 16. CO_2 emissions and Kyoto targets: North America, European Union, and Japan. (United Nations, *Global Challenge, Global Opportunity,* 17.)

with small prospect of these countries coming close to the Kyoto targets by 2012. Even the seeming success stories in such countries as the United Kingdom and Sweden too often reflected the easy achievement involved in upgrading antiquated, coal-fired steam plants. Thus, the estimated greenhouse gas emissions for Europe, Japan, and the United States in 2010 will be 17 percent higher than in 1990.

In 2003, two senators, John McCain and Joseph Lieberman, forced a Senate vote on an amendment to an energy bill that would have required the United States to reduce greenhouse emissions to 2000 levels by 2010 and to 1990 levels by 2016 (they eventually dropped the second and much more intimidating target). As they expected, this amendment lost in the Senate (and was not a part of the energy bill finally passed in 2005), but it revealed a growing consensus, even among corporate leaders, that the United States would have to reduce its greenhouse emissions, particularly CO_2.[7]

One emerging technological fix—the capture and storage of CO_2—

may allow the United States to gain a leadership role in reducing green-house emissions. Since in the near future fossil fuels will continue as the main source of electrical generation, any major reduction of CO_2 emissions depends either on much more efficient energy production (such as conversion to natural gas) or some way to keep the CO_2 out of the atmosphere. Three countries have already begun capturing and storing CO_2 underground, in well-capped geological structures. For commercial purposes, most countries already capture some CO_2. The problem is storage. At present, the most feasible of these are the geological formations from which we have extracted oil and natural gas. In some cases, the CO_2 captured from steam plants or, even more cheaply, from natural gas processing can be injected into oil wells to enhance the recovery rate, thus in part paying for the cost of such capture and storage. The capture, transportation (by pipe lines), and storage will add to the price of electricity, but at a cost much less than that for developing renewable energy by wind or solar generation. Other possible storage options are pumping it into deep oceans (which promise a very slow leakage to the surface and back into the atmosphere) or in abandoned mines (which are difficult to protect from leakage).[8]

MITIGATION

What can humans do to avoid the worst-case warming scenarios? In one sense the answer is simple—reduce the emissions of carbon dioxide and other greenhouse gases and increase the vegetative sinks for carbon dioxide. Achieving such goals may be all but impossible. Present global trends all war against any early reduction of CO_2. Global energy consumption is rising at 2 percent annually, and in the all-important developed countries, which use over 50 percent of the total, by 1.6 percent. It is rising most rapidly in Asia and the Pacific, or at 4.6 percent annually, with China the greatest concern. The global average would be much higher if it were not for the productivity declines in the former Soviet bloc, where energy use has declined by 4.6 percent annually since 1990, but may soon begin to increase once again. If present trends in energy use should continue until 2100, the world could use up to a third of the estimated storehouse of available fossil fuels, and all of the conventional sources of oil and natural gas. Thus, mitigation strategies require major shifts in production and consumption, and could involve high costs and diminished consumption in affluent countries, and low growth or even declining incomes in poor countries.

The IPCC, in its 2001 assessment, has a large volume of data on all aspects of mitigation (*Climate Change 2001: Mitigation*), which only documents in elaborate detail the challenges facing the present century if it is to lower greenhouse gases. The IPCC has tried to provide likely costs, in money and in shifts in the gross domestic product, for various mitigation strategies, and has for the first time tried to consider the major equity issues that accompany each strategy. Just reading this long book invites pessimism. One feels that the political obstacles are so immense that the nations of the world will do very little to reduce warming over the next few decades. The wealthy countries will indeed do a great deal to find ways of coping with warming, leaving the poorer countries to bear most of the burden.[9]

One critical issue reveals the magnitude of the challenge. In 1996, the last year with anything close to firm data, the world released around 6 billion metric tons of carbon into the atmosphere, and by most estimates it released at least 6.5 billion in 2003. This is over one ton for each person, per year (see figure 17). If present trends in population growth and carbon use continue, this will rise to 9.8 billion tons in 2020. Of the 6

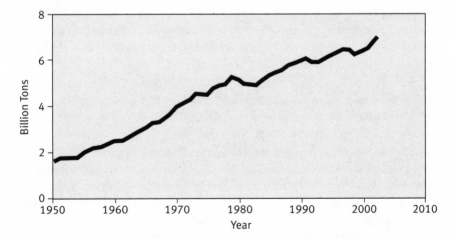

Fig. 17. Carbon emissions from fossil fuel burning, 1950–2003. (Worldwatch, *Vital Signs* 2005, 41.)

billion tons in 1996, the industrialized countries were responsible for 64 percent, or over three tons per capita, six times as much per capita as in developing countries. The United States alone emitted 1.463 billion tons, or almost 25 percent of the world total (and fully 35 percent of the total among industrialized countries). If the world should meet the most optimistic target for CO_2 levels by 2100 (490 ppm), then it would have to reduce annual emissions to 3 billion tons of carbon, or less than half as much as in 1996. Because of population growth, this would mean a reduction by three-fourths on a per capita basis. If, in behalf of equity, the present developing countries were allowed more leeway for increased energy use, and thus were able to cut carbon emissions by only one-half per capita (almost all the added population will be in these countries), then the most affluent countries, like the United States, would have to reduce their carbon use by up to 90 percent. In other words, they would have to decarbonize their energy systems.

Such a worldwide reduction would benefit more than climate. It would diminish air pollution and extend the date when most available fossil fuels will be exhausted, and thus allow more time to find substitutes. But are such reductions possible? If not, the lowest estimate of warming (1.4°C) may not even be a remote possibility. Note that the first reductions will be easiest. In fact, the ancillary benefits of such reductions could make them cost effective. In the United States, the best way of promoting such reductions will involve issues other than climate, which has only recently mobilized intense public concern. Promoting such goals as clean air, improved human health, and less dependence on imported oil may be the better catalyst for action.

Any mitigation will, above all, involve policies in the United States (for a detailed analysis of American energy policies, see chapter 4). As other countries almost gleefully point out, the United States and China are the key culprits in recent increases in greenhouse gases. And despite concern, research, and promises, the United States is presently not reducing, but still increasing, its annual output of CO_2, even as a few western European countries have stabilized or reduced such emissions. For the first time in a decade, the emission of carbon fell in the United States in 2001, due to a sharp decline in industrial activity and a very warm winter, but rose again in the next three years with economic recovery. From 1990 to 2001, carbon emissions rose by 17 percent. The United States, by the most conservative (EPA) estimate, is responsible for at least

20 percent of all greenhouse gas emissions (the President's Council on Sustainable Development sets the American figure at 22 percent). If all the people of the earth released as much carbon per capita into the atmosphere as Americans, the annual total would more than quadruple, and the annual rate of growth in atmospheric carbon dioxide would probably move up from approximately 2 percent a year to over 7 percent (the increase was an unprecedented 3 percent in 2003). This will not happen, cannot happen, for before 2100, during the lifetime of a few who are alive today, the atmospheric concentration of carbon dioxide would approach a level that would seriously endanger human health. This creates a dilemma, for clearly the people in the underdeveloped or developing parts of the world, who burn only one-twentieth as much energy as Americans, aspire to the living standards of the West, and do not easily accept the admonition that they must attain such standards in environmentally safe and more costly ways. Why not emulate the West, follow the same path of least resistance in resource use and growth? (They are already following this path, but are not very far along it.)

As a result of the Rio and Kyoto accords, the United States established a national Climate Change Action Plan (CCAP). This was the implementing tool for the still unratified Kyoto quotas. But it did not receive even half its needed funding. Over and over again the Congress denied adequate funds for this program, deceitfully justifying this lack of support by the claim that it had not yet ratified the Kyoto Protocol. In fact, there was never a large and powerful public demand for lower emissions, while well-organized lobbyists from negatively impacted corporations were very successful in Congress. Officially, before the Bush Administration ended our participation, the United States professed its full intent to meet the quota set for 2010–2012. CCAP thus set targets for emissions that even exceeded the mandated reductions, and worked to get voluntary reductions in emissions (the Bush Administration has continued this effort). By CCAP accounting, such voluntary agreements reduced emissions below what they would have been otherwise. Most major reductions so far have involved cost-effective shifts to more efficient energy use, with the most important dovetailing with mandated changes in air quality. Presently, Bush Administration officials rightly applaud U.S. leadership in developing new technologies, and the country's role in transferring such to underdeveloped countries. As late as 2000, CCAP officials still argued that a spectrum of studies, new tools, and planned incentives (such as tax breaks, tax penalties, and the imposition of quotas) would finally do the trick, and this by 2012. But its mandated reports to the Conference of the Parties were, in effect, a confession of failure. Other factors supporting more energy use simply overwhelmed its work, and it is difficult for an observer to take seriously its projected reductions in the first decade of the new century (2001 to 2011), even if the United States had remained a party to Kyoto.

Other questions loom ahead. Given the failure, so far, of most industrialized countries to move close to the Kyoto quotas, will underdeveloped countries be willing or able to reduce greenhouse emissions? Because of U.S. insistence, the three COPS after Kyoto moved toward targets for underdeveloped countries. But not very far. At COPS 11 in 2005, many discussions involved frustrating efforts to get India and China to accept targets for greenhouse gas reductions. At present, the effort is to help such counties gain the techniques needed for an accurate survey of existing emissions.

Even if the more developed countries, with less than a fourth of the world's population, should meet the Kyoto goals, the total amount of CO_2 might still climb at close to the present rate, or within a decade at an even higher rate. This is because of the aspirations and present growth efforts of such developing countries and regions as India, China, and much of Southeast Asia and Latin America. Such are the immediate problems of air and water pollution in the republics of the former Soviet Union and former Soviet bloc countries in eastern Europe that they cannot at present make greenhouse emissions a high priority, although some pollution control measures will also reduce such emissions (in total, these countries emit almost 15 percent of all carbon). In the last decade, they have drastically reduced such emissions, not so much because of policy but as a result of rapid declines in productivity. Finally, the countries of sub-Saharan Africa are only now making a transition from wood as the main fuel to coal and petroleum, and are much too poor to expend any funds to curtail still limited greenhouse gas emissions. It is a sobering fact that, today, all the countries of sub-Saharan Africa, collectively, emit only one-seventh of the CO_2 emitted by the United States.[10]

Thus, the dilemma. Is there any way for three-fourths of the world's population to escape poverty and move toward living standards comparable to those in the industrialized world without following the same developmental paths already taken by those countries, including the same evolution of energy use from wood to coal to petroleum? Largely because of new technologies and population growth, the use of fossil energy has increased by up to five hundred times since 1800. For the underdeveloped countries to move toward parity with wealthy countries in living standards, unless magical new technologies appear, they will eventually have to consume fossil fuels at the existing level of western Europe, if not of the United States. In approximate terms, they will have to consume fifteen times as much total energy as today. This is impossible. Energy resources will not allow such a high level of global use. If the industrialized countries, with all their wealth, and their leeway for reducing greenhouse emissions, should insist that underdeveloped countries accept the same restrictions on increased use, then it would seem to be in a position of dooming their people to perpetual poverty. No one has an answer to this problem, although as a substitute for an answer everyone talks, in vague and ambiguous platitudes, about possibilities for "sustained development."

China alone may insure the continued rise of greenhouse gases. It plans to double electrical generation, and possibly also the consumption of coal, by 2020. By 2002 its total coal consumption exceeded that in the United States (although not on a per capita basis). China has terrible, and worsening, air and water pollution, of a type that endangers health and contributes to a higher mortality rate. It is concerned about these immediate, pressing problems. The United States may gain a market in China for new environmental technologies. But none of these will halt the rapid growth in fossil fuel consumption, and with it, as an inevitable effect, the rise in CO_2 emissions. India, with a population now at over a billion, will confront many of the same problems as China. Greenhouse gases simply cannot have a high priority in such countries.

At present, it seems increasingly unlikely that even a majority of the affluent, industrialized countries will meet their now diluted Kyoto goals. Although not goals for the United States, the Bush Administration has announced continuing efforts to lower emissions. It is not clear how much Congress, and behind that the larger public, will be willing to pay for measures needed to reduce CO_2 and methane emissions, or to pursue the possibilities of underground storage of carbon dioxide.[11]

One encouraging sign is the recent outpouring of books and articles about global warming, both in the United States and in Europe. In 2006 no topic was hotter, and the level of public awareness never so high. Many writers, and a few movie producers, have bought into the worst-case scenarios, and added an apocalyptic urgency to their jeremiads. Al Gore, so long a lonely prophet crying in the wilderness, is now the author of a well-received book, which has led to a movie of the same name: *An Inconvenient Truth*. Extreme weather events have aided his cause. And, of course, even the worst predictions may come true. Maybe the earth's climate is approaching a tipping point, with rapid and irreversible warming leading to massive extinctions or even the end of modern civilization. After all, all the great civilizations developed only with the climate stability that followed the turbulent shifts during the Wisconsin glacier. Concern, even fear, may stimulate the type of costly shifts that will be required to lower the level of CO_2 in the atmosphere. The problem is that, like so many environmental predictions of the past that turned out to be wrong, these extreme scenarios may be either mistaken or premature. Even if catastrophic shifts do occur during the next five hundred years, the predictions may quickly lose public credibility when very little happens in the near future. Even in a period of warming, cool cycles may recur and last for a decade or more. What is needed is a fuller public understanding of the complexity of the issues, and the willingness to take needed steps that will have major impact, and visible results, only for our grandchildren. If anything is clear, it is that no policy choices in the present will have very much to do with the warming now taking place. Humans will have to cope with it, and possibly make choices that will lead to something close to climate stability in a hundred years.[12]

The buildup of greenhouse gases reflects not just more emissions, but also a lack of equilibrium. The earth is simply not absorbing enough CO_2 to maintain a balance. This involves the sinks described earlier in this chapter—vegetation and the oceans. Clearly, areas with little vegetation absorb little, and those with the most dense vegetation, such as rain forests, absorb the most. The United States has tried to measure, and emphasize, not total emissions, but net emissions, particularly of CO_2. Thus, if the United States emits 1.65 billion metric tons of carbon per capita, and its forests and other vegetation absorb 0.20 billion tons, then its net impact is only 1.45 tons. The difficulty here is firm measurements. The leeway for a larger sink is not large for the United States, but much larger in tropical areas with the replanting of cleared rain forests. The United States hopes to gain credits for reforestation efforts abroad. Trees are the single most concentrated sink for CO_2. This is most true for young, rapidly growing trees, less so for mature forests. In the eastern United States, reforestation of abandoned farmland continued throughout the twentieth century, more than balancing a continued loss of trees in growing urban areas. But an increasing share of these restored forests are approaching maturity, and thus absorbing less, not more, CO_2. Even though urban Americans may feel that they are helping reduce greenhouse emissions by planting a few trees, the effect is so tiny as to be almost inconsequential, or even negative if they drive a gas-guzzling sports utility vehicle to pick up the seedlings. But no one doubts that the massive cutting of rain forests is adding to the greenhouse problem, even though exact calculations of how much is impossible to make. It might seem desirable to clear cut mature forests and then replant. Not so. The carbon dioxide given off by the stumps and roots of the harvested trees would more than compensate for the absorption of young trees.

What does the future hold? No one knows. Any major shift in nonhuman sources of warming could drastically modify present predictions. Certain natural impacts on warming are inherently unpredictable. The energy from the sun is variable, in part because of the eleven-year sunspot cycle. By most estimates, a small contribution to warming in the recent past has been due to greater solar insolation. Another powerful natural variable is volcanic activity. Super volcanoes push sulfates, and dust, into the stratosphere. Unlike tropospheric sulfates, these do not quickly return to the surface, but can remain for up to two or more years. One powerful volcano can lower global temperatures 1 °C or more for at least a year, or more than added emissions have warmed the earth over the last century. The last such super volcano was Pinatubo in 1991. One necessary condition for the surge of global temperatures in the late 1990s was the absence of any super volcanoes.[13]

The wide range of IPCC estimates simply reflects a continuing problem with the whole issue of global warming. Despite a growing body of research, most of the predictions about the next century are very cautious, not primarily because of continuing uncertainties in the scientific area, but because of the difficulty of predicting patterns of population and economic growth, the degree of convergence in living standards between rich and poor countries, and the political will to adopt mitigating policies to reduce greenhouse gases. Only one conclusion is almost beyond doubt. Temperatures will rise. How much is the question. Will the increase of greenhouse gases raise the mean global temperature by 2.5°

or 10.4°F over the next century? Will the oceans rise by 4 or 36 inches? The computer simulations, the climate models, so far yield such diverse possibilities, largely because of the demographic, economic, and political variables built into different models. And the difference has momentous implications. If one takes the higher figures in each case, the earth is facing what could be a major catastrophe. If one is optimistic and believes that human responses and a low climate sensitivity will result in the lower estimates, then it faces what may be a significant but manageable problem, one that human ingenuity can solve without major disruptions. The high estimates almost make it imperative that the nations of the world immediately initiate costly policies to reduce greenhouse emissions. As a component of a precautionary policy, even the risk of such high temperatures should motivate major control efforts by affluent countries. Yet, if the lower estimates are more likely to be correct, then underdeveloped countries, in particular, should continue to devote all their efforts to economic growth and pollution abatement, with small concern for greenhouse emissions. The low estimates would also allow the people of the United States, now enjoying the greatest consumptive cornucopia in human history, to feast a bit longer without too many pangs of guilt.

PART FIVE

Environmental Policies and Philosophies

So far, I have tried to survey the major environmental problems facing humans in this century. In total, and from a worldwide perspective, they are intimidating. But one positive factor is the large number of people concerned about them, the thousands of nongovernmental organizations that have sought polices to deal with the problems, and the degree to which committed environmentalists have already won broad political support and, in many cases, effective governmental responses. Abetting such activism has been a lively debate about the proper philosophical and ethical grounding for environmental policies. In chapter 9, I consider the role played by American environmentalists who have chosen to work for reforms within the present political and economic system. For lack of a better term, I refer to them as reform environmentalists. Some call them "liberal," whatever the content of that loaded label. In the United States, such reformers have been very successful at the level of federal policy, if not always at the level of governmental achievement. Thus, I end this chapter with a survey of the official environmental policy of the federal government.

But some of the most committed and passionate environmentalists have not been happy with mild protest and reform. It has not basically altered a political and economic system which they believe is the source of an environmental crisis that is steadily worsening despite stopgap reforms. They have also engaged in a lively debate over broad, philosophical issues. Some have taken their advocacy so far as deliberate law breaking or violent activism. In chapter 10, I try to introduce readers to some of the debates over environmental philosophy and to some of the most activist groups who have tried to implement radical agendas.

Reform Environmentalists and American Environmental Policy

Most Americans who have become involved with environmental issues have sought reforms through the present political system. Some have devoted most of their effort to single issues, such as wilderness protection, or pollution control, or the protection of biodiversity. They have thus founded and supported nongovernmental organizations committed to such goals. But, in time, such specialized concerns have led to a broader environmental consciousness, or to what one might describe as an American environmental movement. Such reform environmentalists have been very successful even when they have been dissatisfied with the degree of governmental support for environmental improvement. Most federal environmental legislation reflects their influence.

Historical Prelude

Concerns about the environment are, one suspects, as old as human self-consciousness. All humans have a sense of beauty and wonder, and thus have always rejoiced in the more awesome or pleasing aspects of what surrounded them. They all, at times, have known the dangers of the larger world, or that which was usually beyond their control. They suffered floods and droughts, heat and winter cold, earthquakes and rare volcanoes. Even the earliest farmers, like later ones, shed bitter tears over the crops washed from the hillsides, the soil rendered useless by erosion, the denuded woodlands that no longer supplied fuel, the fish and game made scarce by too much hunting or fishing. Always, the environmental problems that most concerned people were those that most directly affected their welfare. This is still true, but today people have a much better understanding of the causes of problems, have information about more distant dangers, have more powerful tools for alleviating threats, respond to the pressure of environmental organizations, and turn more often to legislation to effect changes.

Our awareness of an environment, of that which surrounds us, is usually quite restricted. Essentially, it is what we can see when we look around us, plus what we have seen frequently and can therefore easily resurrect from memory. It is our home, our workplace, our village or town, our region of a county or state or nation. From reading or travel, we may have images of other places, even distant places, but they are not our place, our home. They are the environs of other people, always to some extent alien. Because of highly specialized production and extensive commerce, we may depend for our livelihood on distant places, but we lack intimate images of them. If we move from place to place, we end up with images of many local places, and also end up to some extent with a confused identity.

In the past, the immediate surroundings of people had to provide them the resources to stay alive: food, clothing, and shelter. In human history, the vast majority of people have had to spend almost all their time and energy to make a living. They have had no alternative but to view what is around them in functional terms. This does not mean that they did not, on occasion, enjoy beautiful vistas, but in the stress of life they often overlooked the esthetic blessings of the world around them, or what some refer to as nature (as if humans are not a part of the natural world). They were much more aware of the painful, frustrating aspects of their world, or those aspects that impeded their efforts to gain a livelihood, or those aspects that caused them to suffer from cold or oppressive heat, from birds that destroyed their crops, from weeds that infested their gardens, from poisonous snakes that threatened their lives, from insects that stung. So often, life was a constant struggle to gain enough control over one's environs to stay alive. Thus, what is around us was rarely valued for the pleasure it afforded at the moment, but only as it supported instrumental goals.

Today, a concern for a range of environmental issues that reach far beyond our primary surroundings is a luxury of people who live in high-energy, high-consumptive societies, who have much leisure time, who do not have to worry all the time about basic necessities. In the United States, it was such people who formed late in the nineteenth century the first organizations to alleviate threats to some aspects of the environment. But the concerns stretch back to soon after the first European settlement, when people in coastal cities soon lamented the lack of trees for fuel or the shrinking yield of nearby game. By the eighteenth century, naturalists in both Europe and America were fascinated by American flora and fauna, and also by its often dramatic landscapes. Esthetic concerns joined economic ones. Amateur naturalists, such as David Thoreau, were early preservationists. Landscape painters joined poets in celebrating an untamed nature, or what everyone would later refer to as wilderness. Economist Henry C. Carey anticipated most of the concerns of contemporary bioregionalists, while George Marsh, at the end of the Civil War, wrote as devastating a critique of the human impact on landscapes and climate as any contemporary environmentalist.

Both economic and esthetic concerns lay behind the first organized environmental movements in America. By movement, I refer to a group of people, however diverse, who join together in pursuit of common goals, however limited in scope. Before the Civil War, large and prosperous farmers joined in agricultural clubs, in part to find better ways to care for soil and prevent erosion. Both the wonders of Yellowstone, and its potential for a profitable tourist business, led to our first national park in 1872. By 1880 a growing number of Americans were shocked by the rapid and reckless exploitation of timber, first in the white pine forests of the upper Midwest, then in the pine forests of the Southeast. Some pursued an academic career in forest management, and sought public support for what they observed in Europe and called scientific forestry. Their concerns lay behind the first forest reserves, created in the otherwise undistinguished administration of Benjamin Harrison in 1888. This was the beginning of our national forest system, with the primary purpose being conservation and a rational use of our forests. By 1900, conservation was the "in" word, with Theodore Roosevelt convening the first national Conservation Congress, with forests still the center of attention, followed by minerals and fossil fuels. As already noted in the chapter on biodiversity, Roosevelt also set aside the first wildlife reserve.[1]

The two oldest of present environmental organizations began in the 1890s. They both, at the beginning, had a single purpose, but today they embrace almost all environmental issues. The present National Audubon

Society can claim priority, although not as a continuing organization. The first Audubon Society formed in 1886, grew too rapidly for easy management, and lapsed in 1888. In 1896, a group in Massachusetts, largely women, were outraged at the continued killing of birds to provide plumes for women's hats, and they formed a local Audubon Society to boycott such a frivolous and immoral exploitation of birds. Within three years, it had expanded into fifteen local societies. In 1899 these societies supported a privately published magazine, Bird Lore, which in 1935 became the present Audubon Magazine. In 1900, these still largely New England societies began a continuing tradition, a Christmas bird count. In 1901 the growing number of societies formed a national convention and in 1905 a corporation, the National Audubon Society for the Protection of Wild Birds and Animals. It won its first major legislative victory in 1910, when New York banned the sale of all plumes. In its early years, the Society primarily worked to protect birds, and had an important role in the development of the Fish and Wildlife Service. Since the 1960s, it has broadened the scope of its concerns to encompass almost all environmental issues, and in 2003 it listed over five hundred local chapters.

The most famous American naturalist, John Muir, helped form the Sierra Club in 1892. Muir, a child of Scottish immigrants to Wisconsin, visited California and fell in love with the Sierra Nevada mountains, and particularly the Yosemite area. For years he hiked his beloved mountains, often alone, and committed himself to preserving them from human development and exploitation. He, more than anyone else, gained national park status for Yosemite in 1890. In the folklore of environmentalism, he is often contrasted with conservationists, such as Gifford Pinchot, who supported a rational use of American forests, not their pristine preservation. But the purported conflict is exaggerated. Muir was indeed committed to the preservation of great scenic treasures, not for what they produced in the way of consumer goods, but for their impact upon the human spirit. He knew that Americans would continue to burn wood and build wooden homes. In fact, he relished his own campfires. The rational use of timber was preferable to its wasteful exploitation. The goals of conservation and selective preservation were more complementary than conflicted. But for his beloved Sierras, and for Yosemite, he was bitterly opposed to major human alterations. He fought for years to block the Hetch Hetchy Dam and Reservoir (water for San Francisco) on the

Tuolumne River at the north of Yosemite Park, and died soon after its completion in 1914.

The first Sierra Club was a group of men who became disciples of Muir. Some were wealthy. They formed their new organization both to preserve the Sierras and to enjoy them. The club organized hikes into the mountains, some large enough and so well provisioned as to compare to African safaris. Even to this day Sierra Club chapters are distinguished by their frequent outings. Muir, unlike some later wilderness advocates, wanted people to come and admire his mountains. The early Sierra Club built trails, and even roads, into the most scenic areas. It was long after Muir's death that club members realized that throngs of hikers, or roads full of automobiles, could love his mountains to death. Sierra chapters expanded first in California, then to the Rockies and throughout much of the West. The first on the East Coast came as late as 1950. By World War II, the Sierra Club was becoming an all-purpose environmental advocacy organization, but it still took the lead in wilderness preservation. One of its close collaborators was the Wilderness Society, formed in 1935, with another famous environmentalist and wildlife expert, Aldo Leopold, as one of its founders. Other, primarily single-purpose environmental organizations were the National Parks Conservation Association, formed in 1919, and the General (later the National) Wildlife Association, established in 1936 and at first largely committed to the protection of species important for hunting and fishing.[2]

In the 1920s and 1930s, economic issues dominated American public policy, while after 1939 World War II was all important. Thus, the focal environmental issues related to the depression and war. In the 1930s, the most focal issue was land erosion, from wind and water. This led to enduring and effective conservation legislation (see chapter 3), while some marginal lands purchased by the federal government supported a new system of state forests and parks. In the war, recycling of scarce resources became a necessity, with strong public support. But other concerns, such as air and water pollution, usually yielded to the one overwhelming goal—winning the war.

First Fruits

A new era began shortly after World War II. A range of developments made environmental consciousness an imperative. Gradually, former colonial dependencies gained independence in both Africa and Asia. New medical advances spread to the underdeveloped world, and assured a population boom. This, alone, added unprecedented demands on basic resources. In North America and Europe, and soon also Japan, a dual development added even more demands on resources. From 1950 to 1970, the United States, and to a lesser extent, western Europe, experienced a baby boom. This joined an economic boom, first in North America, but by 1960 also in a reviving Europe. Rising incomes and consumption meant a steadily growing demand for basic resources, particularly energy, a dramatic increase in waste products, and increased pollution. In the United States, from 1950 to 1970, agricultural productivity doubled, and soon a green revolution spread to all parts of the world. Gains in yields depended more and more on chemicals—fertilizers, insecticides, fungicides, and herbicides. Organic chemicals supported the switch from metals to plastics, from cotton and wool to synthetic fibers. From 1950 to 1970, in the United States, the population expanded by 37 percent, incomes by 50 percent, automobiles by 100 percent, and energy use by 100 percent. Motor vehicles, and what is needed to make them, fuel them, and supply them with roads, have placed greater pressures on the environment than any other consumer product.

As early as the 1950s, a growing number of critics began to highlight the environmental costs of exploding populations, particularly in Asia, Africa, and Latin America, and of economic growth, particularly in North America and Europe. These concerns expanded in the 1960s, and led to the first boom in environmental legislation in both Europe and the United States. The awareness of environmental problems, and the response to them, climaxed in the 1970s, or what many now refer to as the environmental decade. With this concern came a new array of environmental organizations (at least a hundred, large and small, in the United States), and expanded agendas and a more radical posture for the older organizations, such as the Sierra Club and the Audubon Society. These nongovernmental societies mobilized the public, lobbied effectively for new legislation, and litigated in courts to insure enforcement of existing environmental laws. In each decade, the focal concerns shifted, with air and water pollution the one constant, but with atomic fallout and threats to biodiversity a dominating concern in the 1960s, energy shortages and a threat of world hunger in the 1970s, ozone layer depletion in the 1980s, and global warming in the 1990s.[3]

Rachael Carson and Silent Spring

In retrospect, most historians date the beginning of the modern environmental movement in the United States to the publication of Rachael Carson's *Silent Spring* in 1962. It was more than a symbolic beginning. The book had enormous impact, not only on public perceptions but on the focus of subsequent scientific research and governmental regulations. It came at an opportune moment. In the very midst of widespread public anxiety over nuclear fallout, and in the year of the Cuban Missile Crisis, Carson suggested that the earth faced an equal threat from the widespread and indiscriminate use of newly synthesized organic pesticides—insecticides, herbicides, and rodenticides. In only three decades, the unleashing of the atom and the chemical revolution had opened a new and ominous era in the human impact on the natural world, or potentially a more destructive impact than from all human innovations since the origin of Homo sapiens.

Carson, an aquatic zoologist, a former employee of the Fish and Wildlife Service, and a gifted author (her book of a decade earlier, *The Sea Around Us*, became a best seller), wrote in the last years of her life, for she would die of cancer in early 1964. Her central thesis, one she presented with verve and passion, was that hundreds of synthetic chemicals, those that did not exist until humans created them in laboratories, posed a silent, insidious, and still largely ignored threat to the survival of many forms of life on earth. In the perspective of what became clear much later—the threat posed by synthetic halogen compounds to the ozone layer—this insight was even more prophetic than she realized. She limited her warning to pesticides, and more specifically to two families of insecticides—chlorinated hydrocarbons (DDT, Aldrin, Chlordane, Endrin, Lindane, Methoxychlor, Dieldrin, Toxaphene) and organophosphates (Parathion and Malathion)—plus herbicides (two trichlorophenoxy acids, 2,4-D and 2,4,5-T). Her warnings about the widespread threat of herbicides to both plants and animals set the stage for the debate, soon after her death, about Agent Orange (one formulation of the above herbicides) when the United States sprayed it wholesale in Vietnam.

What Carson did not do was suggest a complete ban on any of these pesticides, at least not without further scientific studies, so long as companies took proper care in their manufacture and users applied them carefully at a local level. What she emphatically denounced was the widespread aerial application of such toxic chemicals (it was their toxicity that made them effective), or any use that allowed them to spread over large areas or run off into streams. It was such aerial spraying that led to a silent spring, at least in one or two towns, because of the massive killing of birds. It was such leaching of pesticides into the ground and streams that threatened all manner of good as well as bad insects, fish, critical soil organisms, and ecologically essential plants. Her accounts of massive kills of birds and fish were compelling, even without an exact explanation of the mechanisms at work (she did not anticipate the later discovery of how DDT weakened the eggshells of many birds, and thus at times she incorrectly attributed the fall off in reproduction to chemically induced sterility). She correctly emphasized the high concentrations of such chemicals in the fat of animals that were at the end of a food chain, for in successive predations the concentrations increased. She believed that several of these pesticides were carcinogens, and thus a dire threat to humans. But here her evidence was anecdotal, for she did not have the scientific data to be very specific about the nature of this threat, or have any way of determining what threshold quantities pose a human risk. Carson did not want to go back to earlier and chemically simple insecticides, such as arsenic, but instead lamented the almost casual use of the new organic chemicals because of the mistaken belief that they posed no threat to humans and animals. The fact that they worked internally, in the tissues of the body and in altering enzymes and hormones, made them insidious. Thus the need for her wake-up call.

Pesticides kill. This is their role. They are inherently dangerous, as any farmer or most any housewife is well aware. Even use within a house for the spot killing of insects or spiders can pose health threats if one does not take precautions. Carson was not primarily concerned with such limited use, unless the chemicals escaped into the larger environment and thus polluted the air and water used by the larger public. What she was most concerned about was the use of such pesticides in agriculture and forestry, and in the control of carriers of disease pathogens. Here was the widespread spraying, or what she, in typical language, usually referred to as chemical drenching. In each case, she waded into an area that poses all types of perplexities and dilemmas today. Pesticides were a necessary condition for the surge of population after World War II, for they made possible the food production and disease prevention required for over 6 billion people. Without the continued use of pesticides, along with chemical fertilizers, it will be impossible to sustain the present world population, let alone the 9 billion expected by 2050. Pesticides are just one among many ways that humans have altered and controlled the world around them. The risks are very high. Carson perceived this before most people.

Modern agriculture depends on insect and weed control. To a more limited extent, so does modern forest management. In the past, humans used hands or hoe to subdue weeds, and plucked bugs and worms from vegetable crops by hand. This labor-intensive agriculture survives in some underdeveloped countries, but with an enormous cost to living standards. Just as machines replaced hand labor in plowing land and harvesting crops, so chemicals have replaced it in the protected growth of crops. Although organic farmers argue otherwise, I do not believe there is any way back to a chemically free form of agriculture without either a sacrifice of present yields or much higher labor costs.

The new organic insecticides that came into use during World War II seemed a great blessing for farmers, and for foresters who needed to control the usually alien insects that damaged our trees. They were inexpensive and seemed much safer than older arsenic, zinc, and sulfur insecticides. But, as Carson pointed out, they soon posed new problems. Many insects quickly developed an immunity to new insecticides, requiring, at first, higher doses, and then the substitution of new chemicals. And the massive use of insecticides killed off beneficial insects, including former predators of the target insects, or pollinating insects, or at times the very birds that helped keep insects under control. Soon, farmers felt like they were on a treadmill, with no stopping. They still face this problem. And, as Carson made clear, safety was always a problem, not only for the farmers or forest workers who applied the chemicals, but for the people who consumed their products, for those who drank the water polluted by agriculture or forest runoff, or for those who breathed the air near where the spraying occurred. For the United States, at least, which then enjoyed huge agricultural surpluses, Carson believed that farmers could reduce the use of pesticides, could dispense with aerial spraying, and suggested biological substitutes for chemicals (the use of other enemy insects, such as wasps or ladybugs, or of bacterial insecticides, such as BT, or the sterilization of male insects to end reproduction). Some of these were already used, and quite successfully, but so far they have not been the answer to all insect problems. And in such agriculturally stressed economies as Egypt or India, there is no surplus and no leeway for more expensive insect controls.

Herbicides, first developed by the military during World War II, gradually were adopted by farmers and even owners of suburban lots after the war, at first to control broad-leafed weeds. Since then, companies have developed selective herbicides for certain weeds and grasses, as well as herbicides that kill all vegetation. Gradually, most commercial farmers, at least for row crops, began using herbicides as a labor-saving substitute for the cultivation of crops. These seemed safe, and for the most part they were. The earliest herbicide, 2,4-D, is still widely used. Even Carson suspected only indirect health effects on humans or animals. What concerned her was the ecological consequences of widespread spraying, as of sage brush in the West or along roads, railroads, or utility lines. This could destroy the habitat of animals, or the nectar needed by bees and birds. As it turned out, 2,4,5-T, as originally produced, was toxic to humans, at least in any but the lowest concentrations, because it contained one of the most deadly of a class of chemicals called dioxins. Its widespread use in Vietnam, as Agent Orange, meant that the United States was guilty of a type of biological warfare, not just in its intended use to destroy forest cover or rice crops, but as an agent with possibly severe health effects on civilians. American soldiers who were in areas sprayed, and particularly those who did the spraying, may have suffered some of the dire effects, although endless litigation by veterans, and many scientific studies, were inconclusive about the degree of harm from the relatively low levels of dioxin they absorbed. In any case, they eventually won compensation from the federal government.

As for so many environmental issues, the use of herbicides involves conflicting values and goals. In much of the underdeveloped world, the high cost of herbicides and the relatively low wages there deter their use. But in high-wage countries, they are cost effective and safe if those who apply them use the prescribed methods. They not only save labor, but reduce the use of fossil fuels and allow no-till farming. The herbicides kill the grass and weeds, so that farmers can plant seeds with just a minor cut in the soil. This prevents erosion, and also limits the runoff from fertilizer or insecticides. Such no-till agriculture may become a requirement in certain river systems to prevent water pollution or siltation.

The second issue confronted by Carson was the widespread spraying to control diseases, particularly those caused by mosquitos. More often than not, this involved the earliest, most widely used of the chlorinated hydrocarbons, dichlorodiphenyltrichloroethane, or DDT. Unfortunately, Carson's book is too often associated only with the debate over and ultimate banning of DDT (in 1972 in the United States). On no other issue were as many competing values at stake. The synthesis of DDT in 1873 in Strasbourg made it one of the earliest synthetic chemicals. Since no one knew of its value as an insecticide, it was not commercially produced. In 1939, a Swiss chemist, Paul Müller, reconstituted the chemical and discovered its amazing ability to kill insects, an achievement that won him the Nobel Prize in 1948. It gained its first extensive use as an insecticide during World War II, and became available to the public at the end of the conflict. American troops used DDT to kill body lice in Italy, and to kill malaria-infected mosquitos. Its use soared at war's end, making it the most used insecticide in the world. It was inexpensive, effective at low concentrations, and seemed to have no ill effects on humans in exposures short of a massive ingestion of the chemical. Its widespread use for mosquito control saved millions of lives, mostly in underdeveloped countries. It became an essential tool in public health campaigns around the world. Dangers were soon apparent. It was toxic to fish, but seemingly not to mammals, although it was soon clear that DDT accumulated in their fat cells.

The first proof of dangers to nonaquatic animals came in 1960, in a finding that had a major influence on Carson. At Clear Lake, in California, the annual spraying of DDT to control gnats led to the death of over one thousand western grebes (the pathological evidence was overwhelming) that had fed on lake plankton with high concentrations of DDT. By 1962, as Carson wrote, impressionistic evidence at many sites suggested that DDT was toxic to many species of birds, including the robins that she emphasized in her book. Correspondents in Hinsdale, Illinois, believed the annual spraying of DDT had killed almost all the area's songbirds. Several southern bird watchers reported either the death or exodus of almost all birds after massive aerial spraying to kill spreading fire ants. In these cases Carson had no tangible proof of the accuracy of these observations, let alone a detailed study of possible causes. But in Michigan and Illinois she found rather detailed pathological evidence, gathered by scientists, of high mortality among robins, and low reproductive rates for those that survived, all tied almost beyond a doubt to the DDT concentrated in earthworms after spraying to control Dutch elm disease. Even when Carson wrote, it was clear that the birds that were most susceptible to DDT were raptors, including many hawks and the bald eagle. They gorged on fish that had DDT in their fat cells. Later, it was clear that the greatest threat to raptors was not direct poisoning, but the thinned eggshells caused by DDT. Reproduction all but ceased over large areas, and the eagle population of the lower forty-eight states would move close to extinction before and just after the national ban.

But it was not bird deaths that created enough public and scientific pressure for banning DDT. The obvious benefits of DDT as an insecticide, the human lives it had saved, might well have overridden any concern over birds, although the possible fate of our national symbol was a powerful persuader. An even more powerful persuader were the charges that DDT was a human carcinogen. Here the case was full of ambiguities, with different studies leading to conflicting opinions. In some cases, with high doses, DDT caused tumors in mice. About the only compelling argument for human endangerment is a minor one, and of recent cogency—DDT may increase estrogen levels in women, although much less so than birth control pills or post-menopausal prescriptions, and in this way slightly increase the risks for breast cancer. As a whole, it remains one of the safest insecticides so far as human risks are concerned, and it is still used in some countries in malarial control programs. It is inexpensive, effective, and safe when used within homes to kill mosquitos. Its widespread banning hurt the international effort to control malaria. Ironically, almost all replacement insecticides, excluding biological ones, have been more toxic to humans, more expensive, and more difficult to apply safely. None have posed as many risks to birds, but several have proved more toxic to honey bees and to fish.

Carson's book did not end, or even diminish, the use of pesticides. It did lead to intense scientific evaluations of each pesticide, and beyond that to legislation to control or prevent the use of each. As intended, the book's apocalyptic tone frightened people. They began to take notice of the chemicals in their own homes, or ones they used freely, and often recklessly, on gardens and lawns, or even to kill termites. Her book was also the first to mobilize new environmental discussion groups, and soon new organizations, all in the turbulent 1960s. By the first Earth Day, in 1970, Carson was a hero and martyr to a great cause.[4]

THE CLIMAX OF ENVIRONMENTAL REFORM

In the decade after Carson's book, environmental concerns gradually rose
to the top of American political concerns. By 1970, polls showed that
over half of voters saw environmental stress, primarily air and water pollution, as one of the three top issues facing the country. One event after
another reinforced the concern, including much publicized smog over
Los Angeles, numerous oil spills (by ships or offshore wells), bans on
the eating of lake trout and coho salmon from the Great Lakes, the near
extinction of the bald eagle in the lower forty-eight states, even the publicity over a burning river (the Cuyahoga in Cleveland in 1969). By the
late 1960s, college youth were in rebellion, not only against the war in
Vietnam, but also against the middle-class, liberal culture of their parents'
generation. Thousands repudiated consumerism, moved to rural com-
munes, and flirted with anarchism. Next to civil rights and Vietnam, the
plight of the environment most enlisted their idealism. The first Earth Day,
supported in Congress by Senator Gaylord Nelson of Wisconsin, seemed
to be one tool for enlisting youth in a constructive rather than a violent
and destructive crusade. But the more radical youth rejected mainstream
environmental organizations, and joined in several radical, even a few
violent, environmental groups (see chapter 10).

By 1970, all the older and most prestigious environmental organizations had become more active in advocacy and increasingly effective in
lobbying. Carson's book led to an advocacy group, Environmental Action.
David Brower formed a schismatic and more radical offspring of the Sierra Club, Friends of the Earth, in 1969. It soon branched off into the Environmental Policy Center. The Environmental Defense Fund (1967) and
the Natural Resources Defense Fund (1971) helped insure the enforcement of a series of new environmental regulations. The League of Conservation Voters (1970) lobbied for new legislation. A small Center for
Environmental Education (1973) soon shifted its primary emphasis to
efforts to save whales, and then to almost all issues involving the oceans
(in 2001 it changed its name to Ocean Conservancy). These are only the
largest and best funded of dozens of mainstream environmental groups.
Of these, the two that verged toward the more activist end of the spectrum, like Greenpeace, were Brower's two organizations and at times the
Environmental Defense Fund. Of all the larger organizations, the Nature
Conservancy, begun back in 1959, tried to maintain a broader coalition

across the political spectrum, and also has left a more enduring legacy in all the land it has purchased in order to preserve biodiversity.

Public concern, strong action agencies, and a favorable political environment led to a near avalanche of new environmental legislation. From 1963 to 1980, the bills were so numerous and far reaching that almost no one in Congress could keep track of them all. The bills, and major amendments to them, soon numbered in the hundreds. But about a dozen were, and remain, the most important. Although the political and cultural situation was different, Japan and most western European countries enacted closely related environmental legislation, even as the United Nations tremendously expanded its environmental programs, as has been evident in several previous chapters of this book.

The flood of environmental legislation in the 1960s was soon confusing, and in most cases only an opening to more demanding and encompassing acts in the 1970s. One exception was the Wilderness Act of 1964, which remains the legislative foundation of our system of wilderness areas. This act, passed by the Senate in 1963 under a supportive President Kennedy, was approved by the House in 1964 and gladly signed by President Lyndon Johnson. The legislative history stretched back for seven years, during which several congressmen (one was later vice president, Hubert Humphrey) had supported bills strongly urged on Congress by the Sierra Club, the Wilderness Society, and, less focally, most environmental organizations. In a sense, the act was a belated achievement of John Muir. But, because of several special exceptions in the act, it was not a total victory for wilderness advocates.[5]

The Wilderness Act added protection to what, in many cases, already existed—wild, reasonably well-protected, primitive areas in national forests and national parks. The bill had much to recommend it to Congress, including almost no costs. What it did was provide for wilderness designation of selected areas within national forests, parks, and wildlife preserves (after 1976 it also included Bureau of Land Management lands). Jurisdiction over these designated areas remained within the existing agencies. Thus, the bill established no new agencies and required no new personnel. The areas designated as wilderness were to be contiguous sections of wild lands, those scarcely affected by human action. The congressional purpose was to preserve such wild areas, as a place of solitude and recreation, by excluding any development, any permanent residences, any roads, and the use of any motor vehicles or motor boats. The only development within these areas would be hiking trails and shelters. Over a ten-year period, the secretary of Agriculture was to survey and recommend suitable primitive areas within the national forests, while the secretary of the Interior was to locate contiguous, roadless areas of over five thousand acres in parks and wildlife preserves. Public hearings and congressional approval were required. The president, in order to round out the boundaries of designated wilderness areas, could add up to five thousand additional acres to the areas proposed by the federal agencies. In 1975 Congress mandated the establishment of over fifteen wilderness areas in eastern national forests. In 2003, the United States had 662 wilderness areas, consisting of over 106 million acres, or over 4.6 percent of all land in the country. No other country matches this. But it is important to note that around 55 percent of this is in Alaska, where one wilderness area is larger than the 9.1 million acres first set aside under the original act.

For both legal and political reasons, the original act included some important concessions to private interests. It allowed for roads where necessary for fire control, allowed the continued use of motorboats in lakes where this had been an established form of recreation, allowed access roads to any private land encircled by a wilderness area, and, possibly of greatest significance, honored all existing mineral leases on land in a wilderness area, and allowed not only access roads to such leases, but also timber cutting to allow such road access. Where well established, it also allowed grazing in wilderness areas and access to reservoirs or water used in power production. For all these excepted uses, both federal agencies and state governments could set strict requirements for use, but each exception considerably compromised the idea of a pristine wilderness. In the same sense, the sheer number of hikers and campers in the more accessible wildernesses has subverted the ecological purposes of such reserves.[6]

The Johnson Administration proudly listed environmental reforms as a part of its Great Society legislation. Indeed, three or four environmental bills passed each year from 1964 to 1968. They set important precedents, but most would be superseded by stronger legislation in the 1970s. The Great Society included amendments to the Clean Air Act of 1963, and three bills involving water quality, water resources planning, and an early version of a clean water act. Two bills involved air pollution, another new controls over radiation. A Wild Rivers Act supplemented the Wilderness

Act. A highway beautification law led to some, but not enough, controls over roadsides. Several bills involved consumer protection and the safety of workers, or issues related to, but not central to, the environment. By far the most important of these was the Occupational Safety and Health Act of 1968. Both environmental and safety legislation led to new agencies (for example, a Federal Pollution Control Administration) or advisory councils, with their homes in three or four federal departments. By 1979, all these new innovations had led to bureaucratic confusion. For this reason, in 1970, President Richard Nixon, as a part of a governmental reorganization effort unchallenged by Congress, combined most of these advisory or enforcement efforts into the new Environmental Protection Agency (EPA), which became the largest federal regulatory body.[7]

THE NATIONAL ENVIRONMENTAL POLICY ACT

Before he created the EPA, Nixon signed into law the most comprehensive environmental bill in American history—the National Environmental Policy Act (NEPA), approved by Congress in late 1969 and signed into law on January 1, 1970. At the time, many referred to it as the Magna Carta of environmentalism in America. It did not live up to this billing, but has had enormous influence not only in the United States but in much of the world. As noted in earlier chapters, several United Nations organizations, and most developed nations, have adopted variations on what became the most imitated product of this bill—environmental impact assessments.

The earliest versions of what became NEPA dated from a resources and conservation bill introduced in 1959. Other related bills gained some congressional attention in 1961, 1963, and 1965. One introduced by Senator Gaylord Nelson had the interesting title of "Ecological Research and Survey Bill." By 1969, thirty separate but related bills vied for support. The one that succeeded was a version of a bill first introduced in 1966 and then reintroduced in 1969 by Senator Henry Jackson. John Dingell pushed a near similar bill in the House. The Senate bill first gained a unanimous vote. After a conference committee harmonized the two bills, the final version sailed through both houses in late December with little debate and, probably, very limited understanding of the bill by most congresspeople. Notably, the bill involved only limited new appropriations.

NEPA, with its almost revolutionary implications, remains notable among critical congressional enactments because of its brevity and eloquence. It most closely resembled, in the scope of its policy implications, and in form, the Full Employment Act of 1946, which set a visionary economic policy agenda for the nation (one never fully realized) and established the Council of Economic Advisors. The National Environmental Policy Act first included a declaration of national environmental policy. It then set certain procedural requirements for all decisions made by federal agencies. Finally, it established a three-member Council on Environmental Quality in the Executive Office of the President of the United States.

The policy declaration in the act was as comprehensive and as daring as any environmental activist could have wished. In the preface, Congress stated that it would now be a national policy to encourage "harmony between man and his environment," to promote efforts to "prevent or eliminate damage to the environment and biosphere," and to "enrich the understanding of the ecological systems and natural resources important to the Nation." In its more detailed statement of national policy, it acknowledged the "profound impact of man's activity on the interrelations of all components of the natural environment" and listed the role of population growth, high-density urbanization, industrial expansion, resource exploitation, and technological advances. It committed the federal government to the maintenance of "conditions under which man and nature can exist in productive harmony." To implement these goals, it was the duty of the federal government to use all practical means to "fulfill the responsibilities of each generation as trustee of the environment for succeeding generations; assure for all Americans safe, healthful, productive, and esthetically and culturally pleasing surroundings . . . , achieve a balance between population and resource use which will permit high standards of living and a wide sharing of life's amenities; and enhance the quality of renewable resources and approach the maximum attainable cycling of depletable resources." The Congress authorized and directed that, to the fullest extent possible, the policies, regulations, and laws of the United States "shall be interpreted and administered in accordance" with the above policies.

It is a long way from such eloquent statements of a general policy to the actual implementation of its goals. One of the problems with NEPA is that it did not, perhaps could not, clarify what the federal government had to do, in the way of regulations and appropriations, to come even close to such lofty goals. In a sense, all the new environmental legislation in the 1960s and 1970s reflected some efforts to fulfill what NEPA identified as the national policy. The announced policies in NEPA were, in a sense, hortatory, even a bit of a sermon, since they had no regulatory power in themselves. The courts later ruled that one could not use legal process to hold any government agency responsible for fulfilling such lofty but general goals unless they were embedded in regulatory legislation, such as clean air and water acts. In my estimation, the one subsequent congressional act which came closest to fulfilling these sweeping policy goals was the Endangered Species Act of 1973. It, more than any other federal act, at times forced economic priorities to give way to environmental ones.

As its means of forcing government agencies to heed the new environmental policies, NEPA contained what turned out to be a very important procedural requirement, or what soon became famous as Environmental Impact Statements (EIS). I doubt that many congresspeople who read the bill realized the importance of these provisions. In summary, the act required that all agencies of the federal government, in all planned projects that would have any impact on the environment, integrate information from the natural and social sciences, and from the design arts. They were to develop methods and procedures to insure that they gave appropriate consideration in decision making to unquantified environmental amenities as well as to economic and technical considerations. Out of this process, they had to develop a detailed statement on the environmental impact of any federal action—on adverse environmental impacts that an agency could not avoid, on "possible alternatives to the proposed action," on "the relationship between local short-term uses of man's environment and the maintenance and enhancement of long-term productivity, and any irreversible and irretrievable commitments of resources which would be involved in the proposed action should it be implemented." The agency, in preparing such reports, had to consult with other agencies with overlapping jurisdictions or with special expertise, and with state and local officials, and had to make public all recommendations.

Here was the teeth in NEPA. Unfortunately, in time most people forgot about the substantive polices that made such statements necessary. In a series of decisions, the federal courts upheld this requirement, even for projects already in the planning stage. Agencies had to compile such reports, which had to accompany all proposals through the whole review process leading to acceptance and funding. The act did not clarify any procedure for accepting or rejecting the required statement. Agency departments and heads had to approve projects, and presumably reviewed not just the adherence of the agency to the procedure (that it included all the items required by the act to be part of the statement), but also the environmental viability of the proposed action. But nothing in the act required such substantive review, for the courts ruled that the environmental statement requirement was procedural only. If an agency proposed to do irreparable damage to an endemic species by building a new dam, it had to acknowledge this in its statement, but such acknowledgment did not mean it could not proceed with the dam if approved by the appropriate department of the federal government, and, at least in the case of military projects, this would happen. Of course, in this case such a species probably received protection from the Endangered Species Act, but not from NEPA.

In time, most federal agencies followed a formula, or even leased out the preparation of their impact statements. When they could get by with it, agencies used an environmental assessment report to prove no major environmental impact at all, and thus avoided the longer and more time-consuming EIS. By 1977, EISs tended to be excessively long and full of unreadable jargon. President Carter formalized clearer and simpler rules, leading to shorter reports. And even when an agency wrote a wonderful statement, with what seemed an admirable way of dealing with environmental problems, no one was responsible for any follow-up to determine how well the agency fulfilled its announced plans. Despite these problems, the procedure, to a large extent, achieved its purpose. This was because of the public disclosure and citizen awareness of what was at stake. From the very first statements, the requirement invited litigation. Plenty of new environmental organizations were on the alert, and they appealed to federal courts over and over again to block federal projects, such as highways and dams, because of an inadequate EIS. And even though agencies did not have to favor the environment, but only admit the problems, in fact the public exposure made it difficult for agencies to violate the purpose and spirit of NEPA, except in cases of national security. Agencies that tried this either lost out in the review process or faced intense and embarrassing public exposure. By 1977, agencies had prepared over 11,000 statements, faced 1,052 legal challenges, and lost on 217 of them, which meant injunctive relief for plaintiffs. In the case of NEPA, it was the federal courts that became the enforcer.

At the time of passage, the Council on Environmental Quality (CEQ) seemed the most important product of NEPA. It was modeled on the Council of Economic Advisors, which had gained enormous prestige and influence. The president appointed the three-member council, including one member as chair. Appointments required Senate concurrence. The members of the council had to be environmental experts. The council was to consult with a Citizens' Advisory Committee on Environmental Quality that Nixon had established in May 1969. The council was required to help the president prepare a required environmental report each year. It was to gather information on environmental trends, analyze such information, determine its impact on the policies contained in the act, and submit its studies to the president. It was also to review and appraise governmental programs to determine how well they met the policy objective of the act. The council had a small budget (at first $1 million) to carry out investigations and surveys relating to "ecological quality and environmental quality." It had to make an annual report on the state of the environment. These were important duties. But for several reasons the council has not yet gained the prestige, or the influence, intended by the original act. Most people are not aware of its existence. Had the act given the council the authority to review and, if it chose, reject environmental impact statements, and thus to block projects that failed to meet the policy goals of the act (it could only recommend that the president reject such projects), it might have played a much greater role in our system.[8]

One final aspect of NEPA was innovative. In addition to creating EISs, all federal agencies had to make available to state and local governments useful environmental advice and information, and also, when consistent with national foreign policy goals, support international programs that could help prevent a decline in the quality of the world's environment. Already, many federal agencies were involved in United Nations environmental programs, and since the enactment of NEPA this involvement has increased exponentially. Despite shifts in the level of political support, the United States has provided more funds for international environmental programs than any other country (but not nearly as much as several western European countries on a per capita basis), and on almost every issue American scientists have taken the lead in critical environmental research and in developing new technologies to gather information and to mitigate problems.[9]

Enforcement: The Environmental Protection Agency

The complement to NEPA was the Environmental Protection Agency (EPA). I find many people who link the two, or believe that the EPA was a product of the NEPA. The NEPA did inspire Nixon to create a new regulatory agency to deal with the ever-expanding body of environmental acts and agencies. In his governmental reorganization plan of 1970, which went into effect when not vetoed by Congress, Nixon consolidated most existing environmental programs into the new EPA. Programs in water quality and pesticide control moved from Interior, agencies dealing with air pollution, solid waste management, water hygiene, and radiation moved from Health, Education, and Welfare, pesticide research from Agriculture, and ecological research from the new Council on Environmental Quality. Not included were environmental aspects of work in defense and transportation, and some water and sewer programs in Housing and Urban Development. The only strong criticism was that the change did not go far enough, and that environmental protection deserved departmental status (an idea revived in the Clinton Administration). The Office of Management and Budget worked out the administrative details of the new agency, which opened for business on December 2, 1970, or a year after the enactment of NEPA. William Ruckelshouse, a former congressmen from Indiana, and a just-defeated candidate for the Senate, took over as the first administrator, and as it turned out, a very forceful one. The original staff simply moved to EPA from their former departments, and at first continued to do much the same work as before.

The EPA quickly became the largest regulatory agency in Washington, and the one with the most complex role. It was also the most ambitious such agency in the world, even though France set up an environmental ministry at almost the same time. Not only did the EPA absorb almost all existing environmental programs, but Congress, in the next decade, would assign it the main administrative and enforcement role for a dozen major new laws. By 2003 the EPA would have over eighteen thousand employees, a majority at the professional level. It is, by far, the largest environmental agency in the world. Not even the administrator can understand its many functions. In 1995, an EPA official listed thirty-three major legislative enactments that guided its regulatory work. Actually, one could easily double this number, particularly if one included major revisions or amendments to earlier legislation. From the beginning, it has been a beleaguered agency, beset with criticism from all sides. Environmentalists have bemoaned its caution, its willingness to seek voluntary agreements with major polluters, and at times its ineptitude. Those regulated have chaffed at all the impenetrable rules, the bureaucratic inefficiency, the cost of what seems to them needless regulations or administration decisions. Congress, at times gladly, has passed complex legislation and then turned over the problem of administration and interpretation to the EPA, but never with enough funding or an adequate staff to do all the work.

It is difficult, in a short space, to enumerate what the EPA does, or tries to do. It has extensive rule-making authority, subject to many public hearings before listing. Perhaps half of these rules deal with pollution, which most people saw as the most critical issue at its founding. It has almost complete enforcement authority over our Clean Air and Water Acts and over toxic chemicals. After a series of amendments to legislation dating from 1947 but which culminated in 1997, it has almost complete control over pesticide use. Even Rachel Carson might be pleased at this. It regulates lead, asbestos, radon, types of radiation, oil spills, solid waste disposal, medical hazards, and wetland protection. It supports various recycling programs, has responsibility for some programs dealing with coasts and the oceans, sponsors environmental education, provides advisories on fish contamination, certifies energy-efficient appliances, and has worked out voluntary conservation strategies with many corporations. Finally, in an unwanted duty, it has devoted much frustrating energy in trying to administer the Comprehensive Environmental Response, Compensation, and Liability Act of 1980 (Superfund), which has involved costly efforts to clean up toxic waste sites and endless litigation over efforts to force responsible parties to pay for the cost.

At times, it seems that no one loves the EPA. The agency has seemed to be in a crisis throughout much of its history, but it is important to note that it is often the legislation, not its enforcement, that leads to criticism. But if one reads even some of the thousands of rules enforced by the EPA, one appreciates the enormous task involved in protecting an environment in a highly industrialized, growing economy. The costs are high. The frustrations are inevitable. But, as a whole, the EPA has been able to implement an overwhelming volume of environmental legislation in such a way as to slow or stop the worsening of environmental conditions in several areas, or even improve them in a few. It has not done much to slow global warming, an area in which the EPA has not had a major role beyond some research and public education. So far, the United States does not have laws that effectively regulate greenhouse gas emissions. If Congress enacts such laws, no doubt it will assign enforcement responsibilities to the already overburdened EPA.[10]

Both the NEPA and the EPA reflect the success of reform-oriented environmentalists in the United States. The policies contained in the NEPA, and the breadth of agency responsibilities in the EPA, go about as far as one could expect in a pluralistic political system. But the payoff in each case is in the implementation of the policies. Few reform-oriented environmentalists, despite all the legislative victories, are happy with the present outcome, particularly under the second Bush Administration. But most will continue to work within the present political system to gain further, largely incremental and modest, reforms. This is not true of a much more angry and passionate group of environmentalists, or the subject of the next chapter.

Passionate Environmentalism

For many people environmental concerns have become their control-ling passion, and for some converts to the Gaia theory even the basis of a new religion. A few have become martyrs to the cause, risking and losing their lives in environmental activism. But, as one would expect, these most committed environmentalists are not of one mind. They all have rejected what they usually refer to as shallow, or liberal, or reform environmentalism, which includes most of the better known, and better funded, nongovernmental organizations that are seeking new and stron-ger environmental legislation. But the exact boundaries between these establishment advocates and those who are deep or radical in outlook is not always distinct. And even among those who accept the label radi-cal, the gambit runs from mild, even pacificist theorists to a few well-publicized activists who have resorted to violent protest, often under such newly coined words as ecotage or ecoterrorism. Of the varied groups, the largest but most diffuse are those who have accepted some version of the Gaia theory developed by James Lovelock, but note that not all advocates of Gaia are radical in outlook, and this includes Lovelock himself.

GAIA

The Gaia hypothesis is largely identified with the work of James Love-lock, a British inventor and independent scientist whose major research has been at least loosely in the field of medicine. He gained his Ph.D. for medical research and, broadly conceived, in the field of biochemistry. Environmentalists, as well as New Age religionists, have correctly drawn inspiration and needed knowledge from Lovelock and from his closest associate, the American biologist Lynn Margulis. But Lovelock is not a radical environmentalist and has frequently ridiculed romantics who would like to move back to a simpler past age. He believes the earth faces grave problems, but is irenic enough to believe humans can fix most of them. Lovelock has developed some intense policy concerns based on his Gaia theory, but most of these are in line with those of reform environmentalists, and most involve the development, and appropriate use, of new tools. On some issues, such as the thinning of the ozone layer, an issue that he had helped clarify, he argued that the widespread alarm was overblown and the issue relatively unimportant to the health of the earth. He once testified for the DuPont Corporation, and was for years a consultant for the Shell Oil Company, not the credentials valued by many environmentalists.

Gaia theory, in one sense, is simple, but much like Darwin's arguments in *Origin of Species*, it is speculatively rich and both boosted and confused by the eloquent but often misleading language Lovelock and others have used to defend it. By his own account, Lovelock, in a revelatory moment in 1965, first grasped the theory that he would, by the suggestion of the novelist William Golding, name after the ancient Greek earth goddess, Gaia. In 1960 he became a consultant for the Jet Propulsion Laboratory, and thus for a branch of the National Aeronautics and Space Administration. For two years he even held an appointment at the Baylor College of Medicine in Houston. Most of his work for JPL involved ways of determining if life existed on Mars. In reflecting on this issue, he realized the significance of a point he had earlier stressed: that the easiest way to find evidence of any significant quantity of life on Mars would be to analyze its atmosphere. In fact, its atmosphere was close to an equilibrium, with its energy content all but exhausted. The opposite was true of the earth, where the air was full of reactive gases, and constantly affected by energy flows from the living organisms that used it as a resource and as a repository of waste products. Unlike Mars and Venus, it was a living planet. This type of reasoning led Lovelock to a new insight and what became a mission—to discover all the ways that life interacted with the inanimate earth, shaping it as often as shaped by it, with climate possibly the one most important product of such interaction.

Although Lovelock lamented the lack of scientific attention so far given to the role of life in shaping the earth, he was far from the first to note many levels of interaction. His own speculations suggested a much wider range of such interactions, supported new lines of research, and eventually gained him a great deal of respect from at least a few highly specialized scientists. But it was not the fact of such mutual influences that made him famous, but a further inference that Lovelock drew from them. I want to state his hypothesis in the form of a simile, for in this way I can postpone some of the difficulties that soon bothered critics. He, in effect, said that the part of the earth which contains life is like a huge, self-regulating organism. At times he almost went beyond this, and said that it *was* such an organism, and this view was reinforced by his personification of Gaia in so much of his writing. But in all fairness I believe it more correct to say that, even in the sometimes overly enthusiastic language of his early defense of his theory, he only argued that, in most but not all respects, the biosphere behaved like an organism. For example, it does not reproduce itself. Also, unlike living beings, it does not reflect anything like innate or learned ends or goals. No teleology is present. Yet, like organisms, it is an almost unbelievably complex whole, which receives all manner of feedback data and which constantly makes such adjustments in air, soil, and water as to maintain all the conditions needed for life to continue to flourish. It is as if the biosphere involved a type of metabolism comparable to that of organisms. This theory, in itself, would seem clear enough for testing, although so encompassing in its scope as to never lend itself to any final verification. As a whole, the detailed inquiry in the several fields of science implicated by this theory has tended to confirm aspects of it, in the sense that in almost every area in which Lovelock predicted thermostat-like changes that allowed the biosphere to cope with outside perturbations, such as increased heat from the sun, scientists have discovered life-produced responses.

Lovelock is, by intent, a broad-gauged scientist, interested in what might be called mega theories. He has created a new label for his line of inquiry, geophysiology. He is often impatient with narrow scientific specialization. He wants to address big synthetic or integrating issues. He was not only much influenced by Charles Darwin, but resembles him in many ways. In a sense, his whole theory rests upon organic evolution. If it were not for inheritable mistakes in copies of DNA (mutations), and thus differential survival rates in scarce environments, life would never have been able to change and adapt. Without mutations, early life, which developed, perhaps as a result of pure luck in what Lovelock saw as a relatively brief window of opportunity, would soon have expired. The environment would have gone through the same type of changes that transformed Mars and Venus into dead planets. Darwin emphasized adaptations that favored individuals. Lovelock discovered the same adaptability for life as a whole, which has helped maintain a life-supporting earth. Note that what he calls Gaia, or the self-regulating biosphere, developed not with the first life (it may have represented the embryo of Gaia), but when early life first began to shape its nonorganic environment. Lovelock believed this was very soon after the first life, or at least as soon as early microscopic life became sensitive to light and began early, prechlorophyll forms of photosynthesis.

Unfortunately, both Darwin and Lovelock used the same type of teleological language to confuse their central claims. Darwin had his own revelation, one that changed the world. He believed that some inheritable variations, which he could not explain at a molecular level (we do so explain them now), would in a context of environmental scarcity inevitably favor some individuals and increase their chances of survival and reproduction. Fortunate variations would allow some organisms better to fit an existing environment, or more easily adapt to environmental changes. Cumulative variations would lead to continuous organic change and to new species. In time such changes would lead to two design-like outcomes—ecological richness, as species would emerge that fit almost any conceivable environmental niche, and what he often called higher species, meaning those with the type of internal specialization of parts and the central nervous system coordination that allowed them to adapt to a wider array of environments or do more to shape environments to fit their needs. But design-like does not mean any design, any agency behind the process of change, any selection. The present biosystem is simply the outcome of an unguided and, in most senses of the term, an uncaused process. But the complexity, and often for Darwin the beauty, of the outcome led him, much as Lovelock, to buy into a simile that soon conditioned many of his arguments and almost all his descriptive language. It was as if, or like, nature had selected a series of beneficial outcomes. He thus proudly introduced a metaphorical agent, "natural selection." Lovelock's design-like metaphorical agent is Gaia. In both cases, the metaphor came to have a life of its own, with endless confusion.

Behind the metaphors were the enduring insights of both Darwin and Lovelock. For Lovelock it was the implications of the self-regulating relationship of life and nonlife in the earth's biosphere. Today, few scien-

tists will deny the all-important role of life in shaping the evolution of
the earth, or deny the almost endless feedbacks and cycles that allow life
on earth to bend and mesh with major changes in the nonliving environment. This understanding was bound, sooner or later, to result from
specialized studies, but Lovelock highlighted the issue, pointed scientists
in new directions, and helped create a broad public awareness of the
wonders of our living planet. In two ways, Lovelock contributed to the
new inquiry. First, in 1957 he invented an electron capture detector, a
small device that could detect minute quantities of any gas in the environment. It soon was vitally important in identifying pesticide residues
in the air, and in helping establish the growing concentration of CFCs in
the atmosphere (vital to ozone thinning research). This device led to his
second contribution. It allowed Lovelock and several other scientists to
verify a heretofore unknown feedback mechanism that allowed life to
regulate climate. Minute emissions of dimethylsulfide by mid-ocean al-
gae help create what had seemed inexplicable cloud formations over the
largely aerosol-free oceans (the DMS, when oxidized into sulfate aerosols, provided the needed nucleus for condensed water droplets). Such
ocean clouds, by reflecting sunlight, help cool the earth.

But Gaia, despite all the newly discovered ways that life shapes the atmosphere, has remained an elusive and controversial theory. At one level
the problem is the language used. But when one gets around the seman-
tics, one is still left with a sense that Gaia is a suggestive but at times misleading metaphor for the totality of life, and nothing more. A good place
to start is with Darwin. Everyone talks of natural selection doing this and
that. But if one looks closely, one can never find any "natural selection."
Nothing is there. No selection takes place. Teleology is absent. The same
is true for Gaia. It does not stand for any actor, any source of change, any
cause. It is a simple, personalized, rhetorical device, a way of referring to
the almost magical outcomes of life processes on the planet earth. After
all, people were already acquainted with such language, as when they
refer to "Mother Nature."

Gaia is a word that may help dramatize the enormous range of interactions of life with its physical environment, but Lovelock believed it was
more than that. Like Darwin in reflective moments, he acknowledged the
metaphorical content of labels such as Gaia or natural selection, but he
still talked as if Gaia was an actor. Just as Darwin often stressed how much
more sublime were the products of natural selection compared to hu-

man breeders, so Lovelock celebrated the wonderful adaptive strategies of Gaia. He also, even when denying that Gaia in any sense was a god, or that it reflected the work of a deity, applauded those who wanted to make Gaia a religious symbol, even an object of a type of worship. He personally referred to Gaia as being at the heart of his own religious sensibility.

The issue that still perplexes people is finding the best way to understand the design-like outcomes of what Darwin called natural selection and the earth-wide design-like outcomes of what Lovelock calls Gaia. The two are so linked as to be one problem. Some recent, detailed work in molecular biology suggests that the wonderful feedbacks, the recycling of chemical elements necessary for life, are a product of the endless mutations and differential survival rates that adapt life to shifting environmental constraints. Out of the interaction of organisms, each in a sense serving or fulfilling its own innate or learned ends or purposes, come not only organic adaptability and complexity, but also continuous modifications in the nonliving environment that facilitate the evolutionary process. Unless one believes some divine intent underlies the process, the outcomes are in no sense designed or selected. As Adam Smith suggested in 1776, in characterizing the outcomes of a free market, they are as if a product of a hidden hand. But there is no hand, or, in his case, no real market. Personified terms, like market, or natural selection, or Gaia, are an almost necessary verbal shorthand for types of dynamic interactions which, because of the characteristics of the individual actors and the environment that contains them, eventuate in new forms of order or structure. The differences between Mars and Earth simply suggest the quite different forms of order that can develop where life is present. And it is important to note that certain seemingly wonderful outcomes are, in fact, often the product of many messy detours and a high degree of chaos (the type of life controlled by DNA remains an unexplained given, while copying errors in DNA seem completely random).

The Gaia hypothesis, either in its restricted scientific sense, or in its mystifications, offered a gold mine of possibilities for environmentalists. More than anyone before him, Lovelock demonstrated the range of symbiotic relationships among all forms of life, and with what people had too easily assumed to be a separate physical universe. If he had any message, it was that humans have not begun to understand most life processes, and often by their interventions may risk undreamed of calamities. He thus warned against detailed human strategies to manage the biosphere. This led him, in some cases, such as ozone thinning, to line up against most environmentalists. Consistent with his focus on major chemical cycles, he looked to the overall welfare of Gaia, meaning the whole biosphere, and not to short-term human benefits. He believed that almost all research reinforced his view that, for Gaia as a whole, the most important organisms are not vertebrates but microorganisms, most at the level of bacteria. He was thus more concerned with the health of these minute creatures than with popular efforts to prevent the extinction of threatened birds or mammals. The great thermostatic processes that keep Gaia in balance with an ever-changing external environment, including the ever hotter sun, occur in the soil, in the deeper water of the oceans, in oxygen-deprived swamps and lagoons. Here are the organic factories that carry out most photosynthesis and thus sequester carbon, that facilitate most of the weathering of rocks, that recycle most of the elements upon which life depends, that break down and assimilate all manner of waste products, including much human-produced waste. Thus, Lovelock's environmental concerns are those related to these most basic processes, with his ever present warning that we do not yet begin to have a full understanding of most of them. But any threat to hard-working bacteria, and to their chemical handiwork, is the most dangerous of all to life on earth. Not that he feared a full destruction of life, but rather another of the great periods of massive extinction. Gaia is enormously resilient, but only over extended periods of time.

At the heart of Lovelock's present concerns is global warming and all that may go with it. In a book for popular readers in 1991, he referred to the "people plague." The sheer number of humans, and what they do, amounts to a disabling disease, a pathological distortion. The modern norm for the earth is the cold, glacial eras, which far outlast the brief interims of warming. From the standpoint of the Northern Hemisphere, the present warm interglacial period is a golden age, but not for Gaia as a whole. In the last ice age, or as recently as twenty thousand years ago, the amount of carbon dioxide in the atmosphere sank to around 180 ppm, or what Lovelock believed was just enough to keep photosynthesis going. Such a drop might seem counterintuitive, since so much of the planet was under ice, curtailing plant life and its sequestering of carbon. But the oceans were then over three hundred feet lower than today, the cooler oceans supported a boom in microscopic life, and in many tropical areas, such as Southeast Asia, near continent-size land areas were then exposed, able to support a lush tropical vegetation. Gaia bloomed, and thus the sequestering of carbon in biomass, and the small annual amount deposited on the sea bottom, exceeded the rate of respiration and other modes of recycling carbon into the atmosphere.

Then, for whatever reason, about thirteen thousand years ago a sudden warming began to melt the continental glaciers. By ten thousand years ago most were gone, and the ocean eventually rose by three hundred feet, covering the continental shelves. Lovelock believes the warm interlude is both exceptional and probably pathological. He calls it Gaia's fever, using the analogy of human illness. By processes only in limited ways involving humans, the concentration of carbon dioxide rose to around 280 ppm by ten thousand years ago and remained rather constant until 1900. It then began rising, largely from human inputs, and has soared since 1950 to around 380 ppm in 2006. Methane, in some respects an even more dangerous greenhouse gas, has risen at an even more rapid rate. And a new group of human-synthesized gases, the chlorofluorocarbons, which affect the ozone layer, have risen from zero to ever higher concentrations (Lovelock fears the greenhouse effect of CFCs more than the impact on ozone). Lovelock is not sure what the impact of warming is, in itself. He argues, in his personalized language, that Gaia will work hard to keep a balance in nature, perhaps largely because of climate feedbacks, such as the added plant growth on land and in the oceans caused by extra carbon dioxide, and because of extra cloud cover caused by plant transpiration and more rapid evaporation of ocean water.

Thus, more than most environmentalists, Lovelock emphasizes what is happening to carbon sinks. Like some bioregionalists, he finds the earliest source of the problem in agriculture, and believes that, even today, farming and grazing are doing more to sicken Gaia than manufacturing and trade (he hates cows). He emphasizes the degrading of land, the assault on the precious bacteria and fungi in the soil, the destruction of wetlands and estuaries, but above all the destruction of forests and in tropical areas the desertification that ensues. He even refers to early agriculture as the fall from paradise. He knows that even Gaia cannot quickly respond to so many assaults, and that the present population of the earth cannot sustain its present use of the natural environment. He envisions an early catastrophe without major changes in human behavior, and notes the Malthusian hell already visible in Africa and parts of Asia.

But Lovelock is more hopeful than gloomy. He applauds a recently developed concern for environmental issues, and some already effective reforms. Humans have to stop reproducing at the present rate. They have to reduce the burning of fossil fuels. Most of all, they have to preserve forests, particularly tropical forests. What is needed is not a retreat from agriculture (this would mean widespread starvation), but such new efficiencies that agriculture will require less land and less deforestation. He supports an expansion of nuclear energy to replace oil and coal. I could go on, but in most respects he sounds not like environmental radicals, but like liberal environmentalists who indeed want changes in human values and consumption, but also seek a technological fix for many global problems.[1]

DEEP ECOLOGY

Beyond the Gaia hypothesis, the broadest and most philosophical approach to our environment is deep ecology. It has directly influenced other theories or movements, such as ecofeminism, Greenpeace, and, at the radical extreme, Earth First! Certain themes are common to almost all people who identify with each of these groups. Most believe that humanity, without fundamental changes in beliefs and patterns of consumption, faces an imminent environmental catastrophe. Many are apocalyptic in their sense of coming doom. Most condemn free market or capitalistic economic systems, hate multinational corporations and world trade organizations, deplore consumptive values, are suspicious of modern scientific or linear or rationalistic forms of thought, and blame much of our present environmental crisis on monotheistic religions. They value Oriental, animistic, or neopagan religions, support localized and cooperative forms of production, celebrate preindustrial and primitive cultures, seek a simple life with limited desires, and often move to something close to anarchism in politics. Beyond all this, they seek a complete transmutation of what they believe to be a presently dominant anthropocentric ethic. This is most true of those who advocate a deep ecology.

The label "deep ecology" dates to 1973, to a brief article in a philosophy journal by Arne Naess, a Norwegian philosopher. This article launched a movement. In it, Naess offered an alternative to what he called the "shallow ecology movement." At first, he did not elaborate on the content of shallow ecology, except to note that it included those who fought against resource depletion and pollution in behalf of preserving the health and affluence of people in developed countries. In later writings, he filled in a rather complete ideal type of shallow ecology, one that probably matched no one person, and which was close to a caricature of most reform-oriented environmentalist activists. It involved, above all, an acceptance of most aspects of the present social and economic order, with piecemeal efforts to reform it, to solve various environmental problems, all in behalf of an improvement of human life.

In his first article on deep ecology, Naess offered an outline of its principles. Because of Naess's openness to alternative philosophical foundations, and a certain looseness of language, these principles inspired a continuing philosophical debate, or what has become by far the most elaborate theoretical development among contemporary environmentalists. In a later book, *Ecology, Community and Lifestyle, Outline of an Ecosophy* (1976), Naess advocated a rather formal philosophical position, and summarized this by an eight-point platform that has been widely publicized. To distinguish his philosophy from that of other deep ecologists, he arbitrarily chose the letter T, and dubbed his philosophy Ecosophy T. Its leading disciple in America would be George Sessions.[2]

Perhaps the one central article of faith for Naess was his rejection of what he called anthropocentrism. By this he meant any philosophy that privileged humans over the rest of the natural world, and thus any environmental movement predicated upon human welfare. Instead, he wanted humans to accept a broadened identity that fully encompassed all other life, not because of sympathy or altruism, but out of a sense of mutual interdependence. All species have an equal right to live and blossom. When humans extend their self-image to encompass the whole network of life that is, in a sense, their larger self, then they escape from an alienation from the larger web of life and gain a higher level of self-fulfillment. This fulfillment joins with that of humans who reject the exploitation of other humans, who deplore invidious class systems of any type. Guiding all of his thought was a commitment to organism, total-fields, gestalts, or networks. Such holism did not mean large, impersonal systems, but usually local or regional communities of interacting and interdependent species, often referred to, by his disciples, as ecoregions or bioregions.

When Naess tried to express all this in the form of a platform, he necessarily left much unclear or open-ended. Yet, his platform is worth repeating in full, as the closest approximation of a deep ecological position:

1. The flourishing of human and non-human life on Earth has intrinsic value. The value of non-human life forms is independent of the usefulness these may have for narrow human purposes.
2. Richness and diversity of life forms are values in themselves and contribute to the flourishing of human and non-human life on earth.
3. Humans have no right to reduce this richness and diversity except to satisfy vital needs.
4. Present human interference with the non-human world is excessive, and the situation is rapidly worsening.
5. The flourishing of human life and cultures is compatible with a substantial decrease of the human population. The flourishing of non-human life requires such a decrease.
6. Significant change of life conditions for the better requires change in policies. These affect basic economic, technological, and ideational structures.
7. The ideological change is mainly that of appreciating *life quality* (dwelling in situations of intrinsic value) rather than adhering to a high standard of living. There will be a profound awareness of the difference between big and great.
8. Those who subscribe to the foregoing points have an obligation directly or indirectly to participate in the attempt to implement the necessary changes.[3]

This platform is too equivocal to provide very clear guidelines for environmental policies. It does not clearly separate Naess from reform environmentalists, who often advocate policies that Naess himself supports. His position is one familiar in religious discourse. What he argues is that too many environmentalists have the wrong motivation for policies. It is like the Christian who points out that what is visibly moral conduct may reflect selfish ends and not a love of God. What Naess wants is a change of heart, a deep ecological understanding that will anchor political activism and insure that it not be coopted by the present power brokers who have created the present crisis. Unlike some of his disciples, he tries to avoid dogmatism or absolute positions. This means hedge language, as in his stipulation that humans can reduce the diversity of life-forms to meet vital needs. Who defines vital needs? Or does Naess only point to the obvious—life lives on life. Humans have to eat, either other animals or plants. He notes that too many people live on earth for nonhuman life to flourish, but suggests no way to reduce this population. Such an evasion of the means to reduce the earth's population is typical of many environmentalists, and one that often seems to reduce some of their policy advocacy to pie-in-the-sky dreams.[4]

What Naess proposes is a new ethical imperative or ideal. What has most engaged other philosophers is his belief that humans can, and should, so identify with life as a whole, or even the life-supporting aspects of the inanimate world, as to gain an expanded human identity, from which will flow, naturally and not as a duty, the choices needed to avoid an impending ecological catastrophe. The broadened conception of self-hood, and of relationships to fellow life, will lead to a type of self-fulfillment, for the type of solidarity with life as a whole will mean no separation between the human and nonhuman. For humans with such an expanded identity, the exploitation of the nonhuman world, the use of other life to enhance narrowly selfish human desires, would be self-contradictory. Thus, Naess wanted such a conversion in the reality of being human as to obviate not just an instrumental approach to nonhuman species, but also any moralistic approach, any sense of obligation, any guilt, any patronizing altruism which he found in so many affluent, Western environmentalists. All forms of life are part of one family, all cousins. He found support for this in some non-Western traditions, particularly his understanding of the epics of ancient Hinduism.

This attempt to escape anthropocentrism soon became a test for deep ecology. Some critics accepted the same standard, yet argued that Naess had not achieved it, that his emphasis upon self-fulfillment was insufficiently emancipated from a selfish human bias. But it is far from clear what a deanthropocentrism ethic means, or whether it even makes sense to try to divest an ethic of a human perspective. After all, Naess was trying to persuade humans, not dogs or horses, to buy into a new ethic. Any ethic is a distinctively human creation, for the commitment to such an ethic requires a symbolic language and reflective self-consciousness, or traits that seem absent in all other species. At least at the level of discourse, humans cannot escape their humanity. Equally problematic is the suggestion that humans can somehow choose to expand their identity to encompass all life. Maybe a few humans really do so identify, but it seems inconceivable that such is a product of choice. Like the Christian doctrine of faith, involving as it does the deepest levels of belief and preference and trust, such an all-embracing sense of self, of solidarity with all life, would seem to be, like a complete love of a god, a matter of grace, a gift for which one could be thankful, but not an achievement for which one could take any credit. If this is true, then one might, like Naess, find such a love to be desirable. It might solve many environmental problems. But an intellectual respect for such an expanded selfhood is not the same as being such a person, and like sainthood, one suspects that few ever are blessed with such a gift.[5]

Equally difficult to grasp is what not only Naess but environmentalists of many schools so often affirm—the inherent value of nonhuman forms of life, or the "rights" that attach to such inherent value. It is easy to talk of the right of birds or bees or even roaches to live and thrive. But what does "inherent value" and "rights" mean? The word value is rich, with many different meanings. Clearly, dogs and humans enjoy certain experiences, such as eating. One could talk of food as having intrinsic value for each, for it brings a pleasant experience. But such value in the having is not, in itself, ethical, for it involves no ends embraced, no judgments of worth. Humans can self-consciously stand apart from eating and ask questions about long-term consequences, or about harmful effects on other people. In some cases they would give up on the pleasant experience in behalf of more important experiences, such as living a longer life, or gaining harmony with one's neighbors, or enjoying a sense of moral complacency, of having so acted as to fulfill one's sense of beauty or of justice. Most often, in moral discourse, the word "value" refers to the goal of conduct that one has established through moral evaluations. These, we say, are our values, ones that we commit to and, at times, even fight for. When Naess talks of the inherent value of nonhuman species, he seems to be arguing that humans will, as a product not just of sentiment but of moral criticism, come to value such lives and thus try to protect them. But he means a bit more than just this, for in his system of ethics humans will come to value such lives not because of what they contribute to human welfare or happiness, not for the instrumental values he finds among "shallow" ecologists, but because they are part and parcel of ourselves, extensions of our identity, tied to our own highest level of fulfillment. In a Kantian sense, to not work in behalf of the welfare of our extended self would be inconsistent, as inconsistent as making it a rule that all animals, including human animals, can kill each other at will.

This leads to a cockroach's right to live. Roaches have no legal standing. But Naess suggests that they should have a moral standing. This is not far from a position espoused by William James. Right, in this case, means that a roach, if it were self-conscious, could ask a potential human exterminator what moral justification they could offer for causing it pain and then taking its life. How justify its suffering? If no credible justification can be offered, then the roach can argue that it has a right, meaning a moral claim, to continued life, and that it would be a wrong to kill it. A right is the opposite of a wrong. If one followed Naess, this does not mean that, in all cases, humans would desist from killing roaches. His qualification—vital human needs—might come into play. The roach might spread a deadly disease, as in the past did rats and fleas, and in this case humans might kill roaches in good conscience, despite the possibility that roaches play a critical role in an ecological community. But they would have to place any such killing in a moral context, and thus offer a moral justification, and for Naess a justification that reached beyond isolated human needs. Acquired habits, or acquired taste (a repugnance at the looks of a fat roach), would not suffice.

ECOFEMINISM

A year after Naess first identified deep ecology, Francoise d'Eaubonne, in France, referred to *ecofeminisme*, and thus tried to tie a form of radical feminism to an ecological revolution. Her label caught on among a number of feminists. In most cases, they would agree with the philosophical position affirmed by Naess, although with an insistence that he too often ignored the domination of men, not just over the natural environment, but over women as well. The term ecofeminism identifies a somewhat diverse group of women who have embraced a radical form of environmentalism. They have not tried to develop one formal philosophical position, such as that of Naess, and have different philosophical, and often also religious, justifications for their positions. But at one level, their critique joins that of Naess. They condemn liberal or even socialist feminists as shallow, for in each case they want to reform the present system, to attain equality within it for women, but do not embrace a shared commonality with the nonhuman world. Ecofeminists want a deep or radical feminism that wholeheartedly rejects most contemporary institutions. Thus, they look for a full cultural shift, a transformation of values, that matches that of Naess.

One very common theme among avowed ecofeminists is the linkage, in the present Western and capitalistic culture, between the male domination of the nonhuman world and of women. They suggest that male deep ecologists cannot fully develop their understanding without some recognition and acknowledgment of this long-standing relationship. Feminists, with their own twist, emphasize a perspective that is common among radical environmentalists—that at least males in the West have long viewed nature, whatever one means by that loaded word, as something not only radically different from what is human, but often also as something that stands in opposition to human aspirations. It is wild, dangerous, threatening. Nature, as otherness, has to be challenged, subdued, transformed. And much, they believe, in the Semitic religious tradition has supported the view that men have divine permission to dominate the natural world and to use it for human ends.

If ecofeminists have any distinctive environmental outlook, it involves their belief that male oppressors have often linked women to nature as obstacle, foil, or threat. The oppressors believe that women, who bear and nurture children, are less rational than men, are more passionate and emotional, closer to animality. Unlike liberal feminists, who ecofeminists caricature as committed to equality in a male-dominated world, of becoming more like men, ecofeminists accept and celebrate feminine differences, just as they emphasize and celebrate differences among humans and other species. Indeed, in their view, women are closer to the natural world, more easily empathize with other species, are more soft and nurturing, or the very traits that makes them more open to deep ecology. If the world is to avoid an ecological apocalypse, the values of feminism have to prevail.

Much more than the male advocates of deep ecology, ecofeminists have emphasized what many refer to as "spirituality," another loaded word. Thus, some feminists have tried to reinterpret Christian mythology, and displace its historic hierarchical and alleged antinature biases. Others have identified with nature-oriented or animistic religions, and have provided the most critical membership of neopagan sects or modern witchcraft movements. They have also bought into postmodern assaults on types of linear rationality, and fear an overly scientific mindset, which has abetted a male assault upon the natural environment and also supported types of militarism. They believe that only when men recognize and affirm the feminine elements in their own personalities, and allow such insights to neutralize their present "war against nature," will it be possible for women to end their present feminist crusade and simply merge into a larger and holistic ecological movement.

Many ecofeminists, as well as most other radical environmentalists, believe that the modern assault on the natural environment has roots in the Semitic religions, and particularly in Christianity. Some refer back to a now famous or infamous essay written in 1967 by historian Lynn White Jr., "The Historical Roots of Our Ecological Crisis." What the essay lacked in the way of a nuanced understanding of the varied and complex Semitic religions, it made up for in provocative assertions, few of which have stood up to later criticism. One issue is reasonably clear: it would be in Western, Christian societies that the greatest innovations in science and technology would occur, which in turn supported the type of economic growth that would transform patterns of production and consumption in western Europe and later in North America. What is not so clear is whether rapid economic growth, market-based economies, high levels of consumption, colonial imperialism, and deepening environmental problems all derive, directly or indirectly, either from the ancient Hebrew scriptures, as White suggested, or from various versions of a monotheistic and patriarchal god. White and others even referred to the two creation stories in the book of Genesis in the Jewish scriptures as foundations for a deeply rooted belief that the natural world was inferior to the human, that humans had power over it, and that it was a human obligation to reproduce and subdue the earth. Actually, one can find in the rich and diverse Jewish and Christian scriptures some support for almost any conceivable view of the natural world. And as White acknowledged in the case of St. Francis, one can find Christian examples of environmental awareness, just as many present Christians have embraced various forms of environmentalism.

This critique of Christianity or of monotheism has joined another argument by White and others. In fact, it is a view that pervades much environmental writing from all sides. This is the assertion that pre-Christian and non-Christian peoples had a much more profound appreciation of nature, here meaning the nonhuman world, than did Christians. Because they often held aspects of nature sacred, they were therefore more respectful of the environment. This myth, for in large part it is a myth, has taken the particular form in America of environmentalists seeking in the culture of Native Americans a type of ecological wisdom that they want to emulate. Such was the cultural diversity of Native Americans, and such was their varied and often reckless treatment of their own environment, that these celebrations of more primitive societies amount to little more than a foil for chanting the inanities of the present. Serious scholars, in what is now a vast and growing literature, have undermined any idealization, on ecological grounds, of primitive peoples or pre-Semitic or Eastern religions. But, clearly, one group of passionate environmentalists, the bioregionalists, still buy into this myth.[6]

BIOREGIONALISM AND SOCIAL ECOLOGY

Bioregionalism, or closely related, social ecology, are the somewhat loose names for the more practical, social, or political expressions of deep ecology. Advocates of bioregionalism offer not only a detailed critique of a present world order headed toward an environmental catastrophe, but also try to fill in the contours of a new social order. Here is where their writing is most appealing, for involved in their idealization of small, communal, cooperative social units, tied to a distinctive place with a distinctive flora and fauna, and with no centralized government or hierarchal social organization, is a utopian vision. But since they are weakest in clarifying how present humanity can move to such a new order, or more accurately move back to an earlier and simpler way of life, what they advocate in almost all respects fits the root meaning of "utopia," which is "no place." For example, in none of even the most moderate celebrations of bioregions do I find any realistic explanation of how small, largely self-sufficient, and environmentally benign communities can even begin to sustain a world with 6.5 billion people. Some of the most radical bioregionalists, who want to move back to a hunting and gathering economy, or at least to small agricultural units, envision an ideal world, one indeed friendly to other species, which would, by any fair estimate, support no more than 100 million people worldwide, or one-sixtieth of the present and still growing total. How to get rid of all the others, and who will choose the survivors?

It might make more sense to view bioregionalism as a program for the post-apocalyptic earth, or a type of envisioned new heaven. This is not the view of bioregionalists, for most believe it is not too late to change, to adopt new beliefs, values, and ways of living that can assure a sustainable and fulfilling life. Even if this is not possible, even if it is too late to forestall a coming catastrophe, it is still worthwhile to find out where and how humanity went wrong, and to try to clarify how small, remnant groups—after widespread famine, disease epidemics, and warfare destroy most of the present world population—can begin over again and, as a ravaged earth slowly regains its balance, do it better next time. The new beginning would follow various environmental catastrophes, such as enough global warming to destroy most ocean vegetation and lead to depleted oxygen in the atmosphere, or such resource scarcities as to bring most present production to a halt and to leave a few elites struggling to retain their power against hungry multitudes, or after nuclear war, or after enough pollution of soil, air, and water as to kill off much of the population by cancer and respiratory diseases.

One answer as to when humans first began their rebellion against nature, and their alienation from the source of their being, is when they first embraced what most people have called civilization. The late Paul Shepard, for example, idealized hunting and gathering societies, and believed the domestication of animals and crop agriculture began the human assault on what had been stable and harmonious ecosystems. Farmers cleared the forests for their crops, while sheep and goats denuded grasslands. It was nomadic herdsmen who moved from pantheistic and animistic religions to a monarch-like god who was apart from nature, to centralized political systems, and to expansion and conquest backed up by military forces. Ahead, in such violent cultures, were large cities, class systems, mobile populations, parasitic ruling classes, and eventually centralized manufacturing and distant trade. Ahead were economic systems that depended upon continuous growth in production and consumption, on labor as a commodity, on nature as a resource for human satisfaction, and on value systems tied not to the quality of life in a wilderness home, but to more and more consumption. Almost no one, except Shepard, literally envisioned a return to hunting and gathering, although many wanted a regained appreciation of the values held by such primitive people, a few of whom remain in small enclaves on the present earth.

Bioregionalism combines elements of past communal and even anarchist thought with the concerns of deep ecologists. It has many anticipations and roots. Among them are the celebration of primitive life by Rousseau, the suspicions of both modern agriculture and industrialism by Thoreau, the antipathy to modern industrialism and support of self-sufficient villages by Gandhi, the cooperative anarchy embraced by

Kropotkin, nineteenth-century communalism or utopian socialism, and the regionalism celebrated by southern agrarians in the 1930s. One often overlooked supporter was the nineteenth-century American economist Henry C. Carey, who in his last years emphasized the necessary recycling of all waste products (what he called manure), and the dangers of large cities and distant commerce, which led to the loss of earth's fertility. He idealized the New England village, and local commerce among people who mixed intensive agriculture and small manufacturing.

What was new was the focused emphasis upon environmental issues, and on a sustainable economic regime. The word "bioregional" is a variant of ecoregion or ecosystem. Bioregionalists want to organize society around distinctive geographical areas, those with commonalities in flora and fauna, in climate, and in topography. They have had great difficulty in finding criteria for locating and delimiting such biologically distinct regions. About the only clearly bounded such region is an isolated island in the middle of an ocean, or possibly a valley fully surrounded by high mountains, if there are any such places. Elsewhere, the exact boundaries of a distinct region are never very clear. Definitions can involve certain mixes of plants and animals, or how the proportions make up a distinctive cluster. They can involve topographical features, such as a watershed or a valley or plateau. In any case, the effort to identify regions is an old one, and regional theories have been very important in the twentieth century. But most earlier definitions of regions had as much a cultural content as a biological one. The word "ecology," now overused and far from clear, originated as a way of identifying a field in biology, one in which scientists tried to understand species as participants in larger groups or wholes, and thus mutual interdependencies. Today, as part of wildlife management, government agencies often try to identify bioregions and to adapt policies not to this or that species but to a web of life that, at times, has rather clear boundaries. But, notably, the concerns of regulators help determine what constitutes a region.

Today, biologists have developed a rough nomenclature for classifying different environments, with plant life often the major key. The largest class is often called a biome. This includes such areas as tropical rain forests, deserts, temperate broadleaf forests, grasslands, tundra, and mixed mountain systems. Within each of these one can at least loosely identify bioregions or ecosystems, such as the upper Great Plains, or the southern Appalachians, or the valley of California. At a bit more local level, some try to identify ecocommunities. But it is simply impossible to find any precise biological criteria (rather than political criteria) for dividing up the continents. Notably, in the United States, the EPA has identified, on maps, seventy-six ecosystems, the Nature Conservancy, sixty-three, and a prominent scientist, only forty-seven. At the level of ecological communities, the number for the United States ranges as high as one thousand, and within these some further identify vegetative associations, including those that contain very localized and endemic species.

Bioregionalists acknowledge the problem of boundaries, in some cases try to formulate working criteria, but usually finesse the issue. Locally, people often have a rather clear sense of a distinctive identity, and need not worry about boundary issues. In this perspective, the definition is clearly as much a matter of self-conception, of cultural commonalities, as geography or biology. This is reinforced by the recommendation of the leading popularizer of bioregionalism, Kirkpatrick Sale, that when a bioregion becomes too large and impersonal, it separate into two regions, with somewhat finer geographical bases of identity.

What is central to bioregionalists is that the only way that humans can gain a fulfilling life is to be part of a local place, remain in it, come to know and value its landscapes and wildlife. They need to be safe from the dictates of distant, centralized governments and corporations. In such a region, people can work and produce and exchange goods without becoming a part of large, impersonal markets, and use barter or local forms of script as a medium of exchange. If a bioregion contains cities, then the food and raw materials needed by urban populations should largely come from the immediate area, and city people should come to know and appreciate the regional support system upon which they depend. The quality of life, not the goods consumed, becomes all important. Stability, not an endless pursuit of growth, becomes the norm. But above all, in such a regional context, people can stop the draw down of unrenewable resources, recycle almost all waste, maintain renewable resources, such as soils, trees, or water, and sustain all species of life. As Naess argued, in this context they can identify with all aspects of an environment, and thus join a personal ethic with an environmental one, all as a natural aspect of everyday life. Such people, without any class system, without economic greed, can govern themselves, largely by informal participation.

Normally, such bioregions will be made up of loosely allied local villages or urban neighborhoods, live peacefully with neighboring bioregions, and possibly carry on some commerce with them. In an ideal world, one made up of such bioregions, there would be no room for national politics and international diplomacy, and at least far fewer occasions for internal conflict and aggression, although bioregionalists are not so irenic as to deny the possibility of conflict and the need for local modes of coping with it. Bioregionalists do not emphasize cultural uniformity as a prerequisite of a bioregional society. In fact, they stress the need for diversity, not only in flora and fauna, but in human backgrounds and skills. What they deplore is hierarchal relationships.

The bioregionalist dream, even though in some sense pastoral and reactive, is about as radical as any program one could envision. For this reason, the problem is how to move from a present social order to a new, simpler, and very different one, involving tremendous shifts in both values and behavior. Present societies have developed their institutions, and their belief systems, over centuries. These are always complex, with many interactions not fully understood until someone tries to change them. As the Intergovernmental Panel on Climate Change has pointed out in seeking ways to reduce greenhouse gas emissions, so much of our present social order is all but locked into place. The best example of this is the automobile, now ubiquitous in all affluent economies and eagerly desired in underdeveloped ones. Not only is it built into people's conception of a good life, it is so involved with modern economies that it is difficult to conceive of any rapid transition to a different transportation regime without extreme dislocations, rampant unemployment, and intense human suffering. We can dream of a better system, but in the near future, if we are to prevent global warming, we have to find ways of making automobiles more environmental friendly, not abolishing them. To think otherwise is to flirt with hopeless illusions.

The other problem that faces bioregionalists is a demographic one. It is true that the 20 percent of people who live in affluent societies could live well with less than half their present consumption of goods and services. If they could find a way to engineer a transition to such a society without unbearable penalties to a part of the population (that is the rub), they could dramatically reduce the draw down of nonrenewable resources and the present flood of waste and pollution. But such an option, unrealistic as it may be, is not open to the 80 percent of people who consume less than a tenth as much as those in highly developed societies. At present, for example, much of the world's population would die of starvation without the continuation of a mechanized and chemically buttressed form of agriculture. With present demographic trends, most of the world's people will either have to import food from countries with such a developed agriculture, or else move to the same type of agriculture themselves. In short, no bioregionalist strategy can fit a world of 6.5 billion people.

Such utopian visions do not mean that bioregionalists do not try to relate their ideals to present realities. When they do so, they have to suggest resistance to the present system, or an environmental activism not all that different from reform environmentalists, but with it a continued effort to persuade others to buy into the bioregional dream. Like Christians who dream of a future heaven, they enlist in the cause in the present and, despite all the frustrations, despite cultural trends that seem to all point in an opposite direction, nonetheless gain a sense of community, a quality of enhanced experience in the struggle, as do environmentalists of all persuasions. In fact, as the history of idealism, of utopian aspirations, reveals, the greatest heaven is in the process, not the ever postponed victory.[7]

GREENPEACE

In one sense, the most socially active environmentalists offer a significant challenge to the rest of society, not because of any theory, but because of what they do. Yet, one has to concede that environmental action makes up a continuum from the recycling of household wastes, to lobbying in behalf of new laws, to sabotaging logging equipment. Environmental protest may lead to nonviolent law breaking, or action that involves the destruction of property or the risk of bodily harm. The boundaries are not always sharp, as the following discussion will make clear. In a sense, nonviolent environmental protest, at least on a large scale, began in Canada in 1969 with what soon became Greenpeace. Sabotage began a decade later, with a loosely affiliated group of individuals who referred to themselves as Earth First!

In 1969, a group of Vancouver environmentalists, most members of a local chapter of the Sierra Club, formed a committee to oppose underground nuclear tests by the United States on Amchitka Island in the Aleutians. They reflected widespread concern about the effect of the tests, and widespread student protests, particularly on the West Coast of Canada and the United States. In 1970 and 1971, the growing Vancouver committee tried to raise needed support to send a ship into the closed zone around the tests, and thereby try to stop the testing. The effort gained widespread support and press exposure. In September 1971, the group finally was able to charter a fishing boat, rename it the *Greenpeace*, and sail for Amchitka. In some ways, the effort was a disaster. Bad seas delayed its arrival, the United States postponed the next test, and the crew, made up of volunteers, had to land on an island and were promptly arrested on a technicality. But the effort gained enormous support, particularly in Canada, including well wishes from Canadian prime minister Pierre Elliott Trudeau. In Vancouver, the organizing committee was able to charter a second ship (eventually called *Greenpeace II*), but because of winter weather it never came within seven hundred miles of what turned out to be the final test on Amchitka. No matter. The adverse publicity and worldwide protests helped persuade the United States to end these tests and convert the island into a bird sanctuary. By 1972 the Vancouver committee had incorporated as a new organization, the Greenpeace Foundation.

The foundation quickly grew into an international federation, with Greenpeace organizations in most industrialized countries. The fumbling protests in the Aleutians led to even better publicized, and politically much more influential, protests of French atmospheric nuclear tests (the last such anywhere) on Mururoa Atol in the Society Islands in the South Pacific. In 1973, a retired Vancouver businessman and famed athlete, David McTaggart, agreed to cross the Pacific in a thirty-eight-foot sailboat to try and block the tests. Again, this seemed a futile effort from the beginning. But the publicity for *Greenpeace III* soon had international implications. In July 1974 McTaggart and his crew made it to the restricted area (which largely involved international waters), but a French military ship rammed the small boat. It had to limp into a New Zealand port, its crew now heroes in both New Zealand and Australia. As always, the Greenpeace crew had filmed everything, and McTaggart later won damages from the French government. Even before he could repair his boat, several New Zealand ships sailed for the testing zone. The French boarded such boats and removed them from the area, save for one New Zealand military ship that invaded the area as a token protest and then left.

Greenpeace, by its effort, had helped trigger a worldwide protest of the French tests, and in the process tremendously increased its own prestige. In both New Zealand and Australia, conservative governments fell, in part because the opposition parties had backed the protests. In France, an anti-testing movement almost led to the overturn of the Gaullist government. But by the time of the final series of French atmospheric tests, only a repaired *Greenpeace III* was in the test zone. French commandos boarded the boat and severely beat the crew. However, the resulting film of what happened had its intended effect on world opinion. Another ship, named the *Greenpeace IV*, replaced *Greenpeace III* but arrived after the last test, for in 1974 France, badgered by worldwide condemnation, announced the end of atmospheric testing. It continued to test underground, though, and this led to a much more serious later confrontation with Greenpeace.

In 1985 the now much stronger Greenpeace, with branches in most countries, decided to send its largest ship, the *Rainbow Warrior*, to the restricted area around Morurua. This was part of an effort to halt a series of underground tests. The French government decided to revert to overt terrorist tactics to block the ship. While it was anchored in the harbor of Aukland, New Zealand, completing final protest plans, two French agents planted two time bombs under the ship's hull. The resulting explosions sank the ship, with one death among those on board. The French government at first denied any involvement, but New Zealand captured two of the French agents involved, and newspapers soon unearthed the true story. The French officials who ordered the attack admitted what had happened and resigned their ministries, but the French president, François Mittertand, and the prime minister denied earlier knowledge of the plan and survived the scandal. France, of course, offered its abject apologies to New Zealand, but it continued the underground tests. Greenpeace once again gained wonderful publicity, but in France public hostility soon forced it, temporarily, to close its Paris offices.

A decade before, by 1975, Greenpeace had perfected its form of nonviolent confrontation. It insisted that it would not do anything to endanger human lives and would not sabotage any property. But in its protests it clearly violated local laws or regulations that it considered unjust. It was fortunate in its early targets, and adept at gaining public attention. In 1975 it made whaling its target, and particularly the large Russian whaling fleets in the Pacific. It refurbished two earlier ships, renamed them the *Greenpeace V* and *VI*, and was able to intercede between whales and a Russian fleet, eventually forcing it to leave the area. At the time, whaling was a popular target in the West. Greenpeace later tried to do the same with Japanese fleets. In a small way, it helped gain a moratorium on whaling by the International Whaling Commission, a ban never fully enforced.

Its next target was perhaps even more popular. This was its effort, beginning in 1975, to stop the killing of harp seal pups, largely by Norwegians, off the coast of Labrador. These beautiful white pups were clubbed to death in order to harvest their valuable fur. By now, Greenpeace had the funds to rent a helicopter to locate the harvest crews and land protesters nearby. In doing this, it violated new Canadian regulations. Greenpeace activists were not able to save many pups, but their filming of the bloody slaughter led to an international crusade, which eventually almost forced Canada to give protection to the seals. Ironically, the end of clubbing led to a rapid increase in harp seal populations and new environmental problems. Thus, under better regulations, the killings have resumed—and so have protests by environmentalists.

After 1975, Greenpeace subtly changed its tactics. It continued its nonviolent protests, as at Morurua in 1985, but more and more it sought political solutions to environmental problems, and in Canada was more successful in lobbying Canadian officials than in protecting seals on the ice. Today, Greenpeace, with over 2 million members worldwide, is perhaps best described as the most aggressive of the mainstream environmental organizations. Its membership often overlaps Green political parties. It is often first on the scene of environmental disasters, such as oil spills, and has continued to organize people most affected by air or water pollution, but to some radical activists it seems a rather mild organization.

Not so one still small splinter from Greenpeace. Paul Watson was very much involved in the harp seal campaign of Greenpeace. But he soon despaired of any success without a more violent form of activism and a more active defiance of laws. Off Labrador, he destroyed some clubs used on the baby seals. In 1977 the Greenpeace Foundation expelled Watson, in what became a nasty dispute. He soon outfitted his own ship, the *Sea Shepherd*, and created a tiny organization named after it. He used this small ship for violent forms of protest. It sank two unoccupied whaling ships in Iceland, and rammed, and badly damaged, two Japanese drift net fishing ships in the Pacific. In all such cases, Watson argued that his small society had not violated any laws, but had enforced international maritime conventions when the signatory nations would not do so. By carefully selecting his targets, he was able to avoid arrest because of the elements of guilt, and unwanted publicity, on the part of his targets. But in a sense it was Watson who initiated environmental campaigns based on sabotage. His society is still active in 2006.[8]

EARTH FIRST!

Earth First! is an even more radical, land-based association. It began in 1979 among a group of wilderness advocates, including members of the Wilderness Society. Its leader was Dave Foreman, who would later serve jail time for a conspiracy to sabotage nuclear plants. A small group of deeply committed environmentalists decided to form an action group or circle, but not to create a formal or chartered organization. Its first national gathering, in 1981, was at the much-hated Glen Canyon Dam. Technically, Earth First! has no members and no officers. This deliberate choice of a nonorganization eliminated any target for law-enforcement agencies. All action taken by those who identify with Earth First! is in their individual capacity. Thus, some who support the association do not participate in law-breaking activities. A 1976 novel by Edward Abbey, The Monkey Wrench Gang, inspired the formation of Earth First! and provided a guidebook for some of its tactics. Abbey was a philosophical anarchist, and a fervent defender of wilderness. In his novel, a group of eco-guerrillas destroy heavy road-building machinery at Comb Wash, somewhere in Utah.[9]

Earth First! resembles the civil rights and New Left movements of the 1960s. Its leaders, and its The Earth First! Journal, advocate deep ecology, appeal to eco-feminists, and laud bioregionalism. Its first love was wilderness, old-growth forests, and biodiversity, but it has fought against dams, nuclear plants, and road-building. Most of its activism has been in the American West, with its greatest strength in the Pacific Coast states. Although it has lobbied for legislation, its distinctive method has been civil disobedience, often leading to mass arrests. Like so many of the activists of the 1960s, it has a counter-cultural component. It holds a national gathering each year, at different sites, the Round River Rendezvous. There, serious environmental plotting is joined with a festive-like atmosphere, including protest poems and songs and guerrilla theater.

For many in Earth First!, the limits of protest involve civil disobedience, with no threat to lives or property. Earth First! gained its first national publicity by a series of protests and interventions in behalf of old-growth forests in Oregon and California. This involved blockades of bridges to stop timber trucks, human screens around threatened trees, chaining protestors to trees, or tree sitting in platforms built high up in the branches. Such tactics, as often intended, led to massive arrests, overcrowded local jails, and embarrassed local officials, plus what Earth First! believed to be wonderful national publicity for its cause. On some issues, such as protecting old-growth redwoods in northern California, it won numerous allies and had some success in gaining protective legislation. But, as a whole, Earth First! members do not trust government agencies, and have had endless battles with the National Forest Service.

But what has most distinguished Earth First! is its support of sabotage or what, following Abbey's novel, is most often referred to as monkeywrenching. The most active spokespersons for Earth First!, including Foreman, have been deliberately equivocal about sabotage. Insofar as the association has an official policy, it is that it neither condones nor condemns monkeywrenching. Yet, Foreman wrote essays to define and defend it. The journal carries regular columns on ecotage. It also publishes a field guide on monkeywrenching. Foreman has emphasized that the object is machinery, not people. One tactic—driving spikes in trees to damage chainsaws—has caused some divisions among local groups, because it could cause a chain to break and hurt a worker. But logging equipment and trucks are fair game. Foreman and his disciples believe it is appropriate to attach high cables to trees to prevent cutting. Or to play dirty tricks on corporate officials or compliant government officials, such as throwing manure into air conditioner ducts. The justification offered for such tactics is that wilderness needs help in defending itself, and that those who destroy the wilderness are the true criminals.

Earth First! is not alone. Several smaller, less publicized action groups have resorted to violence in the United States. Others have been active in European countries, where Green political parties have been much more effective than in the United States. But, overall, the heyday of such violent activism seems to be largely in the past. Such activists have been effective in one sense—they have focused broad attention on environmental issues. But their reputation for violence and absolutist policies embarrassed the broader environmental movement and provided cover for politicians who effectively blocked new environmental legislation.

A Personal Afterword

As I wrote this book, over the past six years, I at times felt a sense of hopelessness. I see no good answers to so many problems, beginning with the effects of population growth. What policies can rescue sub-Saharan Africa from an impending environmental disaster? How can India gain the resources to feed a population that could soar to over 1.5 billion before 2050? How can the five most populous nations of Asia (China, India, Indonesia, Pakistan, and Bangladesh), with 2.83 billion people, or 45 percent of the world's total, deal with scarcities of water and energy or mitigate the air pollution that is choking almost all of South and East Asia? I do not know. I suspect no one does.

At present, the gap between the few highly developed and affluent countries (15 percent of the population) and the rest of the world is widening, not narrowing, although the rapid growth in China, if it continues, may soon help close the gap. The gap is twofold—demographic and economic. Almost all the population growth is in the underdeveloped world. Only the wealthy countries have been able to deal effectively with a range of environmental problems. And even the wealthy countries, so far, have failed to make the needed commitments to mitigate what might be the most threatening environmental problem of all—global warming. The high-consuming countries have done the most to stimulate the warming, but it will be the poorer countries that will suffer the most from its effects. It is the wealthy countries that have largely consumed the most easily accessible fossil fuels, including up to half of the accessible petroleum, but it is the developing countries that have the greatest need for inexpensive energy and who will suffer the most from its increased cost.

My failure to anticipate answers to all the looming environmental problems does not mean that humans will not find such answers. I cannot imagine what they will be, but who in 1901 could have anticipated half the innovations that would take place in the next one hundred years? One can only assume that the pace of change, at least in the development of new tools, will continue to accelerate. Great innovations in medicine will extend the span of human life (which might or might not be a blessing). Genetic engineering may double crop yields. Fusion energy may replace ever more scarce fossil fuels. Greenhouse emissions may decline, meaning that near the end of this century the pace of warming will begin to slow. And maybe, just maybe, population growth may climax around 2050, even though present projections suggest otherwise. Maybe, but maybe not. I could paint an even more dramatically dark scenario.

I believe there are major reasons why this century may be one of the most turbulent, and challenging, of any in the last millennium. Human civilizations go back only about six or seven millennia. The great period of growth in human populations and consumption goes back only two centuries. In these two centuries, humans have gained an enormous power to shape the physical world to suit their goals. Never has one species so dominated the earth. What necessary conditions supported this dominance? In one sense, the nature of the earth itself, its temperature range, its oceans and fresh water, its unique atmosphere, all are necessary conditions, but I take those as givens and unlikely to disappear in the future (even when much of the air and water may become more severely polluted).

Also necessary, but likewise a given, is the special nature of humans. We are the only animal that gradually learned to talk and to conceptualize. The key was a symbolic language, and the use of sounds (words) as symbols of not only objects but of relationships. This meant a new form of self-consciousness, a much more nuanced ability to coordinate activities or to create new and better tools, the ability to retain and utilize cumulative memories of events in the distant past, and to project goals far into the future. Above all, language gave humans the power to make enormous changes in the world around them, and thus to adapt to rapidly changing environments. They have adapted with unbelievable success and, at times intentionally, at others unintentionally, have changed the earth more than all other species combined.

What I want to stress are five less secure conditions that I think have been vital. The first and most often overlooked condition has been the unusually stable interglacial climate of the last ten millennia. Only in the last twenty years has research revealed how rare is such a period of climate stability in our age of periodic glaciers. A second necessary condition is the huge storehouse of nutrients that have accumulated in the earth's soils (the great soil bank) and the knowledge and tools and energy that have allowed humans to exploit that soil in the production of food. The third necessary condition is the great energy storage bank—the easily available fossil fuels that have accumulated over the last 500 million years. The fourth condition has been the enormous expansion of human knowledge about all aspects of the physical universe, and the new tools that humans have developed to make use of this scientific revolution. A final necessary condition has been the advance in medical knowledge and in public health management. Of these five conditions, the first three are now less secure than ever before, and a continued enjoyment of the fruits of the last two are dependent upon a social and political order that might not survive severe environmental disruptions.

For at least the last five thousand years, and for the most part the last ten thousand years, the mean climate for the earth as a whole has remained close to 13.8°C (or almost 57°F). Deviations have remained within 1°C above or below this mean, at least until very recently (in 1998 and again in 2005, the hottest years on record, the global temperature soared to over 14.5°C). Even relatively minor shifts have had enormous significance regionally. Shifts in rainfall patterns undermined ancient civilizations. But overall the climate remained close to the mean, while the volume of ocean water has remained near constant for five thousand years (local sea level shifts have been much more dramatic, but these have resulted from tectonic uplift, subsidence, or a spring back of land formerly depressed under the Wisconsin glacier).

This stability may be almost over, as the earlier chapters on rapid climate change and global warming have demonstrated. So far, the average warming has remained below 1°C, or no more than the shift toward a colder climate in the little ice age from the fourteenth to the nineteenth century. But increasingly plausible temperature predictions for this century will entail a break from that small degree of variation, with a warming possibly as high as 3°C. An increase of the present global mean temperature to at least 16°C (or 60°F) is almost assured. Since the warming will be, as at present, more concentrated in higher northern latitudes, the changes could mean rapid and drastic ecological shifts and

massive extinctions. Human adaptations will have to exceed those for
any climate-related changes within historical memory. And because of
the earth's population, such changes will not be easy. For example, massive migrations from areas denuded by decreased rainfall, or cursed with
unprecedented floods, will be almost impossible. And, always lurking as
a dark shadow is the possibility that the degree of warming will cross
major thresholds, particularly involving ocean currents, and thus lead to
rapid climate change in a few years or a few decades.

The earth's great soil bank is now much depleted of its natural nutrients. This is true almost everywhere, particularly in the most productive
agricultural areas. In much of the underdeveloped world, the loss has resulted from erosion and overcropping. Here the soils are often degraded.
In rich agricultural areas, the natural nutrients have been used up, but
replaced annually by chemical fertilizers. No longer do farmers have to
await the recovery of nutrients through natural processes, such as vulcanism, rock weathering, and organic decay. The phosphorus and potash
come from finite deposits, most nitrogen from the air, at the cost of enormous amounts of energy. I am not suggesting that this artificial supply
will soon expire, or that agriculture will have to go through any drastic
changes in this century. It is even possible that genetic modifications will
allow a new surge in productivity. Nor am I suggesting that the earth will
not be able to grow the needed foods for even a much expanded global
population. But across much of the earth, particularly in areas of continued rapid population growth, as in Africa, India, and most Islamic countries, residents will not be able to develop new soils, find enough water
for increased irrigation, or have the money to buy needed fertilizers. This
means increased hunger (as is almost annually the case now in central or
eastern Africa) or massive imports of food or food aid from developed
countries, and in either case increased political discontent.

Few people appreciate how much inexpensive fossil fuels have un-
derwritten modern economic growth and high living standards in the
developed world. Before 1800, biomass provided most hydrocarbons
consumed by humans. This gradually changed with the perfection of
the steam engine, with coal becoming the most used fuel in industrial-
izing countries in the nineteenth century in both manufacturing and
in railroads and shipping. Petroleum became the dominant fossil fuel
in the twentieth century. Oil-fueled engines (gasoline and diesel) not
only transformed the transportation sector (railroads, ships, airplanes,

automobiles, and trucks), but made possible, along with chemicals and genetic research, the agricultural revolution that today enables farmers to feed a population of over 6 billion. Up to 77 percent of productive energy is now based on fossil fuels. Before this century is over, that percentage will almost have to decrease, with petroleum the first to face scarcities because of shrinking reserves. No greater challenge faces humans today than finding ways to make the transition to other sources of energy. At present, no easy choices are available. That is, inexpensive alternative energy sources in the amount needed to maintain the growing number of humans on earth, even at present living standards, are still to be discovered or perfected.

If humans, in this century, are to move closer to sustainable economies (we are far from that today), then two very difficult changes have to occur. I doubt they will occur voluntarily and preemptively. First, the countries with per capita PPP incomes under $5,000 (one-eighth that of the United States) need to raise their level of consumption and do this without what could quickly become growth-limiting environmental destruction. China is the best example of a country that has just now reached such a level of income, but by means that are far from sustainable. China has one leg up on most underdeveloped countries. It has almost attained a stable population. It will be almost impossible for other underdeveloped countries to match the recent achievement of China with a continuation of present birthrates. Or, as in some parts of central Africa, if the population growth ends because of AIDS-induced higher mortality rates, then disease will make higher living standards impossible.

The other change involves the developed countries, and particularly those with PPP incomes above $15,000. They have made the greatest assault on resources, particularly energy supplies and soil fertility. Not only have they cleared the greatest expanses of the earth's former forests, but they now supply most of the market for lumber from the deforestation of tropical rain forests in poor countries. They face no population problem. They have had the means to alleviate the worst environmental problems in their own countries, but they continue to consume up to fifteen times as much energy as the poorest countries and to emit up to two-thirds of all greenhouse gases. They produced most of the halocarbons that threaten the ozone layer. For these countries, the difficult transition will involve major changes in the type and amount of consumption. Without this transition, anything close to a sustainable world economy will be impossible, even if such wealthy countries are able to keep their present pattern of rising consumption, or what they call growth, going for the rest of this century. I doubt that they can even do it for that long.

I think the American economy illustrates this problem. If actively stimulated by effective advertising, it seems that humans have an almost limitless desire for goods and services. What Americans consume would have astounded, and probably horrified, an American of only a hundred years ago. Economists have always assumed that the demand for some types of consumption were inelastic. Food, for example, should reach a point of satiation, beyond which a person would not purchase more of a perishable product. Even this does not seem to be true in America, where obesity has become a major health hazard. It would seem to be good public policy to persuade Americans to eat less. In the same sense, based on worldwide realities, it would seem highly desirable that Americans consume less energy, emit less CO_2, and accumulate less waste.

But how to move from a growth-oriented economy, one that depends on consumer confidence and consumer purchases to keep it all going? How can a country move to a no-growth economy, let alone to an economy with less consumption? One definition of such a move is "recession." One product is fewer jobs, lower profits, less incentives for investment. Individuals who resist the lure of luxury consumption, who adopt a simple life, who have few wants, are often deemed traitors to our system, even though they may be happier than those in the middle of the rat race. What if everyone took a vow to live simply, in small homes, using only public transportation, preparing all food at home, eschewing all red meats, using no cosmetics or beauty aids, buying no jewelry, and ignoring all the silly changes in fashion? Our present economy would collapse. In our system, one requirement of citizenship is to buy all you can afford, or at times more than one can safely afford. Here is the engine of progress.

Or so it seems. Is there any way to reverse the pattern? Can Americans gradually reduce the level of consumption, at least of material goods if not human services? Can they use less resources? I do not know. So much of our present way of life is deeply embodied in learned habits, so integral to our whole culture, so essential to a free-market economy, that it would take a major shift in beliefs and values, a major shift in our economic institutions, to move to a no-growth society. If the total product goes down, then major problems of equity become inescapable.

For any economic justice, even for humane reasons, a smaller economic pie will have to be more equally distributed, or else already low-income Americans will bear the brunt of the shift to less consumption. Also, less American production could have disastrous effects on foreign populations, including those dependent on our surplus food. And with the present economic productivity, based on efficient tools, well-trained workers, and the controlled burning of fossil fuels, any slowing of growth, let alone negative growth, could lead to massive unemployment or underemployment.

American agriculture illustrates the problem. More than any other sector, it has accounted for the economic growth Americans have experienced since World War II. In no other sector has productivity per worker risen so much, although a few manufacturing industries have come close. Less than a million very efficient farmers produce most of our food and a large surplus for export. It seems that the number of farms and full-time farmers could not go lower, but it continues to drop, although slowly. A formerly labor-intensive sector has become capital intensive. Could we go back? Could we really regain the traditional family farm? Could we do without the chemicals that sustain modern industrial agriculture—the pesticides and fertilizers? Not without a large increase in the cost of food (as illustrated by organically grown foods). It seems nothing less than a pipe dream to suggest that Americans go back to an agriculture with less machines, less use of fossil fuels, less chemicals, and more human muscle power.

Some of the same problems confront extractive industries and manufacturing. New tools (capital) fueled by hydrocarbons have created such productive efficiency that a vast majority of people in wealthy countries have to work in service industries. Modern economic growth has been, in effect, the shifting of productive work (the creation of physical consumer items) from human muscles to machines. No end seems in sight, for every year the number of laborers needed to extract minerals and fossil fuels, and to fabricate products, declines. But it is completely unrealistic to expect Americans to move back to local shops, except for a few handicraft products for a luxury market.

It is equally unrealistic to expect Americans to move, in great numbers, back to public transport, and thus to reduce the number of automobiles. So far, it has been impossible to get them to buy small, fuel-efficient motor vehicles. Americans now own over 220 million motor vehicles, or nearly two per family. The number keeps growing faster than the population. In its total effect on resource use, the automobile leads all other innovations. It marked the greatest change in how people live in the developed countries in the twentieth century. It has provided a type of mobility that almost no one would relinquish. One of the compelling desires of people in underdeveloped countries is the ability to own an automobile, and it seems likely that in this century the fastest growth in the number of motor vehicles will be in the developing world. But if anything is clear it is that the earth does not have the resources to permit all humans to enjoy the same number of automobiles as do present Americans.

Economically, the great gap in incomes between affluent and poor countries offers benefits as well as challenges to rich countries. Poor countries use fewer resources, emit fewer greenhouse gases, and out of desperate need almost have to export raw materials and fuels to industrialized countries. Look at oil. Most reserves are in Islamic countries of the Middle East. Such countries need to preserve this precious asset to meet their own future needs, or until it is so scarce that they can exchange it for much more goods than at present. But poor countries cannot afford this luxury, even as they cannot afford new environmental controls. None of the three largest oil-producing countries—Saudi Arabia, Kuwait, and Iraq—are self-sufficient in food production. They have to sell oil to survive. Their oil provides affluent countries with the energy needed to prolong or even further enhance their present living standards, and offers them more time to develop renewable alternatives to fossil fuels. For many environmental problems, such as global warming, air pollution, tropical deforestation, and species extinctions, nothing is more threatening than rapid growth in both population and incomes in Africa, Asia, and Latin America, and particularly in India and China.

Thus, the dilemma. The more the underdeveloped world becomes like us, the worse the prospects for a sustainable earth. It is the lack of rapid economic development in two-thirds of the world that prolongs the opportunity for wealthy countries to continue economic growth and also to mitigate local environmental problems. It is concurrent growth in all countries that will soon force humans to confront certain ultimate limits to the types of economic growth now so valued everywhere.

Here is the moral challenge. Part of humanity has moved in the last century far beyond the normal scarcity that all nonhuman species have always confronted—farther than anyone ever dreamed possible. Almost all humans have moved a bit away from the worst form of scarcity and bare subsistence incomes. But most humans still remain perilously close to such a level of scarcity. They always have. Behind the small gains for most and the immense gains of the few are the nonrenewable resources contributed by past life, whether soils enriched by decaying vegetation or the coal, oil, and natural gas that formed in swamps and bogs and lagoons. The more humans who live at a subsistence level, the more of these resources that are available to those with high levels of human and material capital. But can the affluent rest at ease and continue to enjoy high living standards with the knowledge that there are not nearly enough resources for all humans to join in the feast? And in such a world, how long will the affluent be safe at their banquet?

Notes

1. Our Green Planet

This chapter amounts to a synthesis of an enormous range of scientific disciplines. I have absorbed information from many sources, including even standard textbooks. But my emphasis upon the role of life in the evolution of the earth does reflect a rather recent emphasis among some scientists, and one that is still the occasion of much controversy. I offer a more detailed analysis of these issues in a discussion of James Lovelock's Gaia hypothesis in chapter 10. I will indicate below a few books that offer much more detailed information about our green earth.

1. Herbert Friedman, *Sun and Earth* (New York: Scientific American Library, 1986).

2. Two general introductions to plate tectonics are Jon Erickson, *Plate Tectonics: Unraveling the Mysteries of the Earth* (New York: Facts on File, 2001); Kent C. Condie, *Plate Tectonics and Crustal Evolution*, 4th ed. (Boston: Butterworth Henemann, 1997).

3. An introduction to our magnetic fields is Knoepfel Heinz, *Magnetic Fields: A Comprehensive Theoretical Treatise for Practical Use* (New York: Wiley, 2000).

4. The book that I found most helpful for this chapter is Tyler Volk, *Gaia's Body: Toward a Physiology of Earth* (New York: Springer-Verlag, 1998). This book comes closest to reflecting my emphasis upon the role of life in the earth's evolution, and in an engaging style introduces lay readers to all the chemical cycles that sustain life.

5. Volk's work is supplemented by David Schwartzman, *Life, Temperature, and the Earth* (New York: Columbia Univ. Press, 1999).

6. Volk, *Gaia's Body.*

7. Ibid.

2. Population, Consumption, and the Environment

The challenges enumerated in this chapter make up the issues addressed in much more detail in later chapters. The two exceptions are world populations and world incomes, which are a backdrop to all the issues. The literature on population growth is enormous, as is the often highly theoretical approach to demographic transitions.

1. The data for my brief introduction and analysis came from United Nations Population Division, *World Population Project: The 2002 Review and World Population Project*, February 22, 2004, and *World Population Prospects: The 2004 Revision*, September 19, 2005; Anup Shah, *Ecology and the Crisis of Overpopulation: Future Prospects for Global Sustainability* (Cheltenham, U.K.: Edward Elgar, 1998); K. Bruce Newbold, *Six Billion Plus: Population Issues in the Twenty-First Century* (New York: Rowman and Littlefield, 2002); and U.S. Census Bureau, *World Population Profile: 1998* (Washington, D.C.: Government Printing Office, 1999).

2. Most of the data on national incomes is from the last annually updated profile: *World Development Indicators, 2005*, database, World Bank, April 18, 2006, GNI per capita 2004, Atlas Method and PPP, on the Internet at siteresources .worldbank.org/DATASTATISTICS/Resources/GNIPC.PDF, downloaded on June 2, 2006. This data is generally followed, on a PPP basis, by Infoplease, *Economic Statistics by Country, 2004* (available on the Internet at www.infoplease.com/ipa/A0874911.html, downloaded on June 2, 2006). The particular plight of central African countries is addressed in George Benneh, William B. Morgan, and Juha L. Uitto, eds., *Sustaining the Future: Economic, Social, and Environmental Change in Sub-Saharan Africa* (Tokyo: United Nations Univ. Press, 1996).

3. For the best introduction to the system of national accounts developed by the United Nations Statistics Division, go to its website: http//www.unstats.un.org.

4. The privately developed Daly-Cobb Index of Sustainable Economic Welfare shows a steady decline in individual welfare in the United States after 1976: L. R. Brown, "State of the World 1991," in *Classics in Environmental Studies: An Overview of Classic Texts in Environmental Studies*, ed. Nico Nelissen, Jan Van Der Stratten, and Leon Klinkers (The Hague, Netherlands: International Books, 1997), 320–32.

5. In *The Wealth of Nature: How Mainstream Economics Has Failed the Environment* (New York: Columbia Univ. Press, 2003), Robert L. Nadeau has recommended a new ecologically oriented economic theory that would support a new system of national, and international, accounts.

6. Infoplease, *Economic Statistics by Country, 2004* (available on the Internet at www.infoplease.com/ipa/A0874911.html, downloaded on June 2, 2006).

7. For this chapter, as most others, I have been indebted to J. R. McNeill, *Something New Under the Sun: An Environmental History of the Twentieth-Century World* (New York: W. W. Norton, 2000), which not only includes a wide-ranging survey of the environmental changes that occurred in a century, but also an extensive and useful bibliography of most major environmental publications during that century.

3. Soil, Vegetation, and Food

1. The classification of soils is a highly technical enterprise. This is well illustrated in U.S. Department of Agriculture, Natural Resources Conservation Ser-

vice, *Soil Taxonomy: A Basic System of Soil Classification for Making and Interpreting Soil Surveys*, 2nd ed. (Washington, D.C.: Government Printing Office, 1999).

2. The shift in American agriculture after 1950 is clear in Gilbert C. Fite, *American Farmers: The New Minority* (Bloomington: Indiana Univ. Press, 1981).

3. The status of agriculture worldwide is updated every year in Food and Agriculture Organization of the United Nations, *Statistical Yearbook*, 2004 (Rome: Food and Agriculture Organization of the United Nations, 2005). This enormous body of data is available on the Internet at www.fao.org/yearbook. Also available on the Internet is *Diet, Nutrition, and the Prevention of Chronic Diseases*, Report of a Joint WHO/FAO Consultation (Geneva: World Health Organization, 2003), at www.who.int/hpr/NPH/docs/who_fao_expert_report.pdf.

4. The plight of so many tropical soils is demonstrated in Michael J. Eden and John T. Parry, eds., *Land Degradation in the Tropics* (London: Pinter, 1996).

5. *Diet, Nutrition, and the Prevention of Chronic Diseases*, Report of a Joint WHO/ FAO Consultation (Geneva: World Health Organization, 2003), at www.who .int/hpr/NPH/docs/who_fao_expert_report.pdf.

4. Water and Energy: Will There Be Enough?

1. The following three books offer an excellent introduction to the problem of water scarcity in the coming decades: I. A. Shiklomanov and John C. Rodda, *World Water Resources at the Beginning of the Twenty-First Century* (Cambridge, U.K.: Cambridge Univ. Press, 2003); Mark A. Rosegrant, Ximing Cai, and Sarah A. Cline, *World Water and Food to 2025: Dealing with Scarcity* (Washington, D.C.: International Food Policy Research Institute, 2002); and Alan Richards, *Coping with Water Scarcity: The Governance Challenge*, Policy Paper #54 (Berkeley, Calif.: Institute on Global Conflict and Cooperation, 2002).

2. Richards, *Coping with Water Scarcity*.

3. The following three sources offer a range of views about oil reserves, from the pessimistic to the more optimistic: Colin J. Campbell and Jean H. Laherrere, "The End of Cheap Oil," *Scientific American* 278 (March 1998): 78–83; International Energy Agency, *World Energy Outlook: Assessing Today's Supply to Fuel Tomorrow's Growth, 2001 Insights* (Paris: International Energy Agency, 2001); and U.S. Geological Survey, *World Petroleum Assessment, 2000* (Washington, D.C.: Government Printing Office, 2000). For a list of all renewable energy sources, and a rather optimistic assessment of their possibilities, see John J. Berger, "Renewable Energy Sources as a Response to Global Climate Concerns," in *Climate Change Policies: A Survey*, ed. Stephen H. Schneider, Armin Rosencranz, and John O. Niles (Washington, D.C.: Island Press, 2002), 3–51.

4. Campbell and Laherrere, "The End of Cheap Oil," 78–83.

5. Estimates of the earth's total supply of fossil fuels is in Chauncey Starr,

"Sustaining the Human Environment: The Next Two Hundred Years," in *Technological Trajectories and the Human Environment*, ed. Jesse H. Ausubel and H. Dale Langford (Washington, D.C.: National Academy Press, 1997), 193. A more hard-headed, economic view of energy issues is in Lawrence Gregory Hines, *The Market, Energy, and the Environment* (Boston: Allyn and Bacon, 1988).

5. Pollution, Waste, and the Ozone Layer

1. Marvin S. Soroos, *The Endangered Atmosphere: Preserving a Global Commons* (Columbia: Univ. of South Carolina Press, 1997). This book is clear and open to nonscientific readers. It also contains an excellent introduction to the problem of ozone thinning.

2. Mary K. Theodore and Louis Theodore, *Major Environmental Issues Facing the 21st Century* (Upper Saddle River, N.J.: Prentice Hall, 1997), offers a short introduction to all areas of pollution and efforts to control it. Also see Soroos, *The Endangered Atmosphere*.

3. Norman J. Vig and Michael E. Kraft, eds., *Environmental Policy in the 1990s— Reform or Reaction* (Washington, D.C.: CQ Press, 1997), introduces the political conflict that has marked most recent environmental regulation. Bruce Barcott, "Changing All the Rules," *New York Times Magazine*, April 4, 2004, 38–45, provides a detailed review of new EPA rules that allow utilities to evade one of the most stringent regulations in the Clean Air Act.

4. All of the major antipollution acts in effect in the United States are available on the Internet. The best starting point for the actual acts, or a range of information about them, is the EPA (www.epa.gov).

5. Andrew E. Dessler, *The Chemistry and Physics of Stratospheric Ozone* (San Diego: Academic Press, 2000), offers a recent and clear scientific background on the role of stratospheric ozone.

6. For almost anything one wants to know about the Montreal Protocol, one can do no better than to go to the website of the Ozone Secretariat of the United Nations Environmental Programme (www.unep.org/ozone).

6. The Extinction Crisis

1. Bruce A. Stein, Lynn S. Kutner, and Jonathan S. Adams, eds., *Precious Heritage: The Status of Biodiversity in the United States*, for the Nature Conservancy (New York: Oxford Univ. Press, 2000).

2. International efforts to preserve biodiversity are documented in International Union for Conservation of Nature and Natural Resources, *2006 IUCN Red List of Threatened Species*, redlist.org, downloaded June 7, 2006; United Nations Environmental Programme, *Global Environmental Outlook 3: Past, Present and Future Perspec-*

tives (London: Earthscan Publications Ltd., 2002), which is also available on the Internet at www.unep.org/GEO/geo3.

3. United Nations Environmental Programme, *Global Environmental Outlook 3*.

4. All aspects of the work of the Convention on Biodiversity are on its website (www.biodiv.org). This includes the *Cartagena Protocol on Biosafety: From Negotiation to Implementation*, Convention on Biological Diversity News, Special Edition, 2004.

5. Convention on Biodiversity, www.biodiv.org.

6. Convention on Biodiversity, www.biodiv.org; *Cartagena Protocol on Biosafety*.

7. The text of the *Convention on International Trade in Endangered Species of Wild Fauna and Flora* is available on the CITES website (www.cites.org).

8. *Convention on International Trade in Endangered Species of Wild Fauna and Flora*, www.cites.org.

9. The first American environmental classic is George P. Marsh, *The Earth as Modified by Human Action* (New York: Scribners, 1874), quote on page 144.

10. The history of wildlife preservation in the United States is in Michael J. Bean and Melanie J. Rowland, *The Evolution of National Wildlife Law* (Westport, Conn.: Praeger, 1997).

11. The plight of species worldwide is clear in David L. Hawkswirth, ed., *Global Biodiversity Assessment* (Cambridge, U.K.: Cambridge Univ. Press, 1995). For the United States, one of the fullest assessments of our diversity is Edward T. LaRoe, et al., *Our Living Resources: A Report to the Nation on the Distribution, Abundance, and Health of U.S. Plants, Animals, and Ecosystems* (Washington, D.C.: Department of the Interior—National Biological Service, 1995). This was reinforced by Stein, Kutner, and Adams, eds., *Precious Heritage*. The legislative side is *Endangered Species Act, as Amended through December, 1996* (Washington, D.C.: Government Printing Office, 1997).

12. Stein, Kutner, and Adams, eds., *Precious Heritage*.

13. Ibid.

14. Ibid.

15. Ibid.

7. Climate Change in a Glacial Epoch

1. My very general introduction to the basics of climate summarizes what is present in almost any textbook on the subject. But because my ultimate goal is a better understanding of all the controversies surrounding global warming, I was particularly informed by two sources: (1) Intergovernmental Panel on Climate Change, *Climate Change 2001: The Scientific Basis* (Cambridge, U.K.: Cambridge Univ. Press, 2001), Part 1, "The Climate System: An Overview," and Part 2, "Observed Climate Variability and Change", 85–181; and (2) R. C. L. Wilson, S. A. Drury, and J. L. Chapman, *The Great Ice Age: Climate Change and Life* (London: Routledge, 2000).

2. I found the most detailed scientific analysis of the role of the thermohaline circulation in a series of highly technical, model-based essays: Peter U. Clark, Robert S. Webb, and Lloyd D. Keigwin, eds., *Mechanisms of Global Climate Change at Millennial Time Scales* (Washington, D.C.: American Geophysical Union, 1999). In a very stimulating book, *The Winds of Change: Climate, Weather, and the Destruction of Civilizations* (New York: Simon and Schuster, 2006), Eugene Linden has carefully surveyed recent research on paleoclimate and on the devastating impact of rapid climate change on past civilizations.

3. The history of the earth's climate in the more distant past is still an area of conflicting theories. Much is unknown, and may remain so. An overview of some of the issues is in National Research Council, *Global Environmental Change: Research Pathways for the Next Decade* (Washington, D.C.: National Academy Press, 1999), chapter 6, "Paleoclimate Overview," 237–91. This book is best at revealing what we do not know, and what research is needed to lower levels of uncertainty in almost all climate-related areas. At points it may seem suspect, for it echoes a typical point of view among policy makers in the United States, and particularly in the George W. Bush Administration—wait until we have much more certain knowledge before adopting new climate-related policies, particularly those that might slow American economic growth or place too many burdens on producers and consumers. David Schwartzman, in *Life, Temperature, and the Earth: The Self-Organizing Biosphere* (New York: Columbia Univ. Press, 1999), offers a perspective that draws from Gaia theory. Also see Wilson, Drury, and Chapman, *The Great Ice Age*.

4. Intergovernmental Panel on Climate Change, *Climate Change 2001*.

8. Greenhouse Gases and Climate Change

1. Fortunately, Spencer R. Weart has written an excellent history of the development of concerns about global warming, *The Discovery of Global Warming* (Cambridge, Mass.: Harvard Univ. Press, 2003). An expanded version of this book is available on the Internet at www.aip.org/history/climate. The more distant history of climate change is addressed in Peter U. Clark, Robert S. Webb, and Lloyd D. Keigwin, eds., *Mechanisms of Global Climate Change at Millennial Time Scales* (Washington, D.C.: American Geographical Union, 1999); by two chapters in National Research Council, *Global Environmental Change: Research Pathways for the Next Decade* (Washington, D.C.: National Academy Press, 1999); and by D. J. Beerling and F. I. Woodward, *Vegetation and the Terrestrial Carbon Cycle: Modelling the First 400 Million Years* (Cambridge, U.K.: Cambridge Univ. Press, 2001).

2. At least half the content of this chapter derives from the work of the Intergovernmental Panel on Climate Change (IPCC). It has completed three major assessments of the climate change now under way, with the third completed in 2001. Its fourth assessment will be completed in 2007. The third assessment

was published in four large and at times quite technical volumes: Climate Change 2001: The Scientific Basis; Climate Change 2001: Impacts, Adaptation and Vulnerability; Climate Change 2001: Mitigation; and Climate Change 2001: Synthesis Report (Cambridge, U.K.: Cambridge Univ. Press, 2001).

3. IPCC, Climate Change 2001: The Scientific Basis. The IPCC has synthesized the ongoing scientific research on warming, and its bibliography is almost definitive. Almost all major books on warming accept its data, even if they do not agree with the implied policy implications of this data. The only introduction to the scientific background that is largely independent of the IPCC assessments is L. D. Danny Harvey, Global Warming: The Hard Science (New York: Prentice Hall, 2000), but the content is in general agreement with that of the IPCC.

4. Weart, The Discovery of Global Warming; Beerling and Woodward, Vegetation and the Terrestrial Carbon Cycle.

5. Ibid.

6. IPCC, Climate Change 2001: The Scientific Basis; IPCC, Climate Change 2001: Impacts, Adaptation and Vulnerability.

7. The policy implications of warming and international efforts to control greenhouse gases have attracted an enormous range of opinion and scholarship. I found the following books to be very helpful in these areas: David G. Victor, The Collapse of the Kyoto Protocol and the Struggle to Slow Global Warming (Princeton: Princeton Univ. Press, 2001); Jeremy K. Leggett, The Carbon War: Global Warming and the End of the Oil Era (New York: Routledge, 2001); Stephen H. Schneider, Armin Rosencranz, and John O. Niles, eds., Climate Change Policies: A Survey (Washington, D.C.: Island Press, 2002); N. H. Ravindranath and Jayanta A. Sathaye, Climate Change in Developing Countries (Boston: Kluwer Academic Publishers, 2002); and Barry Holden, Democracy and Global Warming (New York: Continuum, 2002).

8. The most recent assessment of the potential for CO_2 capture and storage is the IPCC "Special Report on Carbon Dioxide Capture and Storage, Summary for Policy Makers," Montreal, IPCC Working Group III, September 25, 2005, and available at www.ipcc.ch.activity/outlineco2capture.pdf.

9. IPCC, Climate Change 2001: Mitigation; Ravindranath and Sathaye, Climate Change in Developing Countries.

10. Ravindranath and Sathaye, Climate Change in Developing Countries; Holden, Democracy and Global Warming.

11. Victor, The Collapse of the Kyoto Protocol and the Struggle to Slow Global Warming.

12. IPCC "Special Report on Carbon Dioxide Capture and Storage, Summary for Policy Makers," Montreal, IPCC Working Group III, September 25, 2005, and available at www.ipcc.ch.activity/outlineco2capture.pdf. As I write, a new, best-selling book by Albert Gore, An Inconvenient Truth: The Planetary Emergency of Global Warming and What We Can Do About It (Emmaus, Pa.: Rodale Press, 2006), has stimulated more debate about global warming.

13. Many books deal with specific topics involving global warming. I found the following to be helpful: Kirill Ya Kondratyev, *Climatic Effects of Aerosols and Clouds* (Chichester, U.K.: Springer-Praxis, 1999); Kirill Ya Kondratyev and Ignacio Galindo, *Volcanic Activity and Climate* (Hampton, Va.: A. Deepak, 1997); and Alan Wellburn, *Air Pollution and Climate Change: The Biological Impact*, 2nd ed. (New York: Wiley, 1994).

9. Reform Environmentalists and American Environmental Policy

1. The best introduction to the first major environmental movement in the United States, in behalf of conservation of resources, is Samuel P. Hays, *Conservation and the Gospel of Efficiency: The Progressive Conservation Movement, 1890–1920* (Cambridge, Mass.: Harvard Univ. Press, 1959).

2. Hays, *Conservation and the Gospel of Efficiency.* A broad, general textbook on American environmentalism is Benjamin Kline, *First Along the River: A Brief History of the U.S. Environmental Movement*, 2nd ed. (San Francisco: Arcada Books, 2000).

3. Much more detailed than the Kline work is Riley E. Dunlap and Angela G. Mertig, eds., *American Environmentalism: The U.S. Environmental Movement, 1970–1990* (Philadelphia: Taylor and Francis, 1992).

4. Everyone should read Rachel Carson, *Silent Spring* (Boston: Houghton Mifflin, 1962), the greatest classic of modern environmentalism.

5. Ibid.

6. As a backdrop to the Wilderness Act, one should read Roderick Nash, *Wilderness and the American Mind*, 3rd ed. (New Haven: Yale Univ. Press, 1982). The Wilderness Act is included in *Digest of Federal Resource Laws of Interest to the U.S. Fish and Wildlife Service* at www.fws.gov/lawsdigest/indx.html.

7. Kline, *First Along the River.* Two anthologies contain selections from a wide array of environmentalists: Lisa M. Benton and John Rennie Short, eds., *Environmental Discourse and Practice: A Reader* (Oxford, U.K.: Blackwell, 2000), with chapter 9, "The Greening of the United States," most pertinent for this chapter; and Sheldon Kamieniecki, George A. Gonzalez, and Robert O. Vos, eds., *Flashpoints in Environmental Policymaking: Controversies in Achieving Sustainability* (Albany: State Univ. of New York Press, 1997).

8. The best survey of the accomplishments of the National Environmental Policy Act is Ray Clark and Larry Canter, *Environmental Policy and NEPA: Past, Present, and Future* (Boca Raton, Fla.: St. Lucie Press, 1997).

9. *Digest of Federal Resource Laws of Interest to the U.S. Fish and Wildlife Service*, www.fws .gov/lawsdigest/indx.html.

10. The literature on the EPA is enormous, including hundreds of its own publications. The best way to gain some understanding of its role is by turning to its website (www.epa.gov).

10. Passionate Environmentalism

1. The original introduction of Gaia theory is in James E. Lovelock, *Gaia: A New Look at Life on Earth* (London: Oxford Univ. Press, 1979); he followed this with *The Ages of Gaia: A Biography of Our Living Earth* (New York: W. W. Norton, 1988); *Healing Gaia: Practical Medicine for the Planet* (New York: Harmony Books, 1991); and *Gaia's Body: Toward a Physiology of Earth* (New York: Springer-Verlag, 1998). I find the most penetrating analysis of Gaia theory in George Ronald Williams, *The Molecular Biology of Gaia* (New York: Columbia Univ. Press, 1996).

2. For deep ecology, one must begin with Arne Naess, "The Deep Ecology Movement: Some Philosophical Aspects," *Philosophy Inquiry* 8 (1986): 10–31; and also Arne Naess, *Ecology, Community and Lifestyle: Outline of an Ecosophy*, translated and edited by David Rothenberg (Cambridge, U.K.: Cambridge Univ. Press, 1989). Also revealing is George Sessions, ed., *Deep Ecology for the 21st Century* (Boston: Shambhala, 1995).

3. Naess, *Ecology, Community and Lifestyle*, 29.

4. Lovelock, *The Ages of Gaia*.

5. The complications and inner controversies concerning deep ecology are in Eric Katz, Andrew Light, and David Rothenberg, *Beneath the Surface: Critical Essays of Deep Ecology* (Cambridge, Mass.: MIT Press, 2000).

6. An excellent, and quite moderate, introduction to ecofeminism is Carolyn Merchant, *Radical Ecology: The Search for a Livable World* (London: Routledge, 1992). A sharper view is in Ariel Salleh, "Deeper Than Deep Ecology: The Ecofeminist Connection," *Environmental Ethics* 6 (1984): 339–45. Excellent essays on deep ecology and ecofeminism are in Michael E. Zimmerman et al., eds., *Environmental Philosophy: From Animal Rights to Radical Ecology* (Englewood Cliffs, N.J.: Prentice Hall, 1993).

7. The most readable introduction to bioregionalism is Kirkpatrick Sale, *Dwellers in the Land* (San Francisco: Sierra Club, 1985). Two anthologies contain excellent selections from bioregionalists, including Zimmerman et al., eds., *Environmental Philosophy*, and Sheldon Kamieniecki, George A. Gonzalez, and Robert O. Vos, *Flashpoints in Environmental Policymaking: Controversies in Achieving Sustainability* (Albany: State Univ. of New York Press, 1997).

8. The publicity for both Greenpeace and Earth First! is immense. A good place to gain an understanding of Greenpeace is its website, http://www.greenpeace.org.

9. The origins of Earth First!, in a sense, are in a novel by Edward Abbey, *The Monkey Wrench Gang* (Philadelphia: Lippincott, 1975).

Index

GE
195.7
C66
2007

WITHDRAWN
From Library Collection

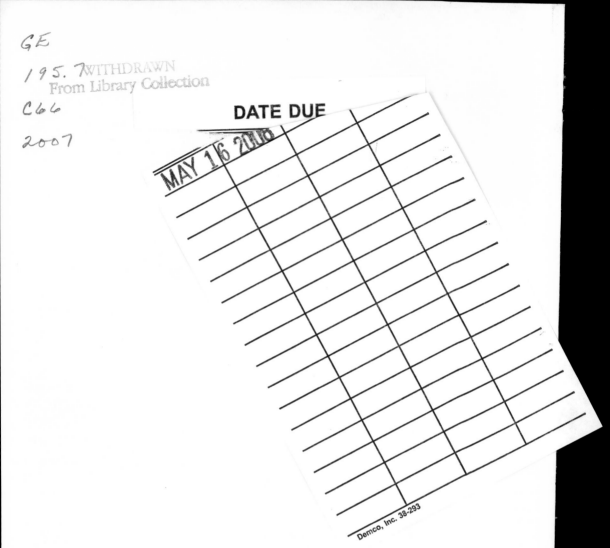

DATE DUE

MAY 16 2010

Demco, Inc. 38-293

WITHDRAWN
From Library Collection

Reinsch Library
Marymount University
2807 N Glebe Road
Arlington, VA 22207